Cross-Cultural Research with Integrity

Cross-Cultural Research with Integrity

Collected Wisdom from Researchers in Social Settings

Linda Miller Cleary
University of Minnesota, USA

First published 2013 by
PALGRAVE MACMILLAN

Palgrave Macmillan in the UK is an imprint of Macmillan Publishers Limited, registered in England, company number 785998, of Houndmills, Basingstoke, Hampshire RG21 6XS.

Palgrave Macmillan in the US is a division of St Martin's Press LLC, 175 Fifth Avenue, New York, NY 10010.

Palgrave Macmillan is the global academic imprint of the above companies and has companies and representatives throughout the world.

Palgrave® and Macmillan® are registered trademarks in the United States, the United Kingdom, Europe and other countries.

ISBN 978–1–137–26359–9

This book is printed on paper suitable for recycling and made from fully managed and sustained forest sources. Logging, pulping and manufacturing processes are expected to conform to the environmental regulations of the country of origin.

A catalogue record for this book is available from the British Library.

A catalog record for this book is available from the Library of Congress.

10 9 8 7 6 5 4 3 2 1
22 21 20 19 18 17 16 15 14 13

Printed and bound in the United States of America

Contents

Acknowledgments

This has hardly been a solitary endeavor. I extend heartfelt thanks:

— to the interviewed researchers who took me through unexpected turns and offered wisdom that sent me beyond my original intentions. Even the few who were not quoted herein added to the collected wisdom that informed this book.
— to those whose wisdom I absorbed before the project even began: Paul Hughes and Thomas Peacock.
— to the highly valued readers, who raised confidence and proffered advice in the harder moments: Liz Mouw, Barbara Powell, Linda Muldoon, Sharon Kemp, John Arthur, Aydin Durgunoğlu, Terrie Shannon, Mary Hermes, Beth Bartlett, Dody Goldberg, Ian Cho, and Magdalena Cho Absher.
— to the research assistants, for their careful transcription and bibliographic work, and other assistances along the way: Allison Krenz, Brandy Hoffman, Avesa Rockwell, Jake La Jeunesse, and Mary Tennis.
— to editor Philippa Grand at Palgrave Macmillan and assistant Andrew James who helped in bringing this project to press.
— to many past researchers, who created the rise in sensitivities that have made a difference. As researchers, we sit on the shoulders of others who began thinking in a sensitive way.
— to the University of Minnesota, for grants for the research from the Chancellor, the College of Liberal Arts, and the McNight Foundation for travel grants.
— and especially to Ed, Jed, and Sarah, and to my grandchildren, who supported me even when my attentions to this project made for my absences from them.

1
Nothing Stands Still

To cross-cultural borders in research is a slippery and complicated endeavor, and good intentions, though essential, are not enough to help researchers make those crossings with respect for those they research and with their own integrity intact. With diversity now a world-wide reality, cross-cultural research has become an endeavor for most of those who research in social settings. Though cross-cultural research has different meanings in different disciplines, it is hoped that this book will benefit any researcher who crosses into another culture to pose questions, formulate hypotheses, accrue new knowledge, or, even better, collaborate with those of a different culture to solve problems.

An increase in the multicultural nature of our regional research populations, due to regional and global mobility and migration patterns, has been further increased by newer notions of culture. Though research used to focus on the cultural difference of race and ethnicity, researchers now see the need to reach beyond those borders that implied travel to different neighborhoods or distant spaces. Now we rarely engage in research that doesn't include participants from different ethnicities, nationalities, sexual orientations, races, religions, social classes, political affiliations, occupations, and/or language groups, all groups with different ways of being. These factors affect research and call for sensitivities that were not deemed as important in previous decades.

In the past, many researchers came to their inquiries bound by their own cultural perspective and intent on their own goals and conclusions. Researchers now investigate and question the primacy of their own realities and have come to value different world views. Furthermore, within the last half-century, ethical concerns have taken on serious consideration in research, and researchers are finding ways to collaborate with communities that have been, with good reason, resistant to research that has been harmful in the past. Thinking through cross-cultural research methodology is necessary to heal wounds and to meet local as well as knowledge-based needs.

Certainly, globalization allows us to learn from other cultures and from other researchers, shifting us away from being a solitary researcher to undertaking team endeavors with "an emphasis on transdisciplinary, multidisciplinary, and multi-perspective approaches...which cross discipline boundaries as well as state and national divides" (Grbich, 2004, pp. 51–52). Traveling, physically or metaphorically, from one culture to another allows us richer perspectives, from richer understandings of different social settings to richer ways of viewing reality. And there is an impetus in the very world problems that face us. As Leung and Van de Vijver (2006, p. 443) note, "Challenges of humankind such as global warming, terrorism, and arms control require the cooperation of many nations." We must understand other perspectives if we are to transact the social change needed to address these problems, and the issues of human suffering and human rights.

The reality of globalization continues to challenge local cultures and their needs. Business and media conglomerates, most often driven by profit, will continue to capitalize on those who have less power in the world instead of learning from local insights and meeting local needs. Walter Ong (1999, as cited in Ladson-Billings and Donnor, 2008, pp. 74–75) "warns of the growing threat of global capital that destabilizes notions of cultural unity and/or allegiance. Instead, the overwhelming power of multinational corporations creates economic cleavage that force people, regardless of their racial, cultural, and ethnic locations, to chase jobs and compete against each other to subsist." Cross-cultural research collaborations can seek to disrupt those competitions and elucidate the "tension between democratic and market values" that disadvantages certain cultural populations (Giroux and Giroux, 2008, p. 181).

This book looks at issues in cross-cultural research, from initiation of research to its dissemination, by tapping the insights of interviewed researchers who were both troubled and pleased, many simultaneously, with their cross-cultural efforts. Some 70 researchers (from four continents, from seven different nations, from different cultures within those nations, and from different academic disciplines) each draw from their geopolitical and cultural contexts and give earnest insights from their cross-cultural research experiences. Those interviewed were themselves varied: some well known in their fields, others working hard at research but who haven't yet made it to the top of the academic ladder; those sitting well on top of their privilege to those fighting on the margins for privilege well deserved. Herein lies a cross-cultural, cross-disciplinary, and cross-national intersection of thought. Interviewed researchers offer their experience, stories, insights, and analyses, but the book also integrates their experience with thought from seminal works on cross-cultural research and with critiques on methodological issues from authors who draw from (and even critique) postcolonial, post-structural, and postmodern ideologies.

Researchers work off one another to create progress in cross-cultural research. Indeed, readers of this book must be active in considering, rejecting, or accepting the proffered advice in relation to their own research agendas. Multiple researchers, multiple stories, and multiple interpretations reach out across the pages to the curious readers as they consider their own research. Many of the interviews for this book morphed into recorded dialogic conversations between the interviewee and me as interviewer, creating, as Grbich (2004, p. 84) describes, "a link between the therapeutic and scholarly aspects of research." As researchers we evolve. Through this gathering of researchers' stories, reflexivity (the researcher's self-examinations of interpretive positions), and resultant insights, we help each other evolve. Nevertheless, perhaps we are arrogant if we think that any absolute truths can outlast a conversation or the reading of a book.

As researcher and author, I take agency in the construction of this text, positioning myself in relation to the topic as the book progresses, allowing my lived cross-cultural experiences to be a part of the whole. The impetus for this book was not dispassionate; it originated in my research association with Julian Cho, the Humanities Department Chair at Toledo Community College. On my first trip to southern Belize in 1996 to study Indigenous literacy, I hiked into a Maya community inland from Punta Gorda. There I witnessed the results of the advent of electricity in the village, which had occurred just days before: one electric pole wired to a thatched community gathering place, a television, and 15 or so Maya children mesmerized by US television. The following day, in an interview with Cho, I described what I had seen and asked him about the possible loss of culture in his Maya village. His response was: "Nothing stands still." We talked about the complexities of surface vs. deep culture, about the tenacity of deep culture, about the place of literacy and schooling in a changing world, about the losses and gains of modernization, and about issues of poverty and power, and gender and culture in Belize schooling. "Nothing stands still" has become a mantra that he has contributed to this book.

I dedicate this book to Julian Cho. Normally a dedication comes before a book begins, but in this case Cho is a part of my research narrative in multiple chapters. Though my formal research about cross-cultural research wasn't to begin until after his death, his phrase "Nothing stands still" has come back to me again and again, sometimes from the mouths of those whom I interviewed, sometimes in what I have read, but often as if the late Cho's contribution was being whispered across the years.

I started with research questions, but they have not stood still and so are hardly worth mentioning. I started with what I thought were some truths, but they quickly dissolved as I collected wisdom from those who had done similar research. Every time I think I have a hold on something absolute to say, it refuses to stay reliably in place. The researchers interviewed for this book rarely touted simple guidelines for a researcher to follow and often raised as many questions as answers. In many cases they posed the very questions that they wished they had asked themselves before entering their own research endeavors. So this will not be a book of absolutes about cross-cultural research, but I feel sure that those who read it, with their own research agendas and minds in tow, will do better research. This is the book that I wish I had had before I began my cross-cultural endeavors.

A not-so-definite definition of culture and identity

In trying to define what cross-cultural research is, I open myself and my readers to an inclusive notion. What Cho had realized wouldn't stand still, Bhabha (1994, p. 5) deemed as the "shifting nature of culture" and, hence, the shifting nature of cultural borders. For instance, Larry Knopp, Director of Interdisciplinary Arts and Sciences at the University of Washington Tacoma and geographer, perceived his crossing of cultural borders to be multilayered. He describes his research as looking at "issues of gender and sexuality, and urban change and verbiage, and cultural politics." In his research he asks the question: "How are gay politics done in a cultural context like Britain, versus the United States, versus Australia, with their different traditions of property ownership or land tenure, like freehold versus leasehold, and the position of these various places in a global and regional economy?" As Knopp and many others point out, cultural borders are layered, complicated, and elusive constructs.

One would think that one region, coastal Maine in the USA, for instance, might evidence some consistency in culture, but Julie Canniff, teacher educator and researcher at the University of Southern Maine, described the complexity she found in studying "concepts of success" there:

> In the six years I spent working with teachers and students on the remote Maine islands, I was fascinated with cultural points of view as those from island cultures talked often about how difficult it was for their kids to go to the mainland school. In ways, the culture of poverty was more salient than ethnic culture, but then again you had Native American, French Canadian, and Catholic populations and all their different concepts of success through many generations. I suppose the notion of "culture" to a Maine islander is simply "the way we do things out here."

I asked Ian Anderson, Director for the Cooperative Research Centre for Aboriginal Health at the University of Melbourne, what advice he gave to graduate students in considering research that crossed cultural borders. He replied:

> Don't look for the border; it may well be seamless. People who are looking for the border trip over things. Be really aware that you carry a whole set

of stereotypes that you will unlearn through time. You may think you are on one side of the border when you aren't. You may think that you are talking about the same thing, but people have profoundly different experiences even if they are using a common language.

The term cultural "border," then, is a geographic metaphor. Cultures are rarely totally isolated from one another. Since time immemorial, they have intruded on other cultures, and groups have been pushed out of what was even formally another group's space (Safran, 1991; Alexander, 2008). In colonization, more powerful groups, often acting beyond their need to survive, have traveled to exert their forceful presence on other cultures around the world, to intrude purposively, with cultural domination, power, privilege, and material gain as motives. Slavery, for instance, was known in almost every ancient civilization and still exists today (Harris, 1999). Hence, oppression has forced most subjugated people to adjust their ways of being by *integrating* themselves into the intruding culture's dominant constructs in order to survive and maintain some of their own cultural dignity, or by *adapting* to the oppressive constructs in order to survive. The Indigenous or other marginalized groups within dominant society often find ways of resisting. bell hooks (1989) noted that "Oppressed people resist by identifying themselves as subjects, by defining their reality, shaping their new identity, naming their history, telling their story"(p. 43). hooks (1989, p. 67) quotes Paolo Freire (2005, p. 67), who makes the distinction between integration and adaptation:

> Integration with one's context, as distinguished from adaptation, is a distinctly human activity. Integration results from the capacity to adapt oneself to reality plus the critical capacity to make choices and transform that reality...The integrated person is person as Subject. In contrast, the adaptive person is person as object, adaptation representing at most a weak form of self-defense. If man is incapable of changing reality, he adjusts himself instead. Adaptation is behavior characteristic of the animal sphere; exhibited by man, it is symptomatic of his dehumanization.

It would be nice if the age of colonization were over, but the motives for gain may have just changed from the quest for gold or chalices to their metaphoric equivalents. Furthermore, as to be discussed in Chapter 2, power comes with privilege; one moves around in the world with both conscious and unconscious privilege and its benefits, or, possibly even more conscious, the lack thereof.

As researchers, we must interrogate our own motives and privileged positions in research as we move across seemingly seamless, multilayered, yet existing cultural borders to determine whether they involve a sort of neo-colonialism. And in studying what we deem to be important distinctions between cultures, many complications arise. "Nothing stands still." For instance, some researchers in this study found their participants had taken on more complicated identities than the researchers had initially considered, due to the absorption that occurs when those of one culture either choose or are forced to disappear into another, abjuring or hiding cultural traces of which they might be proud or ashamed, or sometimes simultaneously proud and ashamed. Boundaries become permeable, further complicating this notion of culture. Rosaldo (1993) says: "In contrast with the classic view, which posits culture as a self-contained whole made up of coherent patterns, culture can arguably be conceived as a more porous array of intersections where distinct processes crisscross from within and beyond its borders" (p. 20). Researchers in this study talk of the intersections of race, ethnicity, nationality, region, religion, class, language, gender, generation, sexual preference, and, hence, political stance. Indeed, some found that being culturally sensitive to ethnicity was actually largely being sensitive to the "intersectionality" of gender, language, identity, and socio-economic issues (Delva et al., 2010). Furthermore, each culture and sub-culture (if indeed that isn't another culture altogether) has its own views of what is right and what is wrong, which further confound researchers' endeavors because, as with most deep levels of culture, these differences are not necessarily visible or discernible. And consistent with porosity, people often go back and forth between different cultures, speaking with a multiplicity of voices depending on their needs at the time, especially when they are of mixed heritage/hybridity. Both participants and researchers may be caught between pressures from different cultures, finding it expedient to identify differently for understandable purposes. Neither people nor cultures exist in boxes.

Once, in 1993, just as the ice was going out of the rivers and lakes in northern Maine, I talked with a Passamaquoddy elder and educator. I told him that I was beginning to see just how complex the cultural issues and literacy issues were surrounding the education of native people. He paused and then said to me: "When you start to see things simply, you will come closer to the truth." Since then, I've tried to think more simply about culture. As researchers have found, starting with the simplest theory about social and cultural behavior may prove to be more accurate. Surface markers of culture, such as group membership, dress, language, food, customs, language, and geographic positioning, may be easy to identify; deep culture, such as ways of being, shared ways of viewing the world, shared bases of social action, inherited ideas, beliefs, and knowledge, are less transparent. Thinking more simply about culture has led me to see surface and deep culture as a construct that people have developed to live in the conditions that their worlds present, ways to survive and thrive. And, of course, the conditions of survival and "thrival" change. The language of a culture evolves, both to allow communication between people for survival and to simultaneously shape, or maintain and articulate, experience. Religion develops to explain the mysteries in the seeable and unseeable world. When people from one culture come into contact with those from another, what Cole (1991) calls "inherently sociocultural-contextual-historical boundedness of mental processes" can be hard to figure out (p. 437). But this lack of understanding is dependent on the relative lack of contact between people who have been inculcated into different ways of being and who use different geopolitical knowledge upon which to thrive and survive. Furthermore, different disciplines use different concepts of culture, indeed different researchers within the same discipline, upon which to base their research. For instance, psychologists Matsumoto and Yoo (2006) note that some definitions allow psychologists to better control variables, eliminating noncultural variables.

And, of course, identity and perspective are inextricably related to culture and sometimes seen as derived from ancestors. As Grande (2008, p. 233) says, "And when I say 'my perspective,' I mean from a consciousness shaped not only by my own experiences, but also those of my peoples and ancestors." Yet, identity is also, in part, a willful thing. One takes on cultural values, perspectives, and behaviors and rejects them, in part due to the way one has been enculturated (the way one has taken on culture non-consciously) but also based on decisions about the way one views oneself in relation to surrounding groups. Identity can also be evolved in rebellion. When we become cross-cultural researchers, we confront the importance of understanding ourselves, our cultural roots, how we live those roots or challenge them, where we are going, and what influences us along the way. Notions of culture thus become intermixed with notions of identity. Shirley Brice Heath, linguistic anthropologist at Stanford University, who has looked at language and literacy development across socio-cultures, stated at the American Educational Research Association (AERA) Conference in 2006 that people hold not just one or two identities but are "bundles of identity." More recently in an interview, Heath referred to "crowded selves" using Shemeem Black's (2010) term. Bundles of identity play out in the multiple ways one presents oneself, determined by one's surroundings at any given moment. Indeed, we construct identity as a way to survive or thrive in that moment. I am a bundle of identities, and I may play out a particular construct of my multiple identities, consciously or unconsciously, as I go about my life. These conceptualizations of myself tie into social identities or collective identities as I move into different groups and arenas (Stryker et al., 2006, p. 26). I present the following because I believe that acknowledging one's complex identity informs the readers of one's values and subjectivities as they affect one's research (see also Denzin, 1998; Lather, 1991; Stonebanks, 2008).

I am a white middle-class university professor. I prepare teachers of English and have taught undergraduate courses in literature, composition, linguistics, and their pedagogy, and graduate courses in literacy and research. That may identify me by class, profession, and discourse community. Before I considered the complexity of culture, I was convinced that I had none as my ancestors were of English, Irish, Scottish, German, Dutch, and French heritage. My ancestry is rowdily European and highly affected by centuries of presence in North America. Being identified as Euro-American doesn't feel right. I hail from the east coast, spent some formative years on the west coast, declare Maine as my home of heart, but work in the Midwest and cherish many Midwest ways of being. I am a regional hybrid. I am a mother, a sister, a grandmother, and still a child of elderly parents. There was a time in my life of single parenting when I used food stamps, had no insurance, and worried about how my children would get through college. I can empathize with what researchers call the "culture of poverty," but I was not raised in poverty. I am, indeed, a "bundle of identities." I am a crowded self. Though I sit in a place of white privilege, I did come through a time of being painfully aware that I was not gender privileged in an academic setting. I am constantly discovering parts of my identity that I haven't been aware of until I have acted from them. Recently, I surprise myself, for instance, when I act with courage in certain situations. It has been a delightful discovery to me that there is more to me than I even know.

It may seem counterintuitive to consider bundles or categories or theories as simpler than a mass of the interwoven, but the Passamaquoddy elder was onto something in saying, "When you start to see things simply, you will come closer to the truth." In this research, one begins to see things more simply by seeing interwoven complexity as the reality. When one sees how really complex the considerations are, one may be jolted into more overarching constructs. In this way one can see identity as simply a version of a self-construction for the purpose of survival and thrival. Cultural borders are where a person's conscious and non-conscious, crowded self meets the surface and deep culture of "others" who have different sets of shared meanings transferred through different symbols and patterns of behavior, and different modes of getting on with life. What one might think of as clear borders may not stand still. As researchers, to become what some deem to be culturally competent, we need to scrutinize our own crowded identities, develop strategies for discerning our own possible biases and privileges, and become sufficiently confident, happy enough in ourselves, to not be intimidated by difference. Researchers need to cross permeable borders, working hard to prepare themselves for departure, and then entering another culture with both curiosity and respect. The purpose of this book is to help in those crossings while placing ethics and actions of right conduct at the center of our scholarly endeavors.

A brief and recent history of ethical issues in cross-cultural research

Humans have long sought to understand the universals and idiosyncrasies of nature, and of human nature and experience, through inquiry. We are curious beings. Researchers, in more organized endeavors, have participated in an unending search into understandings of human behavior and thinking. Robben and Sluka (2007, p. 446) describes this search as a "hermeneutic circle in which understanding was advanced in circular, rather than linear, ways between part and whole, and back again."

Researchers have, perhaps more recently, debated the ethics, the rightness of the methodologies and methods used, when they move beyond their own culture. They have followed a long path to the recognition that all people are moral beings, though those who are culturally different may have had very different circumstances that have informed what grounds them morally. As researchers have become less culturally myopic, they have begun to realize that each culture has different views of the world and of good behavior in research, and most have realized that all inquiry has ethical and political dimensions.

In many countries, the development of ethics protocols became a notable occurrence in the 20th century, perhaps in reaction to medical research in Nazi concentration camps, to the US government's Tuskegee Syphilis Study, to the more recently discovered syphilis study in Guatemala, and to other heinous research around the world. These grievous breaches of respect for humanity have fed world outrage, and ethics procedures surrounding medical research now operate under the injunction of "Do no harm," monitored by rigorous Institutional Research Boards (IRBs) and other ethics reviews at the national, state, and community level (see Chapter 3 for a full view of ethics protocols). The recent publication of Skloot's non-fictional narrative (2010) entitled *The Immortal Life of Henrietta Lacks* presents an interesting (and disturbing) view of the development of medical research ethics in the USA.

Though no one would question the harm done in the research mentioned above, what does and doesn't "do harm" can be complicated due to different takes on what is perceived as harmful in different cultures. As Stanfield and Rutledge (1993) notes, the research rules of procedure and evidence have been historically construed by Eurocentric researchers and have been rooted in Eurocentric hegemony. Stanfield calls for new epistemologies to ground our theories because, in the past, researchers' views of ethical practice have been limited, even arrogant, in their unwillingness to view ethics from other cultural perspectives. For instance, in the past the Western view of research was one in which the researcher remains "under a veil of neutrality or of objectivity; whereas, in Māori culture, research is only considered ethical if there is a 'face-to-face' and continuing relationship between the researcher and researched" (Bishop, 1996; see also Smith, 1999).

Anthropologists have been at these debates since they professionalized their work (see Welsch and Endicott, 2002). They began serious discussions that set ethical standards within the profession of fieldwork in the midst of political turmoil in the 1960s and 1970s, when the USA supported stable governments while ignoring what might be change for the good of the larger population. Anthropologists' debate over their involvement in US endeavors triggered their first code of ethics (see Sluka's discussion of Project Camelot, 2007; Robben, 2007).

Yet anthropologists have been consistent in their empirical studies, long holding ethical obligations not to impose Western culture on Indigenous communities. This complicates, for instance, what might be an individual researcher's inclinations to provide medical assistance in the field from the spirit of compassion and reciprocity (Pollock, 2007). A decade of concern has surrounded Changon's work amongst the Yanomamö in Venezuela. A critique of his work was reported by Tierney (2000) in *Darkness in El Dorado: How Scientists and Journalists Devastated the Amazon*, the book then factually critiqued by the University of Michigan (http://cogweb.ucla.edu/Debate/UMichOnChagnon.html), setting off a debate that involved serious consideration of ethical standards, and shook the American Anthropological Association and the field of cross-cultural research in general (see Borofsky, 2005).

Linguists, psychologists, and educators in the 1960s and 1970s also considered culture and issues that arise when research reaches across cultural borders, becoming responsive to the way ethnicity plays out, for instance, in educational settings (see Bernstein, 1972; LaBov, 1972; McDermott, 1977; Cole and Scribner, 1978; Hymes 1964). They have offered insights into culture, language, and learning that have been seen more clearly in the light of juxtaposed cultures and have benefited from the cautions and ethical insights of anthropology. More recently, groundbreaking ethnographies have been respected as shedding more focused light on crucial issues and relationships with power, respectfully acknowledging the intelligence and literacy of participants along the way (for instance, Shirley Brice Heath's seminal work on literacy, *Way with Words* (1983)). Indeed, postmodern researchers in all the social sciences have critiqued the ethics of research, looking carefully at the complications and fluidity of identity and hybridity in both the researcher and the researched, both when the researcher is an "insider" or "outsider" to the community researched. Post-structuralists have concerned themselves with the power and privilege relationships consequent in the cross-cultural research process, warning of the limitations of positivism (see Foucault's warnings about omniscient statements of truth and his critiques of power in institutional discourse, 1980).

Recognizing the danger of identity simplification has enabled researchers to take another step forward in recognizing ethical issues in research. But as Stacey (1991) notes, a postmodernist approach "acknowledges, but does little to ameliorate, the problems of intervention, triangulation, or inherently unequal reciprocity with informants..." (p. 117). Anthropologist Renaldo Rosaldo (1993) says: "The call for a social analysis that made central the aspirations and demands of groups usually deemed marginal by the dominant national ideology came from the counterculture, environmentalism, feminism, gay and lesbian movements, the Native American movement, and the struggles of blacks, Chicanos, and Puerto Ricans" (p. 35).

Feminist studies, since the 1970s, have critiqued research when it reached across gender, cultural, sexual, racial, and class borders with concern for the care of those being researched. As well as acknowledging multiple voices and ways of perceiving the world, many feminist researchers resonated with what "Gilligan (1982) discerned in the moral reasoning of women and contrasted it with the orientation toward justice and rights which she found to typify the moral reasoning of men" (Friedman, 1987, p. 258). Furthermore, Belenky et al. (1986) led researchers to acknowledge different ways of knowing, to challenge dominant knowledge, to herald different epistemologies, all through this examination of women's ways of knowing.

Though prompted to put the social construction of gender at the center of their research, feminists have also looked at the invisibility of marginalized groups and have critiqued the hierarchical and exploitative tendencies of conventional research, urging it to seek an egalitarian process that is not falsely objective or impersonal (Oakley, 1981; Stacey, 1991). Acknowledging alternative epistemologies, being sensitized to researcher partiality, urging responsibility for authorial construction, and alerting researchers to heed relationality have all played out in what has been termed the empathy and mutuality of the "ethic of care." Feminist standpoint theory challenges "truths" held as universal and demonstrates the effect of biases and perspectives based on sex, class, race, and so on (Harstock, 2004). Though sometimes fractionalized, a broad range of feminisms pull together in discussions of research (Fine, 1992; Spivak, 1993; Cannella and Manuelito, 2008) and find a resultant social justice agenda. For instance, ecofeminism affirms the ethic of care across all cultures, including all people, living things, and the environment, and considers their interconnectedness (Gaard, 1993). Prompted by feminists, these concerns have been much on the minds of all researchers working in social settings as they entered the 21st century, moving research from a "do no harm" imperative to center in an "ethic of care" and respect.

Questions of whether research should even be carried out in a culture that is not one's own have been raised by many researchers in the social sciences (for instance, Patai, 1994), and the most poignant concerns are heard from Indigenous peoples. On reservations, reserves, homelands, and in maraes, I heard a similar, ironic joke that cautioned my inquiry. I first heard it on the Navajo reservation. Question: "What makes up a Navajo (substitute Aboriginal, Penobscot, Māori, etc.) family?" Answer: a mother, father, children, and anthropologist (note the absence of elders). Justifiable anger has fueled the interrogation of past research practices that demeaned participants, intruded on spiritual aspects of life, sensationalized community difficulties, misinterpreted data, and brought nothing back to the communities studied (DeLoria, 1969; Denzin et al., 2008).

Many 20th-century discussions of research ethics have lacked the voices and critiques of Indigenous peoples in considering the very research "done upon" them. Nevertheless, Rigney (2003, p. 9) warns that in becoming credentialed in the eyes of educational institutions and funding agencies, "Indigenous people have had to learn the dominant research epistemologies and methods with precision at the expense of our own [methodologies] whilst recognizing that our engagement in them is the fundamental aspect of our oppression." Recently, Indigenous researchers around the world have weighed in on issues of power, legitimation, benefits, and representation in what some refer to as "liberation epistemologies" or "emancipation epistemologies" and, in some cultures, have re-constructed methodologies and termed them "emergent" (Nakata, 1998; Bishop and Glynn, 1999; Smith, 1999; Hermes, 1998). Many voices are now coming to consider ethical issues in research. Denzin and Lincoln (2008, p. xi) list the critical approaches that have arisen that address issues in research: "Postcolonial, subaltern, First Nation, and Red pedagogies; post-poststructuralism criticism; cultural critique; critical race feminism; critical White studies; Latino criticism/critical theories (LatCrit); critical pedagogy; pragmatic action theory; participatory action research (PAAR); and critical race and queer theories...." Even with this impetus for change and the intellectual understandings for its need, researchers still encounter confusions when they cross-cultural borders, be they distant or local crossings. Research in social settings has moved toward a humanitarian commitment, beyond the previous un-negotiated taking of knowledge, and is now based on the well-being of those researched, emphasizing the reciprocity and collaborative partnerships attentive to the social concerns and local needs.

Need for continued attention to cross-cultural research methodology

Though reconsidered repeatedly, most deem there to be a continuing need for research support from academics whose culture is different from that of those requesting research, but only if that research is done with the self-determination and benefit of those researched in mind (Smith, 1999, 2003). Now institutions and communities have ethics protocols that intercede on behalf of the researched (see Chapter 3). One might align these protocols and rule-bound procedures with the model of morality where justice begets rules. The advent of these ethics protocols is indicative of concern, but some researchers see the rules as oppressive "band-aids" when self-reflexivity and conscience are more to the point.

Because unexamined research reifies traditional methods and methodologies, the need for self-sustained examination is real. The researchers interviewed for this study were earnest in their attempts to fathom the complex terrain of doing research in differently cultured settings and with differently cultured people. All saw that we were in an era of post-positivist social science research. All were reflective and insightful in discussing their histories with cross-cultural research, thinking deeply about what was problematic in their own research. Indeed, many remained conflicted, even simultaneously heartened and disheartened in their practice. It was interesting to collect the vocabulary that differently disciplined researchers used to describe the methods of research they did not respect: "helicopter research," "safari scholars," "data strip mining," "vacuum cleaner research," "smash and grab research," and "hit-and-run interviews." Neither researchers nor research mores stand still.

In considering the researchers' experience proffered in this book, one must suspend disbelief and engage in their stories and thoughts; yet careful reading also demands that the next stage be one of disengagement and reflection. In suspending disbelief, one can enter into the experiences of the 70 researchers and other cited researchers; in disengaging, one can consider how these experiences can inductively inform the research one is doing or is about to do. I have not attempted to evaluate everything that researchers have said. In some cases they disagree with one another. We are all working hard to know how we can go about our work.

Replete with good intentions and misassumptions

Experienced researchers enter research with a developed sense of cultural relativism, but those same experienced researchers, though they may understand the concept of cultural relativism, may have had to stumble across a few cultural borders, or maybe more than a few, before being more practiced at discerning the perspectives of others. "Behaviour in a particular culture should not be judged by the standards of another culture" (Goldstein, 2000, p. 25). To work well across cultures we must become conscious of our own misassumptions, just as we need also to learn of the assumptions another might have of us. Susan Rodgers, an anthropologist from the College of Holy Cross in Massachusetts, USA, talked about the value of mistakes:

> Researchers who are trying to think through how to do their own work with distant cultures often make their most useful insights from mistakes in the field. People should not be ashamed to make mistakes. Sometimes they are useful and illuminating, so if you do make a mistake you can apologize and sort your way through it. [In the end] you're probably going to learn more from that than if everything was going along just fine.

As I know too well, when our mistakes cause discomfort in others, we are obligated to apologize and adjust what we are doing and thinking. Most often, mistakes come when we least expect them, both when we are actually concentrating hard on border crossing or when we have dropped our vigilance and are not searching for the borders that, as Ian Anderson describes, may well be seamless.

Below are some of my earlier stumbles, times when I tripped and definitely times when I discerned my own cultural myopia. Though these events did not all occur in research situations, they did stem from my own enculturated layers of attitudes, behaviors, and beliefs that separated me from a clear vision of others' cultural ways of being, times when the theory of the world in my head needed adjustment and reformulation. In retrospect, I appreciate my mistakes as change agents, and I offer them up to you as examples of how easy it is to make misassumptions with good intentions.

Setting: a four corners, USA, grocery store

In 1993 I had been in Tuba City, Arizona for several weeks, working from there to interview teachers on the Navajo and Hopi reservations about literacy. When I arrived, I craved connections beyond professional contacts but didn't know how to make them. One weekend I was standing at a meat counter in a local grocery store, thinking about the prospects of a good but lonely dinner. An elderly woman in full traditional dress (my memory prompts a picture of velvet and turquoise) was accompanied by a boy of grandson age. She stood next to me as we both selected chicken. She said: "These look like they pecked around someone's door step too long." I laughed, so pleased that she had talked to me. Taken off guard by her English, I asked her advice about how to tell the age of chicken by how they looked wrapped in plastic. I turned to look at her straight in the eye, just as a proper mid-Western white listener should, but it was as if I had slapped her in the face. She turned back to the chicken and went silent.

My misassumption: I had read that direct eye contact might be offensive to Navajo people, indeed many Indigenous peoples. Julian Cho had told me that in Maya communities you "don't look at the person when you are talking to the person. You look away from the person, especially an elder." But there, out of the research context and in that grocery store, my own cultural patterns kicked in. I assumed that I was on my side of the border, but I wasn't. I had simplified this woman's identity. I assumed, given my own ways of being, that her English speaking friendliness, which I craved, was an overture to be relational.

Setting: near a game preserve in Tanzania

In 1996 I was in Tanzania, interested in interviewing at the local schools. My cousin. who ran a safari company, was seeking rights to set up a camp outside a game preserve and was negotiating land use in exchange for a new well in the nearby village. The Masai village chairman was delighted to accept the exchange, as a new deep well would solve health problems for his people. Aware of the remnants of colonialism in this democratic nation, I went with a troubled conscience to the county seat to assist in the permit paperwork. In a trail-worthy Land Rover, we picked up the chief, whose wife had handed me the gift of a chicken with its feet tied together. I held that chicken nervously the whole way. As if in a sort of royal conveyance, the chief waved at people along the route, full of good cheer. We finally arrived at the county seat with an hour to spare. Toddlers playing in the area stared at me until I wooed them with super balls, brought for just that purpose. We bounced some wait-time away, with brief intermissions as they touched my skin and felt my hair. Finally noticing that the chief was uncomfortable with this play, I left them with the balls and took up my "professor" role, sitting by the door with the other permit seekers. When the office opened, I finally walked toward the door, trying to converse with the chief. When the door was opened, I, in my Western female position, went first. I crashed into the chief who, in his Tanzanian Masai village chair position, was also going first. We were both surprised and diminished by the collision. That evening, the chief organized a tribal dance for us as something that might be offered at the future safari camp. Though traditionally they danced under the full moon, due to expected storms, the chief arranged for us to see the dance in the local school. The women had covered their breasts with basketball jerseys and even tattered bras from the local Good Will trove of clothing destined for third world nations. They covered themselves so as not to "offend Westerners" (I was told, that they were told). The men wore fierce lion masks and charged with frightening noises, all in the small confines of cement and thatched classroom, already filled with the noise of beating drums, carved whistles, and with the added contribution of thunder. The village chair explained some of the dances to me. In my concern for the loss of culture, I begged him not to let his villagers stop their dancing on the full moon just because they were dancing for safari participants. He looked at me as if it was none of my business. It wasn't.

My misassumption: As Hall (1973) said, "We are not only almost totally ignorant of what is expected in other countries, we are equally ignorant of what we are communicating to other people by our own normal behavior" (p. 14). My mistakes in entering a new culture were numerous. I didn't ask my cousin enough questions about what would be appropriate behavior for me on this trip. I was uncomfortable holding the gift of the foot-bound chicken and didn't know that I only had to say so. I didn't know that the appropriate demeanor of a signer of documents didn't include superballs. Then I carried my unconscious white ways of being, of privilege, into a literal and metaphoric door-entry collision. Furthermore, I had such heightened misgivings about cultural loss that I didn't fully realize the value of pure water to this community whose children often died of water-related diarrhea and subsequent dehydration.

Setting: in a Maya village

In the cool of an early morning, I hiked in from a bus stop on Belize's Southern Highway, through the bush to a Maya village and beyond it to the grass-thatched school buildings set in a field that was close cropped to keep the dreaded and deadly Tommy Goff snakes well away from the children. I found the principal's office, with its solitary desk and three-foot, three-tiered bookcase, which I later discovered held almost every book in the school. The principal took me off to interview a teacher and left. The teacher greeted me in Creole. She said something like, "Ah, so, you're the English teacher," and then left me speechless with 30 six-year-old children who spoke Kekchi Maya. A child tugged at my skirt and said, "Miss." I thought, "Good, an English word." I turned to the child and asked what English words he knew. He pointed at my skirt and said, "Blue." Colors, I decided. I grabbed a blue pencil, a blue book, and a child with a blue dress. We started. "Blue..., blue..., blue....Children, find something blue?" The child that said, "Miss," pointed to each object and said "blue" in English and Kekchi Maya. He touched the child's flip-flop next to him and said, "blue," and all at once the children were running bringing blue things to me while I was desperately looking around the village for the teacher gone missing, the principal, any handy adult. With no one in sight, we proceeded to yellow: a yellow flower in the weeds at the edge of the classroom, a yellow book (one of a short pile on the teacher's desk), and a school-yellow stubby pencil. Children ran for yellow things. Connections, I thought; these sharp little minds are making vocabulary connections, exposed to several of the 10 to 15 times they would need to hear the word in context to acquire it. I was beginning to be delighted with myself. Reviewing blue and yellow using children's clothing, we began on purple. A purple flower, a girl with a purple dress, sleeve missing. I said, "Find purple" or something like that. Did "purple" sound like the Kekchi word for "head to the bush"? I still don't know. All the children headed out of the classroom, across the field, and beyond the clearing. I was so dumbstruck that it took a while to realize that I now had to admit to the principal that I had lost 30 children. I trudged back to the office with the three-tiered bookcase and made my confession, but the principal wasn't the least bit upset, so different than in my world where the principal would have had police, school officials, and hysterical parents out searching. He laughed and walked with me to introduce me to the village alcalde (mayor) and to tell him that some of the "young ones" were sent home early for lunch.

My mistake: The lesson I learned wasn't just that language similarities and differences make for confusion. What I learned later in this event was that the teacher was reprimanded over the noon hour for leaving and was angry at me for that. I had a tense interview with her later that day and lost what might have been some valuable perspectives she might have had about Maya literacy from her Creole perspective. I don't know how I could have gotten out of this predicament unless I had known that her job was in jeopardy. I didn't have enough information to fully respect that participant for where she was at that moment. I did learn about the mistakes that one can make if one doesn't know the language of those in the communities one researches.

Setting: in a school, Maree, South Australia

One morning in 1997, I drove through the purple haze of the Flinders Range, at dawn. I avoided kangaroos, bouncing across the highway with their early morning business in mind, and passed eagles perched on rocks, bickering over the carcasses of rabbits. Other than these creatures, there was no sign of life, even after hours of driving. No cars, no buildings. Finally I arrived at a community with a few buildings, several satellite dishes, and a school. While the teacher arranged for lunch, I joined his students so I could tell them about Minnesota. I had developed a little routine about how one dressed for the cold, about bears, and about the proverbial water pump and tongue which had amused children around the world. I wasn't about to be as unprepared as I was in Belize. But an adolescent girl interrupted, saying that she knew someone from Minnesota. The others agreed, "Yes, Miss." I was flabbergasted since I had experienced just how far this community was from anywhere. Then she said, and I can duplicate only the gist of her Aboriginal English, "Do you know her, Miss? Her name's Brenda. She doesn't really live in Minnesota anymore; she moved to Beverly Hills, but she talks about Minnesota." I told them that Minnesota and Beverly Hills were even larger than Adelaide. She was very disappointed that I didn't know Brenda. Later I asked her teacher about this visitor from Minnesota, and he laughed saying that she was a character on US sitcom reruns (*Beverly Hills, 90210*) that came in on satellite, and that he was having trouble getting the kids to understand the concept of actors.

My mistaken assumptions: As Hall (1973) said,

We must never assume that we are fully aware of what we communicate to someone else. There exists in the world today tremendous distortions in meaning as men [sic] try to communicate with one another. The job of achieving understanding and insight into mental processes of others is much more difficult and the situation more serious than most of us care to admit. (p. 52)

My friends often call me "media deficient," so I didn't know about Brenda of *Beverly Hills, 90210* rerun fame. I had underestimated the worldliness of the young Aboriginal adolescent's knowledge and was at once thrown by the misconceptions she could have. It was hard for our worlds to meet. Actually, this began a very interesting interview with the teacher, a time when the corrections of misassumptions gave valuable insights. As Rosaldo says,

> The ethnographer, as a positioned subject, grasps certain human phenomena better than others. He or she occupies a position or structural location and observes with a particular angle of vision...By the same token, so-called natives are also positioned subjects who have a distinctive mix of insight and blindness. (p. 10)

My positioned blindness and that of the student brought the teacher a moment of humor, and this illustrates the complications of technology used between people coming from different cultural standpoints.

Setting: in a school on the Mikasuki reservation

One of my final interviews for the book *Collected Wisdom* was with a white teacher teaching at a Mikasuki reservation school in Florida. As I talked with her, I asked her what she had learned about what her students needed to know. She talked about her love for the children she taught; she was thoughtful, clearly concerned about what would help the "beautiful native children" to get along in the world. She said they needed to know how to act in the world beyond the reservation, adding: "More than reading and writing, they need to know manners, how to give a firm handshake. We practice firm handshakes in our class." I looked at her in surprise, and slipping beyond my usual non-judgmental listening stance, my mouth opened, and I couldn't catch the words in time that tumbled out of my mouth: "Perhaps we need to teach mainstream children that American Indians are apt to have gentle handshakes."

My mistake: At this time in my team's research, we already knew that many white teachers care deeply about their students, but, with the best intentions, assume that assimilation is their route to happiness. And though I later engaged effectively in more dialogic interviews with seasoned researchers, I'm quite sure this teacher experienced my comment as a reprimand. When does a researcher enter into a dialog and when does he/she simply listen? The teacher closed down in that interview, and I lost my ability to look further into her well-intentioned reasoning about why handshakes were more important, for instance, than literacy. And this raises an issue that will re-emerge again and again throughout this book. When does the researcher take what is proffered, and when does one assume a more activist stance in research? When does one simply contribute to the standing body of knowledge, and when does the researcher's privilege compel him/her to leverage the knowledge gained to benefit those researched and their communities? Researchers swing between allegiance and empathetic understanding, between critical detachment and empathy in the data gathering of the moment.

Caring and best intentions are not enough

When I was working with the South Australian Aboriginal Education Unit, Paul Hughes, an Aboriginal leader who made remarkable strides in developing culturally relevant educational materials for Aboriginal Australia, addressed a group of Aboriginal Education Workers from across South Australia. His topic was "Caring is Essential, but Not Enough." I've applied his title in relation to rigorous consideration of cross-cultural research. I care about the effects of my own misassumptions. The events above primed in me critical moments of reflexivity. Caring about those of a different culture during the planning and course of research is essential; nevertheless, work across cultures demands constant reflexivity and respectful attention. The narratives presented in this book can prime our own critical reflections about our planned and current research. We can all learn from the narratives of 70 researchers.

Overview of this book

This book raises issues in cross-cultural research by following the progression that research normally takes, from initiation to dissemination and action.

Following a discussion of privilege and the power differential between the researcher and the researched, Chapter 2 considers the initiation of research by consideration of who benefits, whose questions are asked, and how the participants' knowledge is used. It includes discussion of the tension between participatory research and more traditional academic freedom.

Chapter 3 looks at the initiation of research: at the generation of and development of research questions, at the initiation of access and agreements through collaboration, and at the complexities of managing the gatekeeping of ethics protocols and of funding institutions.

Chapter 4 makes the distinction between methodology and methods, takes yet another look at the values of qualitative vs. quantitative methods, and considers the juxtaposition of methods and the blurring of the disciplinary boundaries of traditional research.

Chapter 5 looks at the issues of identity, hybridity, and standpoint in all phases of research. It also considers language differences and discourse differences that complicate meaning-making transactions between the culture of the researcher and that of the researched. The chapter complicates the categories of "insider" and "outsider" in research.

Chapter 6 begins with a description of pre-entry knowledge that is valuable to attain before stepping into a different culture. It advocates entering a community as a respectful learner, discusses whether it is really possible to understand another, and continues to discuss varieties of cross-cultural research partnerships.

Chapter 7 focuses on gathering data while protecting and respecting participants and institutions, looking at the researcher—participant relationship, the maintenance of that relationship through care, and reciprocity while providing safeguards for the participant.

Chapter 8 explores analysis of research data and the ways in which researchers can collaborate in analysis with participants. Postmodern questions addressed here are: "Is there a 'truth' with so many positionings possible?" and "Can one really separate oneself from analysis?" Other topics include analysis as a layered process, issues of power in analysis, and ways of moving from data to theory.

Chapter 9 delves into issues of dissemination and addresses the imperative of sharing gained knowledge in accessible forms with those researched. It returns to the privilege that the educated researcher often has in mainstream society, and, hence, the imperative of using that leveraging action in implementing research for the benefit of those researched.

Chapter 10 again poses the question of how to do cross-cultural research with integrity. It speaks of the value of rich reflexivity of the contributing researchers as they talk both about the stresses that researchers are under and the remarkable richness of their cross-cultural experience. The question is re-visited as to whether researchers from another culture necessarily undercut the self-determination of those researched.

2
Initiating Research: Whose Question? Whose Benefit? Whose Knowledge?

As an Australian friend and I walked in Melbourne's Arboretum on the way to an outdoor family tea, she said something like: "You know, Americans are known for the way they ask so many questions. Would you mind asking a few questions of my family that I haven't had the nerve to ask?" And when we joined her family, I gorged on her brother-in-law's freshly baked scones, clotted cream, and apricot jam, enjoying that vestige of surface culture of commonwealth people while choking on those questions that would have otherwise flowed out in unprompted tumbles. I had no idea that it was so American to articulate any old question that was on one's mind, that some Australians perceived us as bold, perhaps rude, though my Australian friend would never have said that. At that moment in the arboretum, I realized that modes of question asking are culturally inscribed and, subsequently, I found that I was a better researcher when I asked as few questions as possible.

At about the same time I read Linda Tuhiwai Smith's book *Decolonizing Methodologies: Research and Indigenous Peoples*. Before this I had always fueled my research with my own questions. My research questions may have needed answering for the good of the "knowledge base," or for the good of a cross-section of people, or even for the good of people whose voices needed to be heard, but in my mind they were probably still my questions. I know that good research does come from researchers who are intrigued by the questions they study, but they are also privileged to pose research questions. As Mary Hermes, colleague of mixed Dakota heritage at the University of Minnesota, USA, said to me:

> There is irony in the fact that those with the time to ask questions are those who don't have to worry about food on the table, don't have to worry about being taken seriously by mainstream institutions and publishers. Academics have a certain privilege in crossing cultural borders to ask questions; research is an elite activity.

Many of those who have been "researched" have wanted to pose their own questions and to have self-determination over the questions asked of them, about them, and for them; they have wanted the right to ask the questions themselves and benefit from the answers; and then the right to access the resultant knowledge to use for themselves. This chapter is about power in research when it crosses cultural borders and about whose questions should be asked, about who should benefit, and who owns the resultant knowledge.

Researchers in most disciplines and many cultures are now listening to those whose voices have been marginalized in the past. Amongst the strong voices for self-determination in the seeking of knowledge are, for example, the Māori of Aotearoa/New Zealand. Graham Smith, Linda Tuhiwai Smith and Russell Bishop, amongst other Māoris, have insisted upon "kaupapa Māori research," which, as described by Bella Graham of the University of Waikato, New Zealand, is "more about attitude, ethics, and approach, and about the way you work with people than about methods," though enriched methodology is emerging from previously marginalized groups. Perhaps Māori people are in a stronger position for self-advocacy than others in articulating their research questions and positions because they operate rather cohesively, given their common language and the relatively small regional space of their two islands. Nevertheless, their message is reverberating and joining the other voices of those who have previously been marginalized. Russell Bishop, researcher at Waikato University, talked of connecting with the Māori side of his family and how his finding that part of his heritage had led him to think in new ways:

> Over a year or two, I researched the education that my [Māori] grandfa-ther experienced and what that meant to him in the sense of what he had then passed on to his family. I started learning about who asks the ques-tions and sets the agenda, whose voice is being heard, whose world views are being given a priority, and who has the authority to speak. At the time I had seen myself as accountable to the university, but the family members told me that they wanted the whole family to benefit out of the research. So my research started to change, and in my PhD, my first thing was to critique my master's thesis through five issues: initiation, and benefits, representation, legitimation, and accountability. I didn't fully understand those until I became positioned within a Māori world.

This chapter will use the issues that Bishop examined as an organization, but it will begin by examining how privilege has shaped research in the past and how it demands critical consciousness on the part of researchers in the present and future. Cross-cultural research involves political and ethical decisions about "benefit," "harm," and "care," but, unfortunately, decisions are often unconscious about participant care and policy implica-tions. A practice without critical consciousness (Freire, 1970; Giroux and Giroux, 2008; Willis et al., 2008; Giroux, 2010) can lead to unconscious, but no less culpable, harm.

Issues of power, privilege, and critical consciousness in research

Although I have long understood that I have had white privilege, it wasn't until the summer of 1996 that I began to be aware of some of its realities. My research colleague Tom Peacock came to Maine with his family so that he and I could work on *Collected Wisdom*. In the afternoons we went to the beach, but, after several days there, Tom's sons told me they didn't feel comfortable: "People are watching us." I assumed they were self-conscious. That afternoon the tide was low, so I led them around a point of land at Parson's Beach to a deserted beach where we were entirely alone. The boys were joyous and carefree in the surf, something I hadn't seen before. Later that week we went north to the Passamaquoddy reservation and to a nearby store. As I breezed around the aisles, I noticed that one of Tom's sons was being followed by store security; I was distressed with racial profiling of people I so respected. I had not fully recognized the privilege I had to roam in most any setting without scrutiny. Days after the Peacocks departed, a friend told me that he had seen me with some darker-skinned people heading around the rocks and wondered whether he should follow to be sure I was safe. I was shocked. Kendall's (2006) article "Understanding White Privilege" quotes Harry Brod as saying: "Privilege is something that society gives me, and unless I change the institutions which give it to me, they will continue to give it, and I will continue to have it, however noble and egalitarian my intentions" (Brod, 1989). Years ago as a woman in academia, I had certainly known what it was like to be without male privilege, and even later I was over-committed when women, scarce in academia, were sought after as tokens on each and every university committee. We were burdened with service when we needed time for research, just as academics of color are overburdened now.

Those who are privileged often know the concept intellectually but, as with so many things, when one doesn't hold power, that lack of it may be more recognizable. When one holds privilege without recognizing it, all seems right with the world. And power isn't always "white." In a Belizian open market, I noticed that Garifuna and Creole farmers and merchants held the stalls, and it was the Mayas who were more often positioned/seated on the road edge to sell their wares. Privilege is not based solely on white skin; it is wrapped into most social settings. There is, of course, gendered privilege, skin color privilege, sexual preference privilege in homophobic settings, able-bodied privilege, ethnic privilege, and class privilege, amongst others.

Colleague and sociologist at the University of Minnesota Duluth, John Arthur, suggested I check out social conflict theory as a way to think about power and privilege. This theory was generated in the realization that people cannot be happy if a social system exploits them or makes life uncomfortable for them. For instance, in the case above, the discomfort that the boys felt on the beach and in the store was based in a reality, though even if they had just imagined that they were being scrutinized, that perception would have been cause for discomfort and, perhaps, resultant anger. Drawing from Marxian theory, conflict exists between those who have (the 1% in recent lingo) and those who have considerably less (the 99%), between those who hold power and those who are dominated. Criminologists explore crime in relation to conflict theory (Quinney, 1970; Messner and Rosenfeld, 2007), but there are also implications in all social settings and interactions. Indigenous educators, for instance, talk about dysfunction as a result of internalized oppression (Cleary and Peacock, 1998).

In that social conflict theory explains the fact that humans cannot be comfortable in a society that exploits them or that has exploited them in the past, implications necessarily exist for researchers. Almost any research in social settings will have some participants who have less privilege than others, so almost every such research project sits on issues of power and the political, and even legal exigencies that support that power. Furthermore, researchers need to be aware of their own position of privilege. And if one begins research in communities that are differently cultured, one needs to be especially vigilant in recognizing and challenging power and privilege in whatever guise it takes and in whatever way it might tread on others.

Martin Nakata, a Torres Strait Islander at the University of South Australia who had just completed his PhD thesis, used a strong voice in articulating current responses to a long history of research dominated by the mainstream:

> We are trying to deal with the complexities, rather than buy into the corpus that wants us kept in the margins. We are renowned with characteristics of the disadvantaged, the powerless, the hopelessly situated, the colonized, the oppressed, the minority. Well, hell no, we are at the center of our universe. Don't keep giving us this baggage. We are in charge of our own space with an agency that drives us, not something that determines us to always be oppressed persons. If you see research as top down as structuralists do, then you rob us of our agency, effectively rendering us as powerless. And structuralists don't recognize the assets we actually bring: the knowledge, the histories, the experience of tens of thousands of years.

Voices of anger, both well reasoned and heartfelt, came up in interviews, especially from younger academics. Sarah Jane Tiakiwai, a Māori researcher, said:

> The do-gooders, the missionary [types], they are the worst ones because they are the ones that impose their own agendas with little or no respect for what you have to offer as an Indigenous person. I have found senior academics, non-Indigenous, who are recognized in the academic

community as knowledgeable about Māori things, to be alienating and also humiliating. They speak not on behalf of you but about you.

Many mainstream academics are now recognizing and articulating their growing understanding of the power differentials in research. Much of recognizing power differentials is about critical consciousness. Willis et al. (2008) bring Paulo Freire's seminal work to bear on the critical consciousness needed in research settings, noting that being critically conscious of power differentials is essential in collaborations and allows dialog about research problems and solutions (Freire, 1970; Willis et al., 2008).

In a discussion of Foucault's (1980) offerings on this subject, Lather says: "The various feminisms, Marxisms and minoritarianisms have long argued that to politicize means not to bring politics in where there were none, but to make overt how power permeates the construction and legitimation of knowledges" (xvii). Willingness to participate in cross-cultural partnerships and use of critical consciousness in that process work to diminish power differentials. A number of researchers have talked of the power generated when the researcher and researched can work together at a requested goal, the researcher bringing the needed expertise to the researched, who have both knowledge and need.

Considering the previously held power differentials in research, it is essential to be conscious and active in releasing the clutch of power and academic privilege. Privilege, though often accompanied by good intentions, has acted at setting standards, setting values, and defining the rightness or wrongness by which others' values are measured. For the best research, both researcher and community/participant, need to act with critical consciousness, to converse in identification of problems and questions, and to search for solutions, both in the research process and related to the research question itself.

Reflexivity is a word for the active mental process (used by post-structuralists; Derrida, for instance) as a way to deconstruct one's own assumptions, scrutinize one's unconscious motives and actions, or, as Spivak (1993) notes, to "unlearn our privilege." Reflexivity is a fundamental part of critical consciousness and a recurring strategy used by researchers.

Initiation of research: whose question?

Researchers have skills in developing research and in disseminating results to academic audiences. They also have their own interests in inquiry. On the moral high ground, interested researchers can conjoin their interests with those researched, putting control back in their hands.

As above, Stephen May, sociolinguist at the University of Auckland, New Zealand, talked about a need for more "bottom-up" than "top-down research," the pursuit of questions and answers that a community wants. "At a rural marae [Māori community house] out on the coast, we asked: "What is it important to know?" (The use of the word "community" in this and upcoming chapters refers to a group who have common interests, who sometimes reside in the same geographic location, and, amongst themselves, who have shared ways of being.) It seems simple, but this concept is extremely important, especially to those who have drawn the raw end of the power differential in the past. Though some institutional review boards request proposals before the researcher confers with communities, it is important to talk with communities as research is being constructed.

Participatory/collaborative research: a prelude to Chapter 6

In participatory research, researchers and communities join in developing questions, carrying out research, and often implementing action for change. And although this book is not only about participatory or even qualitative research, Janesick (2001) uses Csikszentmihalyi's (1996) term "problem finding." As Janesick points out, "In fact, qualitative researchers are often co-researchers with the participants in a given study, and the participants open up new ways of looking at the social setting" (p. 537). In the fields of social work and public health, for instance, researchers might use what they term "community-based participatory research" using quantitative survey research combined with qualitative focus groups to research a topic of importance to the community, combining information purposes with action for social change (see Delva et al., 2010 for examples). When researchers with emancipatory aspirations collaborate with participants in the initiating research, the power differential does change.

The above is just a preamble to Chapter 6's discussion on many forms of collaborative research that recognize the need for reciprocity and equalization of power in research.

Melding agendas: researcher's academic freedom and community self-determination

For some researchers the melding of the agendas may not have initially been planned. I have begun, as an individual researcher, wanting an answer to the question of how to prepare teachers to work well with Indigenous students in literacy, and I realized early on that I couldn't do it alone. In collaborating with Tom Peacock, an Ojibwe researcher, agendas merged, the scope of the research grew, the perspectives on the research grew, the value of the results grew, and I grew.

Opening yourself up to the questions of others is worthy. David Carey Jr., a historian from the University of Southern Maine, USA, noted the funding difficulties in research that begins with the questions of the researched, especially for the graduate student with a new topic in a distant region:

> To get a grant, it might be difficult to go in without some ideas about what you want to do. It would be really ideal to go and figure out what the

community is really interested in. That was productive for me in Chile, in the sense that I did a lot of listening to people, and in Guatemala, as well. I knew I didn't want to just go down and extract information but rather establish a more symbiotic relationship. You may go with a plan, but mentally you keep an open space in your mind for what the community is interested in and weave in those interests. Having been going to Guatemala since 1994, I can work grants in such a way that I allow community interests to be part of my research even if I'm not articulating that necessarily to the grantor. It is a relatively new concept for historians, this idea of a research agenda coming from the people themselves.

Though the best scenario is to start with the community's question and goals, the concept of open space that Carey raises is important if research is already underway or if distance and money keep one from tapping community interests in initial grant writing. (See also Lincoln and Gonzalez y Gonzalez (2008, p. 787) about graduate student funding for binational and bilingual work). As did Carey, researchers with continued work in one region have found ways to embed the questions of the community in continued lines of inquiry.

A Canadian researcher noted the dilemma in retaining one's own academic freedom in research when communities or research institutes maintain control.

> Pure and applied, social, biological, or political research, are put in the same bag, and we do not make any distinction, but Aboriginal communities want more applied and helpful, and utilitarian research. To the Cree it's an important issue. At this meeting the issue was raised, "How can we make critical research if we have to have that concern, if the Band Council will always set up the agenda of research?" In the discussion it is not a problem for them; it will always be a kind of collaboration. But for the researcher, it's a question of academic intellectual liberty or free liberties of doing our own research, which is called into question, and then there is the control of resource.

Academic freedom has long been a cherished right of the academic and has allowed questions to be asked that institutional agencies and other powerful entities might prefer not be asked, so the debate described above is an important one. A key feature of democracy is open inquiry, both in political arenas and in academic pursuits. Melding interests becomes a way to serve the needs of the researched and continuing with some freedom in scholarly pursuits. Nevertheless, in healthy and effective participation, the researcher gives up sole control.

One of the advantages of talking to many researchers is that they have weighed in on these complicated issues, such as the tension between academic freedom and initiation of research from solely community impetus (see more on academic freedom in Chapter 3), but in discussing "Whose questions?", melding agendas is a start, as is Carey's concept of "open space" through which researchers can go to sites armed with their skills, with parallel questions, and with resilience to the needs of participants.

If one looks at the long history of research, the relatively new use of the questions posed by marginalized groups is heartening. For those in the midst of research, it is not too late to examine where your questions are coming from, without necessarily rejecting your inquiry interests. Is it as simple as going to a community and asking, "What is important to know?" and "How should we go about finding that out?" And researchers still have to consider whether they go to the right person or persons to negotiate questions. Who best represents the community to shape questions, advise about methodology, and consent to research and partnership?

Representation and legitimation

> We, as Māori, have become an object of research in international ethnographies and anthropologies by mainly white men, by those we call Pākehā [paa-key-haa: non-Māori] in this country. The information written is not all wrong, their idea of going to observe other people is not all wrong, but it's about who gets to speak, what becomes the knowledge that represents the Māori people. (Liz McKinley, Māori researcher at Auckland University)

> The act of representing (and hence reducing) others, almost always involves violence of some sort to the subject of the representation, as well as a contrast between the violence of the act of representing something, and the calm exterior of the representation itself, the *image*—verbal, visual, or otherwise—of the subject... You wrench it out of the context of living life and put it before an (in this case, European) audience... What we must eliminate are systems of representation that carry with them the kind of authority which, to my mind, has been repressive because it doesn't permit or make room for interventions on the part of those represented... The alternative would be a representational system that was participatory and collaborative, non-coercive, rather than imposed, but as you know, this is not a simple matter.
>
> (Edward Said, 1985, pp. 4–5)

Issues of representation raise themselves in many chapters in this book. In initiating research, representation may be about *which* members of a community are collaborating in determining questions. When talking about participant selection, it may be *which* participants' information best represents that of the larger community? In analysis, it may be a question of who offers interpretation of the data. In dissemination, it may be *whose* voices are heard and, are they presented in a way that the community feels is consonant with their views of themselves?

One of the thorniest issues in cross-cultural research is representation. When you bring your skills as a researcher to a community, it is hard to proceed until you know the community well, until you understand the politics in the community, and until you know who is respected by the community and who represents the community and its best interests. All this speaks to the kind of collaboration that Said suggested above.

Said noted that our notions of the culturally different are shaped both by our experience and imagination, and by the prior representations of the group that have come to us from other sources than the researched themselves. Furthermore, the researcher (or photographer, or novelist) can have an effect on the way in which people in the future will view the cultural group. Our responsibility as researchers is daunting: we need not only to ignore past misconceptions that we have developed or that others have foisted upon us, but also to work on access, data collection, analysis, and dissemination to prevent misconceptions in the future. Collaboration allows a cultural check in all these phases of research.

Being aware of the diversity in groups that we, at first glance, might think to be of one culture is hugely important. Socio-economic differences, for instance, can cause more dissimilarity within a group than between the group and those without (Betancourt and Lopez, 1993). How do we generate questions when there is such diversity? To complicate that, we must consider the politics that are affected by our representations of others. Eleanor Bourke, professor at the Centre for Australian Indigenous Studies at Monash University in Melbourne, Australia, described Aboriginal concerns about representation and land rights, an area which has required research, in many nations, when claims are questioned:

> We can only speak for our group. If you were asking me very deep questions, I'd have to say, "Well, I don't know about any group but my own." If it is to do with political things like land rights, again the consultation process has to take place. For instance, when academics have made a personality known, but that person was not necessarily the right person to represent the larger group, the community has not had the outcome they wanted. There can be jealously and resentments. We had the Indigenous Working Group who were designated by virtue of the positions they held in the national organizations. The fact that 6–8 people were speaking for the whole of Aboriginal Australia about native title was strongly resented, but the other side is not to have anybody to do it at all. You feel those issues of representation no matter what culture you come from.

Beyond considerations of how people are represented comes the problem of knowing whom to go to as a legitimate source of knowledge that might further your inquiry, how to know who is the correct authority to represent a group, and with whom you should negotiate research questions and agreements. Linda Tuhawai Smith, professor at the University of Waikato, further complicated the notion of who is "legitimate" to give permission and knowledge:

> Do you recognize authority by saying, "Take me to your chief", or "Who is the expert [in whom] that sort of knowledge resides." For us knowledge resides in a collective society. It's not just in people who have particular positions of power. Women have knowledge, particular women have particular sets of knowledge, and particular men have particular sets. The people [that researchers go to] are most often the ones who are in power. Hopefully that view has changed, but I don't know. I've gone through that myself, asking minority people their views on genetic engineering, and you know they don't have a clue what it is, but they think about it, and that's a dangerous approach because you can shape what they think. They are thinking about something over here, and genetic engineering is over there. So the power of the researcher in interpreting the voices of the people and the response that they give is potentially incredibly dangerous.

Certainly collaborative research teams which include local representation assist a researcher in making wise decisions, and there are also academics with substantial cultural knowledge who are respected by certain communities. I sensed local trust in an insider and/or outsider researcher (hence someone I probably wanted to interview) when I heard respect in different people's voices for that same person; from researchers it was lines like "You should talk to _____, he/she is really accepted by the community," and from community members recommendations such as "I'd like you to speak to _____ (most often an elder) because he/she knows more than other people."

Whose benefit?

Vine Deloria in his book *Custer Died for Your Sins* (1969) is humorous though scathing about the work of past researchers' work with Indigenous people: "Academia, and its by-products, continues to become more irrelevant to the needs of people. The rest of America had better beware of having little quaint mores that will attract anthropologists or it will soon become victim of the conceptual prison into which Indians have been thrown" (p. 93).

Sociologist John Arthur talked about his concerns with larger entities managing research agendas:

> I am thinking about what I will call here "intellectual entrepreneurs" who formulate and provide guidelines for the formulation of research, powerful entities in the research process. The concept of "intellectual

entrepreneurs" could be aligned with sociologist Howard Becker's concept of "moral entrepreneurs" who frame the agenda for the legislative process by deciding what constitutes a rule, a law, a norm and the consequences of infractions. In both groups there is an identifiable in-group with the resource and power base and a well constituted out-group maybe with diminished power, resources, or moral authority.

Concern about "Who benefits from research?" can be focused on the single researcher or on larger entities that manage research agendas. For decades we have talked about "reciprocity." That term was all the rage in the debates that we had in graduate school, but researchers are talking about reciprocity differently now. Back in the 1970s and 1980s, most were talking about whether the knowledge and benefits gleaned were enough to justify the means of the research, and whether there was a benefit that justified the time of those you researched. Research was seen as almost a business proposition in which you got what you wanted, and you reciprocated in some way. But the researcher's idea of what was worthwhile was privileged, and it was they who made decisions about the morally mandated "payback."

Though collaborative reckonings of reciprocity are now more likely, reciprocity is difficult in cross-cultural research because the meanings about what is of benefit in one culture may be different in another. Researchers of the 21st century used more positive terms, such as "giving back" and/or "negotiating benefits." As Daryle Rigney at the Yunggorendi First Nation Center for Higher Education and Research at Flinders University, Australia, says, "I think those days when researchers walked out of communities without the communities receiving anything are gone or definitely need to be gone. In the decolonization process, communities need to see tangible benefit for themselves."

Negotiating benefits

Perhaps most important in negotiating benefits is that research, its questions and its possible outcomes focus on what Deloria terms the "needs of the people" and that the process of that very negotiation levels the power differentials embedded in research. Transparency about who benefits and how is essential.

The first rule of thumb that most researchers talked about was that the knowledge gleaned needed to be returned to the participants in a form that was accessible to them. Liz McKinley used a Māori word: "It'll be koha, I'll send off a copy for them to keep, a present. So, it's just that sort of notion of giving it back for them to keep." David Carey Jr., a historian from the University of Southern Maine, talked about negotiating benefits:

Key to me was the history of US-Latin American relations of imperialism, recreated by academics, by anthropologists, historians, and others, who went down to do their research and took their findings away. I definitely did not want to be a part of that. In consulting with different communities, one of the things they thought would be helpful was to have a text book at about a sixth grade level that was written in their own language. I was proud to write this Kaqchikel history book, giving back their oral histories in their own language. Many of the school textbooks in Spanish describe the Maya as being this great civilization prior to the Spanish invasion, then degenerative after it, a cause of Guatemala's backwardness. I didn't anticipate was their interest in seeing how my archival research connected with their oral histories, what contradicted and complemented it. The elders are the keepers of the history. After reporting back, there was a really interesting discussion, people essentially saying that this would become a requirement for all future researchers. Even folks who were illiterate were excited about the Kaqchikel book project because of their fear that many of the younger children were not learning Kaqchikel.

From researchers I heard the words "consulting with communities," "negotiation," and "transparency" in relation to negotiating benefits.

Benefits to the researcher

As researchers we know the benefits we can receive: achieving credentials, gaining status and promotions, and gleaning royalties. We also know, however, that benefits can be misconstrued by participants from other cultures. Joan Metge, a Pākehā anthropologist and honorary research fellow at the University of Auckland working in New Zealand, talked about misconceptions about researcher benefits:

> Most Māori don't know that the sort of books I and other anthropologists write don't make money. In fact, mostly, you have to either put money into it or spend an inordinate amount of unpaid time. Also, considering the difficulty of getting it through the publication machine and the small runs, the royalties are, bluntly, peanuts. In my own case, all the royalties for my books go into a trust fund for educational purposes in the Māori communities where I worked.

Just as those researched don't always understand the paltry financial benefits that academics receive from publications, many also don't appreciate the more substantive gains received in the form of promotions and raised academic reputations. If there has been true collaboration, participants will share in perhaps the most meaningful reward an academic receives: satisfaction from a completed project that adds both to the store of available knowledge and, even more importantly, to mutual understanding.

Financial and gift benefits for the researched: culture and gender considerations

When research is both collaborative and well funded, researchers are often able to pay all community members or participants involved in the project for their time. Indeed, in the agreement process, many Indigenous communities want to know how many research assistance jobs might come to a community; other communities may be less interested in financial concerns. But, funded or unfunded, researchers talked of many ways of benefiting participants. Adrian Blackledge, educational researcher at the University of Birmingham, UK, worked with his team to reward participants by giving their families vouchers for their favorite shops. "But," he said, "that is not the same as actually giving something back to their community, which we do as well." Researchers worked hard to find benefits for the community and, in some cultures, gift giving is of cultural importance. Fiona Cram, Deputy Director of the International Research Institute for Māori and Indigenous Education, said:

> We took an array of gifts to one state because we were dropping in on the same people again, so we said, "Which gift haven't you gotten?" We gave away boxes of Linda Tuhiwai Smith's books, just truckloads of them. *Decolonizing Methodology* is an academic book, but people wanted it because of who she is. At one stage I had a cabinet full of soaps and gifts of all sorts. For the ethics committees there's that tension between a gift and coercion. I get angry. A fifteen dollar CD is not going to coerce someone to do this research. How do we theorize that and convince ethics committees that gifts are important, that the way we do ethics is ethical?

Many researchers found that culture and even gender factors played a part in their decision whether to reciprocate financially. Roy Young, a researcher at the University of Belize, explained differences in the benefits his university extends for health research given the complex and rich mixture of cultures:

> With the Mayas, I was surprised when they asked what they would get paid. This question was not asked in other areas or by any other culture. The benefits of the research need to be made clear. How would you convince a Maya male to conduct an interview for an hour? He goes to the farm, comes back, he's tired. He has to spend this hour with you. We try to work with the local alcaldes [community leaders], let them inform the people that even though they are not going to get pay, it could bring benefit in the long term for their children and their community. For some others, the need for incentive is not there, especially considering focus groups, except perhaps for providing travel money, snacks, or childcare. The Creole group tries to be socially acceptable, and we find in a lot of cases they give you responses that they think you would like to hear

(acquiesence responses). And then for the Chinese, they don't see themselves as an integral part of the social fabric of the society; they generally don't want to spend the time, are more focused on time. A strategy to increase their participation is to use Chinese data collectors.

Considering the complications of any generalization about benefits, Carey, researching across the border in Guatemala, found that he did need to determine a financial reward on the basis of gender in Guatemala for oral histories, distinct from the survey research above:

> When I first started the research, I had some Kaqchikel research assistants, and they were clear that you shouldn't pay people for their time. These are histories and paying them is just not appropriate. You might bring in some bread or soda, but histories shouldn't be a commodity that can be bought or sold. This was very different than when we did the project with the women. Often they would ask to be paid because they didn't have leisure time. So, we were in a sense taking away from their work; whereas, the men, once they finished their work in fields, were at home relaxing. And at first I was sort of resistant to paying women because of what payment might do to the information. If you are paying people, they might give you different stories or tell you what they think you want to hear, but the research assistants did make a lot of sense to me in the end.

I asked Louis-Jacques Dorais, now a retired anthropologist from Universite Laval in Quebec City, Canada, whether getting paid for an interview might skew what or how much participants would say. He said:

> For some elderly people it's a kind of part-time job; they get interviewed by anybody who comes into town. We give them the fixed rate of thirty dollars for an interview, and we said it will be about one hour, and if it is a little less or more than that they will get paid the same price, so they will not try to keep going. They think, "I get paid, I tell what I know; if I don't know, I tell I don't know." Also we say in the consent form, "If after a few minutes you don't want to continue the interview, you will get paid anyway."

Celia Haig-Brown, an educational researcher from the York University in Toronto, Canada, at first negotiated publication as the basis of benefits, but by the time the publication was complete, the school personnel and parents had changed:

> We promised the school there would be a book. About a year went by before the book was ready. The school had been through a huge transition, and a new parent council was ensconced, and they said, "Are these

people going to be making money off this?" We worked our way through that, but it wasn't pleasant. I went back to the non-profit publisher and said, "I know you use the profits to feed back into your business, but this is First Nations. If you're making a dollar on it, you have to give them fifty cents." They would not budge. I said, "Fine, when this print runs out you can't do it anymore." I have never heard another word from the publisher.

Negotiating benefit was something that Haig-Brown had done, but players can change, complicating what you had thought was a tight process: an ethical and transparent negotiation. Nothing stands still.

Beyond negotiated benefits from research: reflexivity and conscientization

Sometimes researchers from the states come exploit us, and they go back to the states and forget all about us. What I have learned is to clarify the ideas. When you came, I thought, I can get a copy of your book, and it goes to the archives, but now I am thinking there is more than that as the end result because in the dynamic of research itself, I can learn a lot of things. And you come and the bread might rise or it might not rise, or it may rise one way and not rise another way. You can't control what I think, but you can make me think.

In the quote above, Ines Sanchez from the University of Belize reacted to past exploitation of his people by taking the initiative to make benefits transparent when a visiting researcher arrived, but researchers themselves should ensure this before research begins. Sanchez, however, recognized a non-negotiated benefit to be had in our interview discussions from the engaged process itself, something that I couldn't have promised. This particular by-product of research—the participants' own realizations—conscientization, as Paulo Freire puts it—can come from research that prompts reflection. When Sanchez was making realizations in our interview, he would often look up and off, and change his voice to something I began to call an "inside voice," one that reflected his inner thinking. I began to be able to tell, in interviews, when people were reflecting, as if they were no longer really aware of my presence, but thinking deeply about their realizations. In talking to Linda Tuhiwai Smith about this phenomenon, she recognized it and said:

When that happens, that's actually fantastic because you know as a qualitative researcher you're facilitating a process where they can reflect and be quite distant about it in relation to you, the researcher. I think that happens quite often, and I think that's part of the strength of qualitative research as an approach. It's a sort of dialogue, but on another level, it's this sort of a dialogue that the person is having with their own experience. I would say that's when an interview is going well.

Lugones and Spelman (1983) say that "Having the opportunity to talk about one's life, to give an account of it, to interpret it, is integral to leading that life rather than being led through it" (p. 593). Patai (1991) both acknowledges this phenomenon and sends a warning:

> I became convinced that not enough people are listening, and that the opportunity to talk about one's life, to reflect on its shapes and patterns, to make sense of it to oneself and to another human being, was an intrinsically valuable experience. But unlike those researchers who believe that this makes the interview a "fair exchange," where each partner receives and gives in equal measure, I continued to be struck by the inequalities inherent in the situation, both materially and psychologically (142)... When is the purported empowerment or affirmation just another psychological surrogate, a "feel good" measure, a means by which researchers console themselves for the real imbalances in power that they know—despite all the talk of sisterhood—exists? (p. 147)

Julie Canniff, who looked at cultural views of success, demonstrated multiple ways of "giving" that equalized imbalances:

> What was interesting for the adolescents is that they took my questions back to their families. One young woman said "I never thought of myself as bi-cultural, but having talked to you, I realized that I do intentionally shift between my home and my school, that I benefit from two languages, two systems, two religions." As she began to feel more confident about that, she became this extraordinary resource in high school and college to other young Cambodians. I think it also benefits her now as a social worker. After the book was published, I became more sensitive to the feminist perspective on "appropriation." I got a doctorate, a professional career, and published works out of their words. I had to find some way to give back to them that was meaningful. I spent quite a long time tutoring, helped Cambodian elders who were trying to become citizens. I helped the mother who was trying to meet the requirements for getting a subsidized loan. So there's a reciprocity as a part of my relationship with the family and community.

Caniff's participants were more than a commodity, and she realized that conscientization was a part of what she had orchestrated. There will be more in Chapters 7 and 8 about ways in which participants can be benefited by having their voices heard in dissemination and how they assist researchers in negotiating the meaning of data and in building theory.

Unanticipated benefits to the researched

There are possible benefits to cultural research assistants in terms of their learning skills that better enable them to navigate in the academic world or to later assist other researchers, but there are unanticipated benefits that others reported. Dana McDaniel, linguist at the University of Southern Maine, talked about one that she hadn't expected to those whose language fascinated her. Her treatment of Romani syntax together with that of better-known languages helped to legitimize Romani as a language.

My dissertation talks about German sentences and Romani sentences, about a structure that has since been studied a lot especially now by German linguists. And they all cite my dissertation. So you'll read these linguists all over going, "In Romani this is the sentence..." You don't have to tell a linguist that Romani is a language, but I got through to the others who challenged it. I think that's probably a contribution to the people.

Many other researchers who reached across cultural borders were surprised by benefits that were unanticipated in the initial negotiations. Those listed below might give researchers ideas for their own negotiations:

- supporting immigrants in learning English by giving them back their life-story summaries translated into English—Karin Tusting
- assisting Māori women in locating their own subjectivities by hearing others' stories—Tess Moeke-Maxwell-Maxwell
- honoring the request of elders who wanted a copy of the book for the local school—Joan Metge
- collaborating with children on a research project and film making for which they received "kudos" and credits—Barbara Comber
- using oral histories to establish legal evidence for land-rights cases—Liz McKinley
- having linguistic conversations with a Roma woman and hearing her declare to others with pride, "I'm a Romani teacher."—Dana McDaniel

Stephen Muecke, mainstream researcher in cultural studies from Australia's University of Technology, Sydney, found a way to celebrate the work of David Unaipon decades after it had been published under another's name. Looking back on his earlier research, he reflected on changes that he made as he discovered new methods of reciprocity: "I scoff a bit at my first fieldwork experiences when the Anthropology Department gave me a stock of chewing tobacco to pay people for stories." Some years ago he took "informants" on as co-authors and then talked about what he called "repatriation." Muecke said, "We found this manuscript that had been stolen by a white fellow and never published under Unaipon's name, so we were returning it to its own authorship and returning it to its own people in South Australia." Repatriation is catching on in other areas as museums return artifacts and even human remains to the cultures from which they came. Family friend and anthropologist Helen Codere (1970) repatriated masks and other cultural artifacts that had been given to her in the 1960s by the Kwakiutl.

Another non-negotiated benefit that researchers have managed to create is access to materials or opportunities for the participants, unrelated to the data that they've helped generate. Barbara Rogoff, a cognitive psychologist from the University of California at Santa Barbara, talked about the gifts of photos in Guatemala:

> I've gathered photographs that people in town have appreciated, putting them in the library, in the town museum, giving them to people, even photographs taken by other anthropologists in 1941. In working on a book with a local midwife about her life and changes in San Pedro over her lifetime (using earlier anthropologists' field notes, as well as my own field notes [Rogoff, 2011]), I went to visit another midwife in her 80s, who said that anthropologists who worked in the town in 1941 had taken a picture of her deceased mother. I thought I knew which photograph that was, and so I made 8″ × 10″ copies of it and brought it to her the next time I was in Guatemala, and she burst into tears. When I have access to something that's appreciated, not just giving a lecture on my research, it's such an easy gift. Several people have commented about the new book, which contains many photos: "What you're doing contributes so much to our history." That's probably more important to many local people than the details of findings of how mother and children interact, which is what I am interested in.

In other cases, researchers talked about providing access to resources that those in the target culture did not have: tertiary education for community members or family members of their participants (for instance, tutoring, assisting with applications, or searching for scholarships), and even material things for the community (hard-to-come-by office supplies or locally unavailable conveniences). Gifts like these come from the heart of the researcher, beyond the consent forms and other negotiated benefits.

The price of unmet promises
Some researchers talked of the risk of promising the benefits that they hoped would result from their research. Roy Young from the University of Belize said:

> An important thing is not to promise anything to the respondent such as: 'After this survey we will "build a health center" or "have better roads." '

We tell our researchers not to promise because if, three months down the road, you need more data, they'll say: 'You came here before, and we have no new health center.' We don't want to lose respondents' trust.

Thinking of research as part of an ongoing process is important to future researchers. There have been so many breaches of faith that we undermine our future ability with unmet promises.

Considering long-term benefits: applied vs. pure/blue-sky research

While sitting on committees that make decisions about funding of research grants, I have had to decide whether funding a colleague's pet project (for instance, on the ancient tombs of Turkey) should have the same priority as Aids research in an impoverished country. Should funding be allocated for "pure"/"foundational"/"blue-sky research" (different terms in different nations) when "applied research" is desperately needed? What are the short-term and long-term benefits of research and how should they weigh in? In Belize, Ines Sanchez noted: "Everything in this small country is determined by money. We need good valid research by which to make essential decisions. When researchers do projects here, the applicability of the projects needs to happen here."

Cross-cultural researchers who collaborate with communities beleaguered by dire local needs must give serious consideration to the priority of applied vs. pure research in the contest for funding. Eleanor Bourke talked about the university status of applied vs. pure research and how that plays into both funding and career issues. "If you are in a mainstream university, you don't get the same points for applied research that you get for pure research, which translates into dollars for your university. It is hard for Aboriginal people to break in as researchers because we want to solve real and immediate problems." Relating to education, Foley et al. (2002) note that researchers of color "generally eschew the positivist dream of a universal, 'scientific' explanation of ethnic school failure. Instead, they do policy-relevant studies often labeled 'critical ethnography' or 'action research.'" Aydın Durgunoğlu, a Turkish-born psychologist now at the University of Minnesota, was more future oriented considering the debate over applied vs. pure research:

I talk about this conflict in my experimental methods class all the time. These types of research feed each other. Your research may make something clearer, down the line. I love being part of the research community with everybody contributing a small piece to the whole jigsaw puzzle. The example I often use is: every car made now has the third brake light. That research involved people sitting in front of the computers, lights flashing, buttons being pressed, reaction time measured. I mean talk about blue-sky research! And now the knowledge from that is part of a bigger picture.

There is no doubt that the third brake lights save lives. Ian Anderson helped to put this controversy in some perspective:

> I have had to think a lot about research policy and development. What is a priority-driven research agenda and what is the role of curiosity in a priority-driven research agenda? Research is a critical set of tools for social change. The benefit of research is part of the ethical dimension: theoretical, blue-sky research vis a vis participatory action research projects. To me it is not about the type of research, but where it fits in a broader agenda. For example, some work done looking at genotyping of scabies/mites, you might think: "How relevant is that?" But for nearly two decades it was believed that dogs had been critical to the ecology of scabies, and there were dog eradication programs and prejudice against Aboriginal people in remote communities who had camp dogs, an important part of culture and companionship in community life. Then genetics research with scabies demonstrated that the scabies that infect humans and the ones that infect dogs are not the same species. That is the most brilliant piece of foundational, straight down the microscope research that actually had a practical value. In Aboriginal funded research, I want to see where that research project fits into a program that is really concerned about finding a health care outcome.

The applied vs. pure research debate will likely continue as long as resources are limited, but there is an imperative for clear negotiation as to the benefits to those researched. Perhaps most important is the ethic of attending to the *implications* of both applied and pure research when the research is complete (further discussed in Chapter 9).

Whose knowledge? Whose property?

The Western world's knowledge has held preeminence as the center of what was deemed to be known and true, but in the postmodern world it has been acknowledged that there are more than one culture's way of knowing and truth. Quests for absolutes and certainty are now tempered with an awareness of the complexity of knowledge and its different cultured and gendered conceptions (Foucault, 1980; Belenky et al., 1986; Lather, 1991). Furthermore, cultural groups act on what they believe so that understanding ways of knowing and culturally valued beliefs furthers our ability to comprehend human behavior. The Western conceptions of intellectual property often take an economic bent. But knowledge is cherished in different ways by different cultures; different kinds of knowledge hold different power levels and are protected by different degrees of secrecy. It is hard to understand what others value as knowledge and how they appreciate it without interrogating your own value systems surrounding knowledge. In postmodern times we need not be paralyzed in this relativism but should use it to challenge universals. Views of knowledge and property within a particular culture are different across generations as well, and researchers are hence challenged by what they don't understand and by what they haven't even suspected.

Generational loss

In communities destabilized by colonialism and its sometimes resultant dysfunction, there may have been a change in accessibility of knowledge and loss of the cultural knowledge previously held by elders.

There has also been a past misappropriation of knowledge by researchers, resulting in mistrust and pain. Perhaps Eleanor Bourke talked most poignantly from her own experience:

> Who actually owns the final product in research is a pretty vibrant debate. We [Aboriginals] were always giving up knowledge. For example, in the linguistics field, non-Indigenous people know languages that Indigenous people don't have any more, making Aboriginal people feel so bad. Young people don't know because we don't operate our own education anymore. My grandmother was an informant for a number of researchers when I was very young. Now that we are adults, we've found her voice on tape telling stories, only some of which we know, and talking about music and language. Someone else knew more than I and from my own grandmother. It's a very emotional thing, a demeaning thing, an angering and embittering thing. It's our language but the researcher's copyright. Now we have to buy this book. Ownership in Western law is a double-edged sword. I have explained to our people, "Well, copyright can be a protection because at least knowledge is written down," but in our culture it is still a misappropriation of knowledge. Knowledge is a group thing. Does any individual have the right to give away cultural knowledge? Something is not working here. We guard knowledge more jealously than ever before.

Recording knowledge for the young, to offset cultural loss, has been one rationale that researchers have used, but Joan Metge, a Pākehā anthropologist, set this and other motives in a historical context:

> When I started, my [Māori] mentors' attitude was [that] the more widely this [cultural knowledge] was shared and known, the more respect that would be taken into account by government. There was a strong feeling that the difficulties Māori were facing were because Pākehās didn't know enough. What happened in the 1970s was a young angry Māori resurgence of emphasis on the *Iwi* [tribal] identity: having a language, a dialect, a history, and knowledge, theirs and theirs alone. Māori

themselves became protective of their own intellectual property rights, not something I struck early in the field.

A new irony is the appropriation of ethnicity as a commercial enterprise. For instance, eco-tourism is currently popular. In the best situations it benefits a community in need and enables self-determination; in other instances an ethnic population recreates itself in the image of corporation; and in even other situations it most benefits marketing firms as they target an ethnic culture for a removed profit (see Comeroff and Comaroff, 2009, for an interesting discussion of the commodification of ethnicity).

Linda Tuhiwai Smith talked about the misappropriation of knowledge with another disturbing twist:

> The Human Genome Project has a sub-project using about a hundred Indigenous communities which are deemed to be self-contained. In the Indigenous world it's known as the "Vampire Project" because they take blood. Now it's our bodies and our DNA that get exploited because biomedicine is interested because these communities because have resistant genes to this or that disease. We won't see the benefits that come from this recent research done upon us, yet US, Australian, and New Zealand Indigenous communities still suffer from third world health conditions. Before it was being exploited because we weren't considered human, which was the 19th century. It's a different kind of engagement, but it's neo-colonialism. Are scientists naïve? They might have good intentions, but they operate on a principle of implied consent, that they have the consent of the New Zealand community to pursue science. That's hegemony.

It is easy to see why there is such anger and emotion over issues of knowledge and property.

In negotiating issues of property gleaned from research, from whom does one request permission? Ted Glynn, a researcher at University of Waikato University, further explained the communal ownership of property:

> Māori communities much prefer being approached tribally. The government would like a nice tidy collective single Māori body that would say, tell us what "the Māori position" is on this issue, and of course they resist that. While you could say the tribal Polynesian world views are similar, each tribe has got its own particular stories and positions. And Smith's DNA example [as above] is a really good one because giving up knowledge or [DNA] is actually betraying everyone that's come before you. The whole ethic is different. I might say: "If I want to give my fingernail for an analysis of the accretion of pollution I've been exposed to, so you [the researcher] can compare it with fingernails from people in other cities

around the world, I'd make that decision for me. But from a traditional Māori point of view, they are not just your fingernails to donate; they belong to the genetic strain straight back. And you can imagine how well many of our Western science communities tries to cope with that.

From just these examples, we can see how the gathering of stories and data, even the analysis of nail clippings, can entwine a researcher in a mixture of ethical dilemmas. Furthermore, transparency in research permissions and agreements may be occluded by cultural misunderstandings. Careful collaboration can enable the researcher to understand cultural understandings of property, knowledge, and permissions that communities may or may not give.

Material knowledge: the weavers

Susan Rodgers gave an example of what kinds of unanticipated infringement on the rights of participants might occur in relation to material objects:

Material culture issues are somewhat different than the intellectual property issues related to oral and printed literature. The [Indonesian] textiles that I'm working on are quite beautiful. I have these three student research assistants, and for the whole year they'll be the docents at the college art museum. They'll probably ask, "Why can't we make little postcards?" for, in fact, some museums do this, and I am going to let the students think through this. For instance, taking an image from Flores [weavers] and putting it on a tee-shirt to sell, would be terrible. Even though I am a consumer of postcards that I see in other museums, I think that the museum at Holy Cross shouldn't get into this kind of business because we don't have the formal permission from the Batak weaver.

Spiritual knowledge: the bridge

I first went to Australia shortly after interviewing an native teacher whose father had been the chair of her tribe. He believed deeply that if the new generation did not take up the spiritual and linguistic knowledge of the tribe then the culture and language was better gone than to have that knowledge available to others. Just miles away, an entirely different tribe even allowed their language to be taught in the local public high school. This was a lesson to me about the variability of beliefs, even in tribes that were close regionally, but it is also about the nature of knowledge. Whereas some Westerners are still translating the Bible into new languages with missionary zeal, some cultures feel their knowledge, including their language, which to them can be inextricably linked with things spiritual, should be theirs alone. In southern Australia I heard about a debate over the building of a bridge by developers in a sacred cultural landscape. It was distressing to many Aboriginal people but especially to the Ngarrindjeri women, who held spiritual knowledge connected to that land. A few years later, when I returned to that part of the world, I asked Daryle Rigney to update me on the issue of the bridge over which Western and Aboriginal values had clashed. He said:

The Hindmarsh Island (Kumarangk) Bridge has been built to increase access to the island from the mainland thereby offering greater opportunity to "develop" the island through housing, land sales, and the construction of a marina. The Hindmarsh Island Bridge affair was about power, "development" and money, in which Ngarrindjeri spiritual beliefs were questioned and "tested" for their authenticity in the non-Indigenous political and legal system. The testimony of the members of the Ngarrindjeri community and its oral traditions and histories were considered secondary to the colonial archive and print literacies. Citizens of our community were trying to stop the bridge because the majority of the women argued that the area was an important cultural and spiritual landscape for Ngarrindjeri. A smaller group of women said, "We don't know about the knowledge related to this site." Powerful interests exploited this difference in knowledge base. The state used the knowledge difference to fracture the Ngarrindjeri by questioning whether particular Ngarrindjeri women fabricated cultural and spiritual knowledge to prevent the bridge from being built. There were a number of inquiries; including a Royal Commission, one of the highest forms of legal inquiry. The women who asserted cultural and spiritual knowledge refused to participate in the Royal Commission because they would have had to name the secret "women's business" [sacred knowledge linked to physical space]. The Commonwealth Minister of Aboriginal Affairs placed a ban on the bridge for a 25-year period and commissioned a non-Indigenous anthropologist, who had a relationship with the women, to write a report for the Minister. Unfortunately, those documents were inadvertently sent to a Minister within the opposition. The Shadow Minister opened them and then distributed some of that private, sacred, women's business. The Commonwealth's ban was overturned, and eventually the south Australian state government said, "We have an obligation; we signed a legal document to say that we will support the bridge and fund it." For many Ngarrindjeri this situation led us to ask under what circumstances and conditions would we be prepared to share information to honour our responsibility to care for country and protect our cultural landscapes and sacred sites? More recently the Ngarrindjeri have determined that our strategy is to avoid situations where our knowledge is subject to tests of authenticity, not to rely on legislation to protect our interests but rather to enter into agreements through contract law to protect our interests. Each site of struggle to care for Ngarrindjeri *ruwe/ruwar* (land, body, spirit) needs to be approached individually—it is therefore situational, contextual and Indigenous community by community. What some communities would be prepared to share, others would not. It still is a sensitive point when I talk about the bridge and about knowledge some 20 years later.

The case of the bridge also brings up the issue of legitimation. As one beginning an inquiry, how do you tell who it is legitimate to go to in considering the acquisition or use of knowledge. Though crucial with sacred knowledge, issues of legitimation in regard to all knowledge needs to be scrutinized. Also, the case of the bridge brings up the issue of ethics vs. legalities. What was deemed legal may have been legal due to precedents in Eurocentric Australian law and courts, but what might be legal in one culture might not be deemed as ethical in another. Did the Australian developers take the high moral ground or just enough high ground to build a bridge?

The role of colonization in lost knowledge and epistemologies

In colonization, attempts have been made to assimilate whole generations of people. Though some culturally proud youth have attempted thereafter to reclaim cultural knowledge, as above, cultural loss has often occurred. Daryle Rigney discussed generational loss of knowledge:

> There is a point of tension because all of us are affected by colonization. It's a reflection of a long process in history, and unless you understand loss of knowledge and other things, research will always be hard. Always be hard. In the case of the Hindmarsh Island Bridge, the state was able to fracture us around a set of knowledges. And I argue that if we had broader sharing of knowledge in our community, if everybody had known this area was important to Ngarrindjeri women, regardless of age and gender, then there wouldn't have been an intra-Ngarrindjeri questioning of the source of that knowledge in the dynamics of intra-community politics.

Researchers and bankers both need to understand that rifts occur in colonized communities in terms of lost knowledge. Without being sensitive to the possibility of those rifts and without being aware of alternative ways of knowing and cultural epistemologies, misunderstandings can effect researchers' ability to work effectively. This awareness can also affect researchers' ability to find the right people with whom to initiate and collaborate and to find "legitimate" participant informants, both groups being those who can then assist them in knowing which knowledges may be made public and which cannot.

Unanticipated misuse of your research

No matter how hard you have worked to make sure that your research will do no harm, sometimes things go in directions that you hadn't any possibility of imagining. Susan Rodgers, who had carefully thought about the possible misuse of weaving designs in museum work, told another story. She held up a beautifully illustrated book she had written and said:

> This book came out in 1988, *Power and Gold*, about ritual jewelry in Malaysia, Indonesia, and the Philippines. It was not two years before fake copies of these pieces [she points to illustrations of jewelry in her book] were being manufactured in Bali and sold to unsuspecting would-be European collectors as the genuine article. Perhaps I was naïve not to predict that that would happen. I have been told that certain unscrupulous art dealers in Bali have copies of this book under their table and when a likely would-be collector person comes along and looks at whatever the person may have in the case, the proprietor brings out this book as evidence. You'd have to look hard to find dishonest researchers, but you've got a whole business community out there who are absolutely into fraud. Publishing field photos presents opportunities for fraud, even when we don't think of that when we launch into a project.

Such art fraud and other inappropriate uses of research will only multiply as knowledge is more available and easier to find, say, on the internet. We may not even have fathomed a whole new level of misuse.

Avoiding another round of colonization

Indigenous researchers are very aware of neo-colonialism in academia. Sandy Grande (2008) asks, "Is it possible to engage the grammar of empire without replicating its effects?" (p. 234). Denzin, Lincoln, and Smith (2008, p. 1) note: "By virtue of living in the Whitestream world, Indigenous scholars have no choice but to negotiate the forces of colonialism, to learn, understand, and converse in the grammar of empire as well as develop the skills to contest it." And Cannella and Manuelito (2008, p. 49) say:

> We believe that the contemporary world will continue to use the research-as-power construct. Rejection of research as practice is most likely not an option; therefore, reconceptualization is of great importance. The Eurocentric error that assumes that scientists have the "right" (and ability) to intellectually know, interpret, and represent others should, however, be eliminated.

Though initiation of research when it crosses cultural borders can be fascinating, constant reflexivity in the cross-cultural research process is essential. Whether next door or around the world, cross-cultural collaboration increases researchers' ability to think through the histories and epistemologies of others, their ways of being and the values that they hold, and it gives them a base from which to collaborate in consideration of questions, benefits, and issues of intellectual property. How do researchers do all this without replicating or recreating colonization? The prosaic answer: "Very, very carefully." As Daphne Patai (1988) writes, "Whenever someone is used as a means to another's ends, the dominant social paradigm is affirmed rather than challenged" (p. 36). Jo-ann Archibald (2008, p. 36) looked at the Western tradition and tried to move beyond the "negative legacy of research history":

> Ignoring or remaining mired in collective colonized history is like staying near the fire. Going away from the fire and finding ways to move beyond the history of colonization is hard but necessary work. Staying near the fire and trying to adapt qualitative methodology to fit an Indigenous oral tradition is also problematic because Indigenous theory does not drive the methodology. Finally, I figured out that in order to find an Indigenous methodology and address the aforementioned questions, I had to go back to the elders.

If the researcher is "other cultured," listening and planning with elders or collaborating with those of the culture who have access to elders' advice is an important step in avoiding another round of colonization.

Legalities vs. ethics

As Martin Nakata said,

> There is always concern about the rip-off of intellectual property. It concerns us deeply because we need to enter into the realms of the legal disciplines, frightening because you find yourself relegated into yet another domain you have no control over. We have institutionalized processes and protocols in universities for getting research work scrutinized to avoid exploiting people and intellectual property, but it doesn't stop others. Even in universities though, people can be very clever with their wording. People in research work, at times, have gotten around things by giving honorariums to participants to compensate for time and taking this to also mean the purchasing of intellectual property. This is a real concern for us all.

Some researchers bringing Western assumptions to research have "set no limits on what can be researched and/or explored" (Smith, 1999; Cram, 2001, p. 39). To be legal in research is one thing (and in an upcoming chapter, legal protocols are discussed); however, to be ethical, one must work hard for the cultural understandings in order to respect participants and their communities.

3

Getting Started: Questions, Community Agreements, Consent, Institutional Approval, and Funding

Given the increasingly multicultural nature of much of the world and the multiplicity of sub-cultures recognized within a culture, it would be unusual for a researcher to enter any research study without some cross-cultural issues being present. This chapter covers what one must consider when getting started in cross-cultural research: one's motivation, the generation of questions, establishing connections, receiving consent for entering another culture, and the funding to do so.

Examining your reason to research

As Shirley Brice Heath, indicated, examining one's motives for doing research becomes increasingly important if you cross those cultural borders:

> What is important in working where other people might say you don't quote "belong"? I'd say the first is to figure out what your motivation is. My motivation when I began fieldwork in the Piedmont Carolinas at the end of the 1960s was to figure out why all these white teachers and black teachers were saying they couldn't understand the "other" kids. I knew they'd grown up talking to one another. Why, suddenly, when we had a deseg [desegregation] order, could they not understand each other? This was a real language puzzle. I realized I had to research when Mrs Hinton, the black woman who took care of my children during my work hours, said: "You've got to help figure out what's going on because our kids are miserable." So the motivation came from the felt need of the local people and my own curiosity. The need in any long-term ethnographic research has to be other people's need, not my published article or book.

Motivation to do research can come both from within and from without. Intrinsic motivation can be fueled by curiosity and by questions that have haunted prior practice. As professors, as graduate students, and as professionals, we are also fueled by the extrinsic pressure to hustle through academic gates as fast as possible to achieve credentials or become tenured, or to accrue professional clout.

Unlike the intrinsic motivation underlying curiosity, motivation theorists (for instance, Deci, 1985) tell us that extrinsic motivation can actually decrease intrinsic motivation to get things accomplished. Extrinsic academic pressure, family pressure, or any other motivation that comes from beyond can be additionally burdensome. But, in fact, as researchers, we do research for complicated mixtures of both extrinsic and intrinsic motivations, the most motivating of which may be deep curiosity related to knowledge either needed in our field or needed for those we care about. When intrinsic motivation keeps us at our research, graduate students and junior academics are more apt to meet their goals of advanced degrees or tenure. Later intrinsic motivation, fed by intriguing research, keeps our scholarship active and sees us through to the dissemination of the results.

Lugones and Spelman (1983) call for cross-cultural research done from a motive of friendship. Rather than operating out of the motivations that can set the researcher in a dominant position, they say: "From within friendship you may be moved by friendship to undergo the very difficult task of understanding the text of our cultures by understanding our lives in our communities." This calls researchers to the ethics of care and reciprocity. When we cross-cultural borders, conscious and reflexive awareness of our impetus is the way to avoid the disrespect possible in our own unexamined motives.

Finding and focusing research questions

Curiosity is a deep human motivation for many kinds of learning. Michael Rosberg, an economic anthropologist and currently Director, Institute for Social Entrepreneurship and Equity, University College of the Caribbean, Kingston, Jamaica, talked about questions that came from his curiosity regarding human actions that didn't make sense from his cultural perspective:

> From the time I was abroad, I was consciously and emotionally affected by the paradoxes that I would see. [For instance,] the nuns would take a taxi and say to the taxi drivers, *"Que Dios le pague"*: "God will pay you", and then they would walk away. That struck me forcefully. Why would the driver simply drive away? The anomalies were interesting to me, and I assumed that there was logic behind what people were doing. Was there the assumption that the nun wouldn't have to pay the bill; God would? The assumption there would be deference on the part of the taxi driver, and she represented the church, and she was on the winning side. I didn't know what her assumption was, but that was my question. And on the taxi driver's side, why did he allow that to happen if driving was his bread

and butter? Perhaps he was Catholic, and that would explain it, or perhaps he was Baptist; that certainly wouldn't. It was yet another complex interaction that I was curious to investigate.

As Jerome Bruner notes (1990), if one is to understand human behavior, one needs to begin from the premise that human behavior is shaped by intentional states steeped in "participation in the symbolic systems of culture" (p. 33). This is what Schein (2012) terms the third level of culture in which shared assumptions are deeply embedded and mostly unconscious. As opposed to cultural artifacts and espoused values, the third level is the essence of deep culture that one acts from without being conscious of its presence.

Part of what is so fascinating about cross-cultural research is discernment of those symbolic systems and their effect on human behavior. Joseph Wood, cultural geographer and currently Provost at the University of Baltimore, USA, talked of another fascination he brought to inquiries that derived from his own lived experience:

> One of the beauties of being a cultural geographer is that you get to study using a remarkable disciplinary lens. We are influenced by events in our lives to answer questions that interest us. After Vietnam I went to graduate school and began to study American landscape topics. While I was happy to come home from Vietnam, and for a while after never wanted to go camping again, I nevertheless also began to think about how Vietnamese shaped landscape differently. The discipline I had come to make my own offered an intellectual lens I had not had when I was in Vietnam. At the same time, I have hundreds of slides of Vietnam landscapes that I took flying around in helicopters, landscape scenes as simple as rice paddies. My experience in Vietnam actually fed my interest in landscape studies without being consciously aware of what was happening. Now, I go back to Vietnam with a great intellectual appreciation of what I see.

Each discipline has its own interests and processes for developing research questions, or hypotheses based on those questions. For instance, in criminology one might look at criminal behavior as a result of the weakening of individuals' bonds to others or to their cultural connections with a social-psychological perspective (Messner and Rosenfeld, 2007), and, as above, as a cultural geographer one might look at the effect of culture on landscape. In education and social work, questions are apt to be more problem-based— for instance, about the effect of culture on educational, social, or economic success. In anthropology the approach may be more eclectic, entering a culture and "picking and choosing" a topic of interest or theory as a focus (Robben and Sluk, 2007, p. 5). Collaboration to seek transmediation between the researchers' expertise and the community's questions and local needs opens up new perspectives and adjusts questions before the research even starts.

As anthropologists tell us, being on the outside of a culture or community can enable the researcher to generate questions that those on the inside might not see the reasons to ask as they live with deeply embedded and mostly unconscious cultural ways of being. For instance, Rosberg's nun and taxi driver above may be so inculcated in the calling on God to pay fares that neither party questions it. On occasion it may be the "outsider" who is better able to see if there are inequities and call them to question, but then it's possible that neither the nun nor the taxi driver truly wants them called into question.

Lather (1991) talks about the importance of "recognizing systemic oppressive forces" (p. 4). Marilyn Frye (1983) uses the metaphor of the cage to describe barriers to recognition of inequities or limitations:

> Cages: consider a bird cage. If you look very closely at just one wire in the cage, you cannot see the other wires. If your conception of what is before you is determined by this myopic focus, you could look at that one wire, up and down the length of it, and be unable to see why a bird would not just fly around the wire any time it wanted to go somewhere... It is only when you step back, stop looking at the wires one by one, microscopically, and take a macroscopic view of the whole cage, that you will see it in a moment. It will require no great subtlety of mental powers. It is perfectly obvious that the bird is surrounded by a network of systematically related barriers, no one of which would be the least hindrance to its flight, but which, by their relations to each other, are as confining as the solid walls of a dungeon.
>
> (Frye, 1983, pp. 4–5)

What makes some insiders far enough outside of a system to see more clearly where there are systemic and metaphoric bars? What keeps others from a wide enough focus to see systemic oppression? In any case, focusing a research question far enough out to be able to see systemic dynamics of an issue or situation may be the real challenge for a researcher but perhaps less so for a cross-cultural team. Inadvertently extending Frye's metaphor to photography, Martin Nakata told me that disempowered people might not have "pulled the lens back far enough to see what is really happening":

> A study may be small in focus, but your own lens needs to be wide enough to be aware of the political and power influences upon what you are studying. We Torres Strait Islanders have a very distinct background from Aboriginals but similar histories, ours not as devastating as Aboriginals'. Aboriginals have really copped abelting from the early Commonwealth settlers. The conservative governments have been very clever, deploying

resources in a way that invokes division between our different Indige-nous groups, and we haven't pulled the lens back far enough to see what is really happening.

A process termed "photovoice" is an example of the process that a commu-nity might go through to identify their own questions and concerns. The participants take pictures of things in their community that bother them and use the pictures to analyze their "frustrations and hopes" in the com-munity. Presenting pictures in a community space for discussion might allow those in the community to come up with agendas for research and action. Using this process to "pull back the lens" may allow some communities to begin to see their problems in relation to more systemic socio-political and economic concerns rather than attributing them to individual or commu-nity failings (Jacobson and Rugele, 2007; Delva et al., 2010). As I talked this over with Mary Hermes, researcher of native language revitalization, she sent out a warning: "We know exactly what is going on. Don't minimalize our understandings."

In developing research questions, then, discernment of the systemic is, in part, about focus. One strives for a question that is narrow enough to be able to generate answers that can inform and be acted upon and, yet, large enough to take in contextual factors that might affect the dynamic, situ-ation, or event. To extend the photography analogy, the questions, which you generate initially, may need to be refocused as you proceed in the study. You may need to zoom in for a better view, but in doing so you might cut out too many of the contextual factors that affect the dynamic, event, infor-mation, or issue being researched. Too far out and the study and data may become unfathomable; too far in and the study may tell you less than you want to know and may be intrusive or offensive to participants. For instance, if you are looking at the spread of AIDS, doing in-depth interviews with the women in a society may only give a partial view of the scope of what is going on. Doing a survey of health officials might give you a view of num-bers but it might not give a full view of cultural dynamics and movement of individuals that imperil the population.

Researcher and educator Chris Winch from King's College in London gave insight into problem solving vs. problem generation. He talked about the then complicated grant writing linked to the European Union's attempt to standardize vocational skill qualifications:

> For example, the word "skill" doesn't really have a ready equivalent in German. And that's a very interesting question in itself. And terms like "qualification," which *look* the same, actually carry a very different cul-tural baggage. They are, in a way, substantially different concepts, even within the quite close Western European countries. In Germany, social identity is more constituted by one's occupation than it is in the UK. And that is a significant issue in terms of what a qualification represents. There

is political capital invested in this. Yet, as far as the [funder] is concerned, they don't want problems; they want solutions. So we're actually seeking funding from an independent charity for this work. But they, too, want to have something, which is of a problem solving rather than a problem-raising nature. I have a feeling that people have a reasonable idea of what the problems are, but there's a certain amount of preferring to ignore them because they're difficult problems. So I guess you are, inevitably, uncovering problems as well, even as you're trying to find solutions to more general ones: a delicate exercise.

Scoping out questions in cross-cultural research is easier for the more experienced researchers, like Winch, because they can spin off from prior research and refocus for more useful results. He is to be applauded for seeking another source of funding for what was needed. There is always the temptation to do only research that has the propensity for being easily funded.

Whether you are in the process of problem solving or problem finding, your first question or set of questions is not apt to be the final set. Revision or refinement of research questions occurs simply because questions and curiosities evolve, especially when researchers reach across cultural borders. Nevertheless, questions are the standard way to enter into research in social settings. Seeking the right question is a way to bring a research team into a dialogic collaboration. Hypotheses often proceed from questions. Sometimes a set hypothesis, upon which research is planned, limits what it is possible to see, much as the metaphorical telephoto lens might cut off contextual factors. In other cases, a well-considered hypothesis might be just what you need to limit variables for the purposes of your study, especially if it needs to convince those who will be convinced by experimental research.

Having questions that are generated and meaningful to participants can ease access to a participant pool. John Arthur has come up with a method to tap research impetus straight from immigrant/refugee communities:

I have gotten to the point where my preference is to be quiet and allow the respondents to formulate the issues and the subject matter. Then what I do is to come up with paradigms in their presence to find out from the researched subjects whether my categorizations are on or off the mark. Only then do I construct hypotheses or research questions to investigate from their own cultural prism to inform my data collection. I am able to step outside of their community by giving them the center stage, or what another sociologist describes as the front stage of the research enterprise. Then the respondents are not subjects from whom we squeeze information.

Working with individuals, as one does when gaining participants from universities, for instance, or from multiple venues, requires individuals to decide whether they want to be a part of the research process. However, in working within a community, one needs to forge agreements, collaborative agreements, in which all phases of the research are negotiated with community members.

Community agreements: an essential precursor to access

Coming to agreements at the community level requires developing face-to-face relationships, in the best-case scenario with a respected elder who can act as a trusted liaison in generating a research proposal, which then may be reviewed by a number of groups. This section will focus on permissions and agreements at the community level. In Australia, I talked with Eleanor Bourke who summarized what was needed in such agreements:

> Years ago researchers just went somewhere, did what they wanted, and our people were disturbed, angry. With a federal grant, we were lucky enough to have time to think about processes and philosophy about how people should engage in research. Each project should have some basic understandings: first, there should be an agreement that particular groups would be pleased to be involved; second that there should be an agreed-upon set of protocols; third, there should be some benefit back to the community; and fourth, if possible, there should be some development within the community.

Organizing research around local needs leads to productive and useful research.

Benefits, property, and accountability

Articulation of benefits, and agreements about intellectual property, need to be clearly stated in an agreement to eliminate hard feelings later in the research process. Furthermore, community approval should go beyond an individual approving research for their community. An individual giving permission may not necessarily represent the community or its best interests. Indigenous groups have been more effective in demanding accountability than multicultural groups in research because they are beginning to operate from an organized base, but in doing research with diverse and multicultural groups, researchers still need to take it upon themselves to build accountability into agreements.

Voluntariness

Most important, as Bourke said above, is the voluntariness of the community and/or individual. Since the Nuremberg Code, adopted by the United Nations after the violations of human rights by the Nazi medical experiments, there has been a demand that research be voluntary (Seidman, 2006). In cross-cultural research, it may be complicated for participants to perfectly understand what they are volunteering for, to understand the language/jargon in the agreement, and to fathom how the community will benefit and how the researcher will use the information. With accessible language and explanations in place (see Chapter 5 on translations), the community will more likely volunteer for something that is understood.

Clarity vs. miscommunication

Just when you think expectations are clear, if they remain unwritten or unapproved by the right people, there's the chance that they haven't been clear enough. Aydın Durgunoğlu, psychologist at the University of Minnesota Duluth, told a story of the need for written clarity in research agreements:

> We did an evaluation study of a transitional bilingual program for an urban school district. The assistant superintendent said: "Would you evaluate the transitional program?" So we looked at a first-grade transitional bilingual education program that had Hmong classes in the afternoon, and one without any transitional program. So the worry was: are they losing out on English if we take some time from school in Hmong? I sent the results off to the superintendent, saying, "Here are the results, and I want to publish it," because basically we found that the two groups were not doing any differently from each other and the one had the Hmong experience as well. But their research department said, "You did this research without permission from us." Because the assistant superintendent was the one who requested the research, I assumed it was approved in the system. They said "No, no, no, we didn't analyze your materials." I think I got caught in the middle of some turf issues and was unable to disseminate.

Community approval from multiple groups

And just as one needs to get clearance from regional oversight groups or community approval groups, as illustrated above, one might need also to seek permission from layers of groups within the institution or community one studies. Celia Haig-Brown, who was doing curriculum work for a First Nations adult school, said:

> I said to the administrator, "I'd really like to do my doctoral research here, so do look at how I do my work, and you can decide whether it would be okay." So I did ask permission from the administrator. Then I had to go to a directors' meeting, present my work and be approved by them. Then, I had to go present to the full staff and get their approval. And I had to go to a student meeting and get permission there. So they did let me in.

Given researcher anecdotes about problems that crop up if permission is not sought at multiple levels, Haig-Brown's patience in getting approval at multiple levels was savvy. Careful agreements with all affected parties delineating process, accountability, benefits, and dissemination plans clears the way for successful research and access to participants.

Beyond agreements to access

There is often a history that makes gaining permission from a community and/or access to individual participants difficult. As L. E. Rigney notes, knowledge of the history of research in the community is essential: "Anger is very much alive; therefore, connection with cultural communication, contextual behaviour, issues of representation and knowledge appropriation are pivotal to safe access... Practitioners who are involved with mutual respect can begin to negotiate misrepresentations, assumptions within the literature and the research design itself" (2003, p. 15). Many researchers talked about challenges in making connections. Eleanor Bourke had been observing this process for some time:

> You often don't know where to start to find good contacts inside the community. Often you start with a person in another group all together, and a chain of contacts may put you in contact with someone from the insider group. That's always the key thing to look for. You've got to be a bit aware that both group politics and strong family groups exist and not to act as though they don't exist. It takes time.

I found that both time and presence overcome naïveté. When I first interviewed native and non-native teachers for what was to be *Collected Wisdom* (Cleary and Peacock, 1997), I thought I had laid the ground work for permissions before even arriving at reservations and that I could sail in, ready to interview. I soon found that I needed time on site to make careful, knowledgeable, and sensitive connections. Knowing ahead of time the stigma that might follow one as a researcher, knowing the political position of the contacts that one has managed to make, and even knowing of the possible coercion participants might feel due to the power of the person who has been your contact—all these knowledges and more are important in seeking representative access to participants. More than once my research has been compromised, for instance, by the very place that I have found to reside in a community. When interviewing at a reservation school, I jumped at the chance of free rent in the home of a teacher, but I realized when I started interviewing that the teacher was unpopular with both native and non-native teachers in the school. Yet on another occasion I paid expensive motel fees as I resisted an invitation to live in a convent with the nun who was the principal of a reservation school, knowing full well the history of missionaries on reservations. As it turned out, the sister was much-beloved and I stayed at her convent on my second extended trip.

Many researchers had already learned the value of knowing about local language and gender issues in a culture to ease contacts. David Carey Jr., historian from the University of Southern Maine, talked about his increasing ability to make contacts and about the complications that gender brought to access to participants:

> The alcaldes' assistants [assistants to the mayor] initially would bring me back to these rural communities where I couldn't just show up. Later on, speaking the Kaqchikel language was like an instant connection. Teachers were also cultural brokers. Many of my assistants were teachers, and there is a tremendous respect for teachers in the highlands—a sense that, okay, we can trust this person because they are associated with a teacher. And later there were organizations, religious brotherhoods and sisterhoods, groups in the community, and I could branch out from there to friends and family. But as a white male and for reasons of propriety, I couldn't sit down and have conversations with women, and that was part of why I hired Kaqchikel women to do interviews for me.

David Carey Jr.'s contacts grew with language knowledge and with time in the area, but he sought an "insider" interviewer when his accessibility to participants was lessened by his gender.

Researchers talked about being ethnically similar but not from the same community, *iwi*, or tribe, or having such likeness but having their academic affiliation act as a cause of separation. We will come back to this topic when talking about identity (in Chapter 5) and those concepts of "insider" and "outsider."

Finding a question of interest to the participants when drawing from multiple communities can also open up avenues of access. John Arthur, sociologist of Ghanaian and Jamaican heritage, was doing research on African immigrant groups in the USA:

> If I take a keen interest in the activities of the community, I have found that people are willing to talk because they see that I see that they are different than the native black people. They welcome the chance to talk about it. And I have noticed that the more I get to know these communities, I find myself better able to understand the full depth of their unique cultural nuances. And sometimes in the narrative section of what I'm trying to present, sometimes I need to go back and seek further clarification so I don't misinterpret or offend.

Initiating collaborations in research can ease the process of access by having those on the research team with cultural connections able to explain resistance. If potential participants say "No," or if they say "Yes" and circumvent questions, or then use absence as a mode of resisting the research, the like-cultured member of your team may understand the reasons why. Of course, letting your research question guide the selection of research sites and participants is the route to follow (Heine, 2011, p. 113), but if the questions address local needs and collaboration is involved, the way will be paved for access.

Institutional ethics approval and review boards: beyond the community

When I first arrived in Adelaide, South Australia, in 1994, I was eager to learn more about how those from more traditional oral communities developed literacy. I had completed the Human Subjects Review (ethics protocol) for the University of Minnesota, and I felt approved and ready to begin my research. Yet those first few days were replete with disorientations. My hostess enjoyed my north—south hemisphere disorientation when the cold water was on the hot water side and vice versa, when I was awestruck when the water swirled the wrong way down the drain, and when traffic was going the wrong way down roads. But most disconcertingly (and jet lag didn't help), I was told the next day that I had to write two more research proposals replete with ethics protocols in unfamiliar formats, one for the state and one for entry into the protected Pitjantjatjara homelands, a place where white Australians couldn't ordinarily go. And I had to write these proposals on a Mac, which, given my PC-centric consciousness, didn't even have the keys in the right place. Graciousness on the part of the staff at the Aboriginal Education Unit helped me see that their interests meshed with mine, and I was impressed that Aboriginal oversight institutions were so careful in protecting their communities.

Institutional review boards' control over research: help and hindrance

Ethics protocols and written consent forms are those institutional and legalistic documents required of researchers which protect the researched by insisting on ethical approaches to research and which protect institutions from litigation. Institutional review boards (IRBs) become gatekeepers, in both the positive and negative sense of the term, for research that affects human subjects by guiding researchers through review processes and by controlling whether the research can proceed.

Researchers may have to fill out different forms for the state, for the funding agency, for a university, and/or for the research organization that provides oversight for a particular cultural group, and some have to add perhaps the most important document—one for the community itself. Every interviewed researcher honored the need for these documents, and still others valued these processes because they had come to see the benefit for themselves in planning their research. This was most simply stated by

Daryle Rigney, who was directing work at Yunggorendi First Nation Center for Higher Education and Research:

> We understand that it can be an onerous, but you need to be thinking about your project carefully and clearly; you need to be thinking in advance because of our history and the impacts of colonization. We need to regulate that research in order to be able to protect the community and to allow for the agency of the community to protect themselves to emerge. It might be onerous, but that's the way it is.

Though honoring the necessity and benefits of the ethics process, many interviewed researchers were frustrated. We will start with the benefits and then move to the frustrations.

Benefits of ethics protocols: sensitizing researchers and communities

Protocols have the positive effect of sensitizing both researchers and communities, of insuring accountability, and of structuring researcher and/or team planning. Writing documents to put before review boards (as well as funding agencies) can scaffold clear thinking about the research and prompt articulation of research intent and process. Furthermore, if researchers are lucky, there will be people on the committees experienced in working in other cultures or who are other-cultured themselves. In contrast with what was seen by some as the "big brother" stance, Wendy Holland, Aboriginal Australian researcher at the University of Western Sydney, who did a three-year stint on such a committee, recalled the way the committee had helped her prior to that:

> The role of UWS Human Research Ethics Committee (HREC) is not to 'stand over' and/or reprimand researchers but rather, to offer suggestions that will strengthen the research. Feedback and advice is offered to the researcher for their consideration. In most instances, researchers are appreciative of such support and will re-work their ideas and approach. For example, I had submitted a small project to interview some other Indigenous people. The HREC asked, "If something came up in the process of the interview that was painful for the interviewee, how would you handle it." I responded by informing the HREC that I would not attempt to act as a counsellor, but would instead offer the name and contact of a trained counsellor within the local Indigenous community that they could maybe speak to if they wished. Something else that I hadn't even thought about that came back from the committee: "Maybe you want to give the interviewee the chance to have another relative sit with them." And I thought, "Fantastic." I was really appreciative of that advice.

Many professional organizations that support research have ethics codes even though developing them may have been a struggle. Berreman (in Robben and Sluka, 2007, p. 274) discusses struggles that the American Anthropology Association went through in ethics development. Hence, he advocated "that paramount responsibility is to the people studied, the censuring of covert research, the principle of accountability for ethical violations, and the commitment to public duty rather than private interest."

Though the researcher's own reflexivity will best guide him/her in scrutinizing the ethical aspects of their work in progress, the most important thing about ethics reviews is that they "lead researchers to a heightened awareness of important ethical issues embedded in their proposed research" (Seidman, 2006, p. 59) before that research begins.

Challenges in individually informed written consent

In the application for ethics clearance, there is usually a requirement for the submission of the written consent form that will be used with individuals. Informed consent forms are usually designed to afford full information about the research to potential participants and to describe the guaranteed protections. Anthropologist Louis-Jacques Dorais said: "The university and also research councils that give their money have very strict rules, so we just have to follow the rules to prepare consent forms, and so once you have people sign the form, the main ethical problem is solved, and we are protected legally." It sounds simple, but a number of researchers talked about the difficulty of requiring written consent before trust is established. Wendy Holland talked about her research into her Aboriginal grandfather's experience with the circus:

> I have been faced with a number of dilemmas in contacting some of the descendants of my great-grandfather's siblings. I had this incredible experience one day when I realized that the sharing of my research findings was somewhat a healing for this distant family member. It was a very moving experience. All too often, research has actually worked to the detriment of many Aboriginals' lives and struggles. I maintain that whatever research I undertake it must be respectful and have benefits for all involved. In 'doing' family history research as part of my work, I would have to go through a whole consent process. But at this stage it seems premature in my relationship with particular family members. I might have to get permission a little bit down the track.

In putting ethical considerations before legality, a few researchers sidestepped the required process by doing oral explanations of the research and the benefits, and delaying the actual consent form until the majority of the data collection had occurred. One researcher said that he had researcher friends who, though he deemed them exceedingly ethical, knew that they couldn't possibly do fieldwork if they had to get somebody to sign a piece of paper first. And so they might give the form to them to sign after a level of trust had been created. This is an example of the conflicts between what is legal and what is ethical. Susan Rodgers talked about circumstances in which oral permission was necessary but for which her rationale was accepted:

> In Indonesia there's a political/historical reason you simply cannot use a consent form. Before 1965 the Communist Party was trying to increase the number of people on its rolls, and they would go into the rural areas where many people had never seen a letter or a questionnaire. They would say, "Come the revolution, the store downtown that sells the soap, you'll own all that. Isn't that great? Put your signature here." Unsuspecting peasant farmers in the hills of Sumatra would put their signature on the roster of the Communists. And then in a military coup, goons used the list from September until the end of 1965. In Indonesia, our State Department estimated that at least 100,000 people died in the violence. As part of my first fieldwork, I used a little questionnaire on kinship relationships. I thought I was being economical with my time, and I quickly discovered that it was just terrifying people who had been happy to deal with me before. The use of a typed questionnaire in itself was, in fact, frightening to the people I was talking to. So in concrete fieldwork situations sometimes you can't use texts where people have to sign their names.

This kind of resistance to ethical protocols by researchers lets us know that the process, at all levels, needs to be resilient to the situation.

Creating written consent forms in cross-cultural research

Written consent forms should give participants the same clear information about benefits, voluntariness, accountability, and rights that community agreements should include. Trimble and Fisher (2006) reported on problems they found in written consent forms: these were often written at three grade levels higher in reading than the participants could handle, the explanation of the research was often in jargon which might not have been understandable to the participant, forms had inadequate language translations, and, finally, they did not always make the right to withdraw clear. Guarding against these problems is especially important in cross-cultural research.

The researchers I interviewed talked about the need to assure cross-cultural participants that there would be a mutually agreeable time and place for research. Finding this time and place as part of the consent and appointment process, they felt, allowed the researcher to discern what was comfortable for the participant. Lugones and Spelman (1983) used a term "non-coerced space," but this meant more than just a comfortable place for the research to take place. Rather, they were advocating comfort between the researcher and participants.

Problems with ethics protocols and approval systems

Of course, it would be difficult to find people who would say: "We don't believe in being ethical," but, as already stated, researchers can get frustrated with these procedures. Most, however, have learned to work carefully, collaboratively, and respectfully through these requirements that satisfy ethics clearance. Nevertheless, when ethics protocols become duplicative and restrictive or when the legalistic parameters for research belie what is ethical or practical, these well-intended procedures can be onerous. Some have even given up research that crosses cultural borders, perhaps, as Patai suggests, because the researchers have lost their autonomy, a commodity "that is perhaps the prime value in contemporary Western culture" (p. 22). The most common complaint of researchers in the ethics review system was of the duplicative and bureaucratic nature of ethics documents. Rhonda Craven, Director of the Centre for Positive Psychology and Education at the University of Western Sydney, articulated the frustration of many: "We have just submitted an ethics application on the university's lightest form, 55 pages long! But it's not just getting the university ethics approval; you've got to go to other organizations. So I think we're bureaucratizing the ethics process." Paying attention to streamlining documents, so that the same one might be given to several agencies, perhaps with a few added questions, would resolve some of this duplicative work.

Many ethics approval systems at universities operate for all disciplines and are derived from Western constructs of legality in medical fields. Brian Street, linguistic ethnographer at King's College in London, commented on the inability of the ethics required of social scientists there to transcend their beginnings in medical research:

> All the ethics stuff created for the medical sphere has found its way into social science. With that said, I know we need the ethics. When you have centralized faculty meetings, a lot is dominated by the medical paradigm, more positivist, evidence-based. So when you start talking about ethics, you have to talk not about some universal but about a particular ideological framing. We probably need an ethnography of ethics. The central ethics committee says things like, "You're not allowed to do research in your own environment," and "It's no good asking to use video." It imagines that all research is like research on patients.

Continents away, Ted Glynn, a mainstream researcher at the University of Waikato, noted the inadequacies of institutional ethics committees in making judgments without fully understanding the cultures of researchers and research participants:

> In the Māori world there's this concept of *tautoko*, where individuals or tribal organizations may wish to have their support acknowledged.

There are times when it may be important to show that they have been involved, have contributed to, and endorse a particular piece of research. There needs to be room for these things to be negotiated.

A reasonable concern is that institutional approval is so bureaucratic and inflexible that it discourages even community-trusted researchers engaged in the social justice issues of our time. Situational considerations and cultural sensitivities are what committees need in resilient deliberations. Clearly, there is no one procedure that fits all cases.

Academic freedom vs. surveillance vs. protection: an argument for situational ethics

It was Australian researchers who started me thinking about the complicated conflict between academic freedom and ethics "surveillance," as Vicki Crowley, researcher in communications from the University of Southern Australia, called it:

> As I look back into the ethics guidelines for the university, I actually think they're incredibly restrictive, and, in many ways, the ethical dilemma for me is I think they are anti-ethical, antithetical to the way I would want to see research happen. They're into surveillance rather than enabling, and having said that, I am extremely mindful of the exploitation that's happened. Nevertheless, the guidelines don't recognize the importance of the intellectual life of academic freedom. But, of course, you can't just go out and do what you want to do; there does have to be ethical inquiry.

Philip Morrissey, Academic Coordinator of the Faculty of Arts Australian Indigenous Studies at the University of Melbourne, Australia, posed some related and poignant questions about research and academic freedom.

> I'm inhibited by the complexity of fieldwork and the amount of time it requires, the amount of consultation that takes place, the difficulties in satisfying all the members of the community. There are some problems, beyond time, as well. As communities, we have made excuses too long about domestic violence. National media has detonated it in the media. It is intensely destabilizing. If I had time at this stage, I might go through all the processes. You must be able to think freely, and if you realize that the findings are not ones that the community might want, I'd have to make the choice of whether I were just going to walk away from it after putting in a lot of time rather than present something that was compromised. When does it become a constraint on the freedom to think? I agree with Edward Said who said that once you make intellectual activity subservient, you might as well give up. The politicization of thought is the end of intellectuality.

Academic freedom permits research to go where the corporate world doesn't care to go, where existing power structures might not approve. That freedom is a check on power. Sluka notes (2007, p. 302, in citing Bourgois, 1991) that sometimes rigidly defined ethics and the purposes of those in power are "at loggerheads with overarching human rights concerns." In some cases, repressive and powerful groups are in a position to give or deny consent for research with the groups they have oppressed in the past. These are the worst-case scenarios of a convention that is supposed to protect human rights.

Research funding issues: with strings attached

Finding funding for research and stretching it to meet research needs is continually on the minds of researchers. This section will look at power and career issues in securing cross-cultural funding, maintaining ethical control of data, dealing with inadequate funding, and finding ways to research with minimal funds.

We can't ignore the inherently political nature of research funding in cross-cultural research. To return to issues of power in research, any institution that offers funding strives to maximize results from its resources while maintaining, perhaps, an image of success in serving people. It is logical that big businesses would fund research to keep eventual profits in their pockets, and there are other elite and powerful bodies, even think tanks, that support research and frame questions to support an ideological and/or political end. Grbich (2004) notes that "funding monies are in a position to control the research agenda in terms of both content and research approaches. Lack of continuity is created as researchers jump from one project arena to another in the reach to secure financial support" (p. 510). Swadener and Mutua (2008) decry "the cultural imperialism of research funding agencies, particularly in, but not limited to, developing regions of the world and their role in defining 'valid' (read positivist) research." Thus, in seeking to fund one's research, scrutinizing the motives of possible funders becomes important in assuring that the interests of research participants are still central. Funding that serves political ends may be aligned with participants' interests, but it may not. Seeking funding with the question "Who benefits?" is as important as it is in developing questions.

University research agendas ought to be purer in intent, given the usual commitment to academic freedom and the now prevalent commitment to social justice, but still universities depend on the overhead from the funding of big research grants from government and business venues. Faculty are rewarded as a result of their ability to acquire grants. This seems disheartening, but some researchers manage funding from Indigenous or multicultural funding groups, or from university travel, or other smaller research grants. If research is local, time may be more important than money; furthermore, many academic institutions give their faculty release time from teaching and travel support for research. Outside funding, with its strings attached, need not be the sole support for cross-cultural research.

Linda Tuhiwai Smith delved right into all aspects of funding with an excellent summary for less experienced researchers:

> It's not magical. There's an art to writing proposals and part of it is something you can simply just learn. You learn how to do it, and you do it. But then there are other things about getting research grants that are more about career: to what extent does this project lead to something else? How does it fit in with your life's work? To what extent does it bring in money but also bring in one big headache because you're doing contract research, and you don't get to be a free-thinking individual? In this new world you do best being mentored by a more experienced researcher. The pressure to bring in external money is strong.

In cross-cultural research collaborations there is also the issue of who acts as the principal investigators in collaborations. Often funding agencies want those with seniority and track records to take those positions, and in doing so minimalize the role of the researcher from the marginalized culture and, perhaps, create tension within a research team. And once a cross-cultural researcher or team contracts for research, there is the question of who owns the data. Does the funding agency own them? Does the researcher? Does the community? In protecting communities, this can become an issue. Barbara Rogoff said:

> I always resist sharing data from Guatemala. I share data with my postdocs and colleagues that I trust, but it would be easy for somebody with a deficit model to use the data that I have collected and do something damaging to the community with which I've worked. And I think it's my responsibility to protect the privilege they have given me. But some federal agencies are trying to make it so that you can't get grants unless you are willing to share the data. They tend to be thinking of the data in terms of property. They don't think about the impact on the communities, and I think that's crucial.

In contracting with a funding agency, these issues of property rights need to be explored. A number of researchers also talked about the power that funding agencies had to "bury" research that should have advised policy makers. More on this topic will be addressed in Chapter 9 on dissemination.

Inadequate funding can have many results. Some countries have little to no funding for research. In Belize, Julian Cho sought funding and research assistance from abroad to do mapping for the purpose of land-rights work and found assistance from North American and European sources. There would have been no funding from within his government, which probably would have preferred that work to be left undone. Researchers from impoverished countries are careful that every piece of research addressed a serious issue. There is also the issue of underfunded projects skewing the results. Jenny Barnett, ESL researcher at the University of South Australia, said:

> I was involved in a review of ESL for schools in the whole of Australia. It involved talking with students. We tried talking with parents, but the cost of interpreters, research assistants, and/or colleagues from the 94 different language groups here in Australia was prohibitive. Data was untapped for reasons of finance, reasons of management, reasons of time, and there was a sense of dissatisfaction for me in having to accept that and publish a report that did not do justice to the voices of the group, losing the perspectives and insights from those on the receiving end of the program and perhaps more useful action. We would be naïve if we thought that funding agencies didn't have their own ends in sight.

Of course, the value of having ample funding is great so that one can do more comprehensive work and actually pay collaborating contributors (Delva et al., 2010), but the cost may be more than financial, and all that needs to be weighed up by the researcher and the collaborating team.

Call for reflexivity and a morally engaged practice

> It would be dangerous and arrogant to think that there are definite answers to any of these ethical/moral questions. We need to discuss them and think about them in both practical and theoretical terms. Meanwhile, however, as all of us (without exception) wallow in a phenomenological swamp of signs and symbols we should not forget that our "informants" continue to be crucified.
>
> (Bourgois, 2012, p. 328)

In a way, research should always be composed of two inquiries: the one from which you want to gain information to answer research questions, and your inner, reflexive one that constantly critiques your own ethical and research process. When the protocols are complete, that is just the beginning. I conclude this chapter on institutional approval for research with an important admonition from Ian Anderson:

> There is a need for external regulatory mechanisms to stop really bad things from happening. But it is probably going to impact on the extremes, but I don't want that consciousness being shackled by a bureaucratic process. Not: "I'll just say it the way I think the ethics committee will pass it." I would hate to think that regulatory mechanisms would be

a substitute for being critically engaged in research practices. Do we stop making moral judgments in other parts of our lives? A morally engaged practice is one of the qualities of good research.

Cross-cultural research will continue to improve as researchers become reflexive in their own practice and as institutional review boards, funding agencies, and other gatekeeping panels become more flexible in their mediation between researchers and differently cultured groups, listening carefully to researchers' rationales for culturally sensitive approaches.

4
Choosing Methods

You shouldn't have a method and then go find data to match your method. You shouldn't have a theory and then go find your method and data to match your theory, and then forget, oh, by the way, there's a question over there. I favor methods appropriate to the circumstances, situation, and research question. To do otherwise is like thinking that every time your kid gets a briar or a thorn in his finger, you're going to take out a butcher knife. I'm known as an ethnographer, but I'm using multiple methods all the time to try to get different angles on the questions I'm asking.

(Shirley Brice Heath, linguistic anthropologist,
Stanford University)

Researchers who enter into the social settings of another culture come from many different disciplines, most often using methods related to their questions and methods that have proved useful in their discipline. Yet, in cross-cultural research, when one starts with a negotiated question that acknowledges local needs, there is the added challenge of finding methods that are comfortable, effective, and productive in that culture. This chapter will look at issues common to all disciplines as researchers seek methods in research that cross cultural borders.

When I first started researching for this book, I assumed I might find remarkable uniqueness in the methods that researchers implemented when they reached across a particular cultural border. In the first few years of reviewing the literature, I was surprised to find so little. Except in a few cases, cross-cultural researchers were using variations on the methods of their discipline, adjusted, as Heath notes above, to the negotiated research questions, to the ethic of care, and to the comfort of participants. Before traveling to New Zealand, I read Linda Tuhiwai Smith's book *Decolonizing Methodologies: Research and Indigenous Peoples* with great interest, searching for the methods preferred by Māori people. Later, Bella Graham, Māori researcher at the

University of Waikato, explained why I was not finding so many specific methods: "Kaupapa Māori research is not necessarily a method, it's more about attitude and approach and how you work with people. If you think of post-colonialism, it's not a methodology, it's more like an attitude, and it is proactive; it is about trying to reduce researcher in position."

Certainly the distinction between methodology and method is useful in this discussion. Willis et al. (2008) says in describing critically conscious research that "Our view of critical methodology (the philosophies that underlie research) and methods (the processes and techniques of collecting data) recognizes that inquiry begins with critical consciousness of the researcher" (p. 50). Methodology informs method, and though this book is more about methodology than method, this chapter will address some of the common themes in considering methods without focusing on disciplinary-specific ones.

Of course, there are intrusive and invasive methods that are anathema to humane research in social settings, but the interviewed researchers wished those to be methods of the past. Methods, no matter what the culture, are *not* politically neutral. As with all aspects of research, method choice needs to be considered, even scrutinized, for unintentional possibilities of harm or of misrepresentational results, but there are cross-cultural methods that pose little interference. Theoretical study of archival materials, for instance, allows us to discover that libraries and collections can tell us about those who are not of the same culture, though David Carey, Jr. will warn us later why there can be differences between what is archived and what really happened. Also, observation from some distance also has both unobtrusive value and limitations. Alan Kellehear (1993) describes the value of non-obtrusive methods: "safety, repeatability, non-disruptive, non-reactive, easy accessibility, inexpensive, good source of longitudinal data." He also talks about the disadvantages: "Unobtrusive methods are dogged by the usual emic/etic problems. This means that interpretation of physical traces or observations may be from the point of view of the stranger, or outsider (etic) and therefore may fail to grasp important in-group meanings (emic)" (p. 9).

As the research for this book lasted a number of years, I was impressed that during those very years, more and more researchers were developing research methods by taking their lead from elders in a community, and from collaborating researchers and field assistants, in deriving methods emerging from the culture's own ways of coming to know. Collaborating with those to be affected by the results and from whom one wants to collect data is certainly the best way to minimize the researcher position and to generate more useful and "care-full" results. Starting with a question and purpose, and moving to method selection is, of course, logical. This chapter starts with a consideration of more traditional disciplinary methods but moves to looking at recently emergent methods.

Weaving of the qualitative and quantitative with purpose in mind

Though paradigm wars of the past are still revisited in the present (Lincoln and Guba, 1985; Shavelson and Towne, 2002; Seidman, 2006), most disciplines have begun to see qualitative and quantitative methods as mutually revealing, especially in cross-cultural work. Qualitative and quantitative research can weave together to pose alternative explanations, and an ongoing process of investigation and self-correction.

Several researchers whom I interviewed talked about the preeminence of quantitative research in their university setting, and the difficulty they had in convincing some approval committees that their qualitative methods were important given their research question and the culture that they were researching. In my university, this battle has been fought, and the purposes of this type of research are now recognized and valued. In other universities, the full value of qualitative research has yet to be recognized. Researchers talked about different notions of knowing, and how quantitative research has held sway in past Western ways of knowing, seeking knowledge, and understanding the world. Though quantitative research might point out problems, qualitative research has a different means of understanding problems. Rhonda Craven further developed the values of both forms of research:

> Quantitative research often involves imposing a structure to what you are asking; whereas, qualitative research is often very open-ended in terms of what you can get back. The design of research surveys can actually limit that richness of responses that come back, but you can find out trends, very important trends, which I believe are absolutely fundamental to making advances in research. Qualitative research can help you take a look at these trends to work out what people are thinking.

Before the advent of easier transportation and multi-sited studies, qualitative, ethnographic research was often a favored mode for anthropologists who crossed into single-cultured settings. In looking closely at human experience, there is a need to understand beyond if something happens, why it happens. As Lather (1991) says, "The methodological task has become generating and refining more interactive, contextualized methods in the search for pattern and meaning rather than for prediction and control" (p. 72). This helps researchers to understand why there are unequal results given equal delivery to differently cultured people, especially in the fields of education and social services. In "experimental" inquiry, the context is "controlled" since it is seen as a distraction from what is happening. But that is indeed the nature of contexts: they affect how things go. To exclude them excludes a part of the reality.

Hence interviewed researchers saw the purpose and the question as defining the method or methods. Both qualitative and quantitative paradigms have results to offer, and both have weaknesses that can be strengthened by the other. When using quantification, the cross-cultural concern can be not so much about the method itself but how the numbers are interpreted and used by the dominant culture. For instance, at the US federal level, the elimination of all but "scientific" research negated the richness of information that qualitative research might have lent to the No Child Left Behind Act (Miller Cleary, 2008), especially in issues of motivation for native children. "Objective" data both deserve attention and require critique, as do qualitative data, especially when researchers measure non-dominant cultures on the basis of the dominant culture without regarding culturally bound values and socially constructed motivational factors. Most important in this discussion is the need to align method and question with the need for a consultative process between the researcher and the participants. In all research in social settings, researchers learn more by using multiple methods and studies. All research thrives in consideration and critique of research that has come before, the formulation of new hypotheses or questions, gathering and analyzing data, and suggesting further research derived from unanswered questions. The best research is that which doubts itself and re-questions itself.

Method concerns in comparative research

Though the main concerns about cross-cultural research in this book are methodological, there are aspects of methods which deserve discussion. For instance, a distinction in research in cross-cultural settings should be made between an "emic" approach to method selection, appropriate to working within one particular culture, and an "etic" approach, when a culture is studied in comparison with other cultures in search for universalities and specificities. Whereas in the past the single-site emic inquiries were more common, now, with easier transportation and more sophisticated statistical analysis, multi-sited fieldwork about cultural practices and problem solving are expanding in number (see Robben and Sluka on "Multi-Sited Fieldwork," 2007). Many of these studies use multiple methods, mixing qualitative research and quantitative research with quasi-experimental design.

In using that etic approach, one can't assume that one method, or methods, will automatically transfer to another culture (Greenfield, 1997; Goldstein, 2000; Cohen, 2007; Delva et al., 2010). "The etically oriented researcher approaches the question of a cross-cultural psychology from a trans- or meta-cultural perspective while the emically oriented researchers attempt to view phenomena through the eyes of their subjects" (Helfrich, 1999). As Helfrich notes, it is hard to establish independent variables given that culture is not outside the individual but is embedded within. Nevertheless, these studies are fascinating in their attempts to find universals in human behavior as singular from cultural specificities. Psychology and sociology often favor the quantitative method for its value in drawing inferences from analysis. Difficulties, nonetheless, abound. In participant selection, for instance, "Though culture is often an independent variable in cross cultural research, we cannot randomly assign participants to different cultures…In other words, culture is a variable that is beyond the experimental control of a researcher. This inherent difficulty makes it hard to evaluate causal relationships in cross-cultural studies" (Leung and Vijver, 2006, p. 443). (See Leung and Vijver, 2006, and Ember and Ember, 2009, for more on experimental methods of comparison.)

Furthermore, in all research, be it empirical or ethnographic, cross-cultural or not, issues of bias exist. For instance, in survey methodologies used in the social sciences, cross-cultural biases in survey development and the analysis of results are an important concern (see Heine, 2011, for a summary of response biases, moderacy and extremity biases, acquiescence bias, reference group effects, and deprivation effects).

When doing etic research, when one is unable to use the same methods in different populations, the problem of obtaining equivalent data arises (see Best and Everett, 2010, for more about this). Methods for one population cannot be duplicated exactly in another. This is a concern during all phases of the research process. Goldstein (2000, pp. 64–65) lines up some of the questions that researchers need to consider concerning different sorts of equivalence of consequence in all social settings: "Conceptual equivalence: Does the primary phenomenon being investigated have the same meaning in both cultures? Sampling equivalence: Does the method of recruiting research participants yield individuals who are similar on dimensions other than culture? Item or task equivalence: Do the questionnaire or interview items or experimental tasks that participants perform have the same meaning in both cultures? Equivalence of the test situation: Is the test situation likely to be perceived and valued similarly in both cultures?" (see also Leung and Vijver, 2006, pp. 444–445). Even when using the same method, the possibility of having that one method perceived in identical ways in cross-cultural research is slim. Some researchers establish equivalence by using comparable cultures (for instance, industrialized) or comparable populations (for instance, college students across industrialized cultures) (see Heine, 2011, p. 118). Matsumoto and Yoo (2006) talk about the progress in the development of cross-cultural theories. They note that though methods to measure dependent variables are more sophisticated, the methods need to keep up with evolving theory that looks at the linkage between culture and psychological processes. Given all these concerns, there is impetus for further sophistication in comparisons between cultures.

Juxtaposing multiple methods and perspectives

As above, juxtaposition of different methods and different perspectives is particularly important in cross-cultural settings. Researchers who have been working in cross-cultural research for some time have learned the value of multiple methods, both those that have been used in their discipline and those emerging from the research setting itself. As Tomaselli, Dyll, and Francis note,

> We aim to develop methods in situ, from the guts of our field experiences, not only to take predigested reified text methods "to go." However, one should of course also work with conventional approaches as they offer complementary analysis via different, related, lenses and cast light on what we think we are doing.
>
> (Denzin et al., 2008, pp. 347–348)

One method, then, can inform another, especially for those trying to move between dominant and diverse cultural groups (Denzin and Lincoln, 2000; Cresswell, 2003; Delva et al., 2010), and one method can inform the choice of the next method. As above, different methods answer different sorts of questions and satisfy different sorts of purposes, and, to extend the photography metaphor, different angles and lenses on the topic expand our ability to understand.

Just as researchers value multiple methods of inquiry, they also value the method of bringing in multiple perspectives to an investigation: different disciplinary perspectives, different cultural perspectives, different team members' perspectives, and multiple researchers' perspectives. Even a single researcher can enrich results with multiple approaches. Historian David Carey Jr. noted the value of juxtaposition of oral histories and archival material in Guatemala to recreate history:

> I spent eight months or so in the highlands doing oral history interviews because I wanted those to guide my research in the archives. And so the challenges came. I found things that contradicted each other. In the historical profession, oral history is still sort of poor stepson, not respected like traditional archival history, particularly with postmodern scholars saying memory is highly flawed. The Maya perspective for many of the elders is different. If you say that memory is so flawed and oral histories aren't valid, then essentially you are saying the Maya have no history. Elders were suspect of written materials when I came with information from the archives; they don't hold the same authority that oral history does; whereas, from our Western culture, the written word is much more powerful. So there is natural tension there and some good reason on

the part of the elders. Even in things like [archived] court cases, there were scribes who wrote it down, and there were translators, so you were going through all these different filters. So I was using the oral histories and archives, helping me navigate, getting to closer reconstruction of the past. Most historians will admit that you're just trying to get as close as possible to what actually happened because there are so many different perceptions of the same event.

Social scientists have long acknowledged that objectivity is rarely possible, that perceptions vary. For instance, Singleton and Straits note that:

> Social psychologists have demonstrated that we do not see the world simply "as is." Rather we learn to see. The light waves impinging on our eyes must be interpreted by our minds, and our interpretations depend on the sum total of our past learning and present experiences— including everything from our culture and language to our beliefs and expectations...Clearly, then, our observation, or more properly–our interpretation—of the world is inevitably distorted to some extent by factors not under our conscious control.
>
> (2010, p. 36)

When working cross-culturally, there is value in perspectives from "insiders" as well as from those outside the culture. Though researchers can consciously strive for lack of bias, multiple modes of acquiring data and multiple perspectives on it are so important. Even within the same-cultured group, perceptions are varied, and researchers have valued focus groups because participants weigh the similarities or differences between their experience and that expressed by others in the group, often explicating their experience in the process. Layers of articulation of experience and reflection are unearthed, juxtaposed, and considered in the same group session.

Liamputtong (2010) talked about the value of images, display boards, and music to prompt conversations. Other researchers talked about starting interviews or focus groups with individuals writing or listening to case studies and then beginning their dialogical process. Some researchers moved from focus group to more private interviews for talk about sensitive issues; others moved from interviews to focus groups to provide deeper probing for understandings and mutually generated solutions to commonly experienced problems.

Researchers needn't be strangled by multiple perspectives and how they play out when different studies show different things because, as Heine (2011, p. 142) says, "Just because there are alternative explanations for every study does not mean that every study is worthless. Each study still provides us with a valuable perspective; however, no single study can provide us with a complete picture." Having multiple perspectives on a question and multiple sources of data is one of the great values of the juxtaposition of multiple methods (Patton, 2002).

Blurring the boundaries of research

In considering and defining postmodernism, Grbich (2004, p. 18) says that "Any borders (disciplinary, research approaches, country and culture) are also constructions that can be crossed, incorporated or reconstructed." In cross-cultural research, blurring traditional method boundaries may move that research closer to important understandings. Mary Hermes saw the value of complicating the issue of methods. She felt herself "continually recycling thought, action, reflection, and writing to point to new methods and to new theoretical directions." For instance, in thinking out of the proverbial box, some researchers investigated "good" case scenarios to find strategies that were working instead of investigating things that weren't working. Researchers I interviewed from four different continents talked about analyzing effective social support institutions or schools for what was working well for non-mainstream people within those institutions.

In another blurring of boundaries, I talked with Jenny Barnett, a mainstream ESL researcher at the University of South Australia, about dramatization as a blurred method. I commented to her, "I suppose modeling after Freire, one could have participants dramatize the ways that they feel powerless." She responded:

> It would be a powerful methodology. If the community was willing and you could use that in research, it would be hugely powerful because their voices would be there, and the images would be there. What keeps happening is that we, as researchers, come up with questions, and questions in Aboriginal communities can be [perceived as] aggressive, so it needs a different construct for research. Through the Reconciliation [a nationwide attempt to heal the wounds and division between the Aboriginal and those of European heritage], stories have been told to different groups of people by Aboriginal people. That process has been documented, but in a way it could be part of the research process. Whilst it's healing, it could be reconstructed as a research method.

Practitioner research is another way in which the boundaries of traditional research, initially practiced only by those highly trained and qualified in research professions, have been blurred. Honoring and training practitioners as researchers has long been a useful staff-development strategy, but this avenue has also produced valued research results. Brian Street acknowledged the negative stance often taken to the research of one's own setting;

nevertheless, he and others have found different sorts of information being gathered in that very process. He said:

> In the notion of teacher inquiry, there's a difference between an ethnographer coming in from the outside and researching the classroom, as I've done quite often, and the teacher themselves learning the tools of the trade, doing ethnography, and researching their own practice. And one theme they argue is that [the practitioners] get a different kind of knowledge because, however much the outsider can problematize the sea they are swimming in, they can't have the depth, the 25 years. Your friendly ethnographer coming in is not going to pick up on all of that.

Practitioners in cross-cultural worlds are learning a lot about their own practice by blurring and defying traditional disciplinary boundaries of methods, and they have valuable information for others. They are also receiving training in seeing beyond their own perspectives to minimize bias.

Finally, when researchers involve community members in research, other boundaries usually established around methods are blurred. For instance, Delva et al. note the value in having tribal participants adapt survey questions "so that they would more accurately portray reservation home life" and having them "adapting measures to the needs of the Indian community" (2010, p. 27). More about participant involvement with data will be covered in chapters 7 and 8.

Wandering between the dialogic and the dialectic

In my research training I was told that listening was the most important factor in interviewing. "The more you say, the less you get from your participant." There is, of course, wisdom in that maxim. Except for asking some follow-up questions in my early research, that was the main path I took. In the interview study for this book, however, quite a few researchers talked about a two- or three-phased method of interviewing. The most common example was doing interviews, then giving the transcripts back to participants for revision and reflection, which precipitated a more conversational follow-up interview. Researchers described variations on this more dialogic method after using an initial research method. In cross-cultural research, this allows you to make sure you better understand an observation, or interview comments, or results of a survey, or a focus-group interaction, or an interview/focus-group combination.

Patti Lather (1991) talks about the move back and forth between positions, as she says: "evocative as opposed to didactic." Using dialog to achieve further understanding has become an integral part of more current research, and the research that has informed this study:

There is a dialectic between people's self-understandings and efforts to create an enabling context to question taken-for-granted beliefs and the authority culture has over us. There, in the nexus of that dialectic, lies the opportunity to create reciprocal dialogic research designs which both lead to self-reflection and provide a forum in which to test the usefulness, the resonance, of conceptual and theoretical formulations.

(Lather, p. 61)

In interviewing for this book, some of my deepest insights came when I wandered into the dialogic. Psychologist Barbara Rogoff talked of the richness of actually observing discussions between teachers and administrators. For her this became a method of developing research insights. So I offer you our dialog, which pushed deeper into the benefit of the dialogic:

BR: I realized in an innovative school how much richer the information was when I could be present at real events where ideas were being discussed. I interviewed the teachers about their philosophy, about how things work, and I got some good examples. But when something was under discussion in the classroom or in a parent meeting, it had much more solidity and meat to it.

LMC: You mean ideas discussed in the context of what they would affect?

BR: Yes, an example: one part of the school philosophy is that the children's motivation should come from interest in the actual activity and not from "extrinsic" means. And a lot of parents and new teachers have trouble with this. And so it's under discussion a lot, and I got very good interview information on it, people reflecting on it. Then there was an incident in which a new principal wanted to give the children candy for helping clean up the playground. There was a big disagreement between the teachers and the principal. Teachers said: "This is not appropriate. For one thing those candy wrappers are going to go right down on the ground, so they will have something else to pick up, so they can get more candy. They should be helping to clean up the playground because it's their playground, a place where they can play and not have gucky stuff all over it." So, the discussions were around that and around some incidents in a classroom where one of the parents was giving kids prizes for coming to do her activity. Those discussions had much deeper insights involved in them than in interviews outside of the context.

LMC: Is it the difference between what ethnographic research versus interview research can tap?

BR: It's more precise than that because in ethnographic research one might be present for those events, but I am talking more specifically about the *discussions* of particular principles. In both places they were articulating things, but in one place they were articulating them to me upon my request, and in the other situations they were articulating them to people for whom it was essential that they understand, a purpose that was different than just responding. So it's back to the purpose thing again. Doing ethnography gives you access to being in on such conversations, but it wouldn't get you thinking about the opportunity to hear principles being explained to a third party for a real purpose. I do not want to downplay the interviews but rather to play up the purpose of people discussing the principles. It could even be something the interviewer arranges, not necessarily spontaneous. It gets at something that we often miss in psychology when we do interviews only to inform us.

LMC: In the Mayan work, did you see parallels in observing discussions that gave you deeper insights?

BR: I haven't done interviews asking for complex philosophical stuff, partly because I speak Tz'utujil but not very fluently. So I am always working with an assistant who's bilingual in Spanish and Tz'utujil. I have been in conversations with people spontaneously discussing things; some of them have been very influential in my thinking. I was doing a study with toddlers and moms in San Pedro, in the US, and in a couple of other places, and I was struck by how the Mayan mothers trusted toddlers around small objects at around 12 months. US moms were saying, "Two and a half years before I would trust them around a small object." So I commented to my research assistant at the time that we were visiting a Mom's house, and video recording her and her daughter, saying: "It's really interesting to me how mothers here can trust the children with small objects." And my research assistant and the mother started discussing, "Well it makes total sense because from what you tell us, Barbara, your children ... [generalizing to US children in general, but they probably meant middle-class European American families] ... you have the children sleeping by themselves and that would lead to kids not really identifying so much with the adults, creating a separation. So they wouldn't notice stuff that our children, being with us all the time, would notice." They were also focusing on the affective side of things. "They know things earlier because they are around us, and we don't push them away." It was the two Mayan women talking about what they knew of US ways and comparing with Mayan ways. That was really an influential insight. Whether it's a true connection to make between sleeping arrangements and kids' understanding, I don't know, but it was really a thoughtful, interesting discussion that informed me, and it wasn't one in which I planned a question to ask. I had an insight, and they did, too. It wasn't something that they came already fully formed with, although they might have thought about it. They developed it in a conversation, and I got insights from the casual conversation.

The above was a conversation within our interview, and for me as researcher there was a three-layered dialogic thing going on. The third was a self-reflexive conversation I was having with myself over the very value of dialogic conversations. This was researcher reflexivity: reflexivity that Rogoff had herself over her dialogic research conversations, and reflexivity I had during and after my conversation with her. This becomes research method in and of itself. And thus I will use Shirley Brice Heath again, this time as a conclusion: "You have to recognize that you yourself are always the instrument of research. It's not like you're using the interview, or you're not using the survey or the questionnaire, the psychological experiment, you're not using the *anything*, you're always using yourself."

Challenging the traditional: emergent methods

> Indigenous scholars, in challenging traditional research methods, have adopted methods of their own. Their methods consider the whole person, that is, the religion, culture, language, nuances, spirituality, and other values shared by their people... The methods have a primary purpose to liberate and transform the lives of colonized/oppressed people... The purpose is intended to revive their people as opposed to researching them to "death."
>
> (Dunbar, 2008, p. 98)

Most interesting are newly considered methods that are culturally derived. Moving beyond traditional research methods that emanate from Eurocentric ways of thinking, development of epistemologically relevant and comfortable methods allows inside researchers self-determination, and researchers from without to evolve in their own views of methods when they are in collaboration with those inside. What has come to be called "emergent methods" evolve, allowing Western researchers to fathom the ways in which people come to knowledge in other cultures.

Indigenous researchers whom I interviewed learned from their elders appropriate ways to research in their communities: Russell Bishop, learning from his Māori elders how to go about research and dissemination; Sarah Jane Tiakiwai, continually conferring with her elders about the research she was doing; Mary Hermes, learning how to balance her academic self with her native self, taking leads from her collaborating elder in the process of simultaneously opening and studying an Ojibwe language school. Epistemologies regrow through local pursuits. As Mary Hermes says (2010), "Methods are more than the tools to collect data; they are also our reciprocal responses to marginalized communities, responses that have the power to interrupt and intervene in previously invisible forms of Whiteness that have historically shaped research." In *Indigenous storywork: Educating the heart, mind, body and spirit*, Archibald models ways to work in resistance to the traditional, and with sensitivity to community guidance, in developing methods. Noting that elders want to be involved, she advocates listening before questioning. Some of her chapter headings say it all: "Taking direction from elders" (p. 37) and "Establishing a relationship" (p. 52). She finds that the first step is "understanding the 'old philosophies'" and then applying those to her research methods. Denzin et al. (2008, p. x) suggest a list of Indigenous methods of both dissemination and inquiry: "autoethnography, narrative, oral/life history and performance studies, among others." "These performances create the space for critical, collaborative, dialogical work. They bring researchers and their research participants into a shared, critical space, a space where the work of resistance, critique, and empowerment can occur" (p. 5). Allowing for self-determination, Delva et al. (2010) describe the work of Morgan et al. (2008) utilizing the native of "talking circles" as a way of generating research using emergent design. This process allowed focus groups, with a research field assistant, to meet to initiate a plan for subsequent groups, allowing that initial group to actually generate the future focus group design.

Aside from researchers who are "from the culture," those who come in collaboration with those of the culture have taken leads from cultural insiders to adjust traditional ways of collecting data. Experimenting with new methods and then critiquing the results with participants is a strategy that helps all researchers to move forward in both challenging and varying traditional methods and generating new ones.

Though Indigenous researchers have taken (and should take) a lead in developing community-sensitive methods for research, other researchers talked about reflexivity, and then flexibility, when their mind, at its critical best, unearthed problems in the methods used with culturally different populations. For example, in surveys, some researchers realized that rapid-fire questions weren't working and found that slower and sometimes repeated questions had better results. Others found that surveys, though understood by Western cultures and industrialized cities, made for resistance in other cultures to the survey itself. Some cultures may be resistant to formal questioning but may feel comfortable with discussion. Other cultures may be resistant to discussing personal topics or opinions with strangers or those of the opposite gender (see also Greenfield, 1997, cited in Heine, 2011).

Seeking new methods to generate knowledge can be modeled after a community's ways of knowing sometimes through such things as storytelling, dance, drama, other media, or ways as Liamputtong (2010) says to "break through silenced experience of participants." Researchers can take their lead from the context and situations, using reflexivity as a method to determine the research method. In the example below, Larry Knopp gave an example of being conscientiously rebellious with traditional methods of geography when they weren't right for his purpose and population:

It's really hard to see lesbian couples in a census because there are generally fewer same-sex female couples who respond than same-sex male couples. And female couples are a bit less heavily concentrated spatially than the same sex male couples, so you have to vary the scale. You can explain it in terms of the cost of housing and other economics, but if you set the standard of comparison at some other scale, like that of the western United States, then you can start to see much more heavy concentrations in certain parts of Seattle where they don't look that concentrated at first glance. The usual standard is that things should be comparable, that if you have a map of Seattle and you're looking at concentrations, those concentrations should be relative to the city overall as the most sensible scale. We said, "But if our objective of making this map is to locate same sex couples, then you may have to violate some of those cartographic conventions," a huge violation of a standard protocol. Our purpose is explicitly political. Ethically, we think they're great ethics. I don't think I sent the article to any traditional cartographic statisticians for review because they would've said: "You can't do that." However, the paper deliberately violating fundamental protocols of cartograhpic method was well received in a population geography journal. We challenged the dominant mentality as heterosexist, heterocentric. To me probably the central issue is power, and the role of researcher is itself a power play. And it's a place of privilege. And to me the question is how do I negotiate that in a way that doesn't abdicate my ethical responsibility? How do I negotiate that in a way so that I can sleep at night? I mean it is a challenge. And lots of times when I don't sleep that well it's because I haven't figured what's wrong.

And that is just the wonder and disquiet of being a researcher. Sometimes you luxuriate in insight, in the learning about yourself and others from being in the richness of juxtaposed cultures, and yet, at the same time the process of disturbing the traditional can be disconcerting, even troubling. Not following a divergent path might make it hard to sleep at night. Knopp and his colleague had the courage to write an article critiquing a traditional method, providing rationale for their departure. Such articles are more and more interesting to editors as they challenge the narrow ways of viewing things that don't tell the whole truth. Challenging traditional epistemologies and developing methods as a result can bring us beyond previously canned and solely Eurocentric ways of thinking and methods.

The power of narrative

Daryle Rigney talked about the value of reporting lived experience as agency and as a liberatory epistemology validating the experiences of those who have lived it. He said: "A common similarity found within Indigenous and feminist theorizing is that of lived experiences...enabling researchers to speak on the basis of these experiences. They are powerful instruments by which to measure equality and social justice of society." Additionally, Soin and Scheytt (2006) discuss the merits of narrative in reporting the embedded nature of organizations, a methodology that adds a complementary approach in cross-cultural understandings. Jenny Bartlett from the University of South Australia described story gathering, which she suggested as a research method, but also as a means to understanding the lived experience of others:

> We sat around a fire in the community center in Freemantle with a number of Aboriginal people, who told their stories one by one, the stories of being forced to camp outside the town, of taking kids into school and being told they couldn't go to that school, or they could sit in the back row, with the white children who were being punished. They needed a lot of courage to tell their stories. There was government funding for these activities all over the country to help the process of reconciliation, and Aboriginal people saw one of the key factors was they hadn't been heard. And others hadn't felt the pain and the anguish of their stories, heard them talk in the ways that the suffering was visible. And some white people in the audience would tell their stories, one from an adult who told how she felt as an eight-year old when a grandad has let the dog go bite the heels of the Aboriginal people walking. You then had some white peoples' anguish as well, which was very moving to the Aboriginal people. The exchange of pain. Then whites who said, "I didn't know," and "I hadn't opened my ears to find out."

We have long known the power of narrative to open the minds and hearts of others. Life histories, oral histories (as collected through in-depth interviews), written narratives, even dramatizations and storytelling can generate powerful data. Timothy Black (2009) in his book *When a heart turns rock solid* used sociological storytelling, a method "to connect the inner life of individuals to larger social historical structures" (p. xii). He tells the stories of three Puerto Rican brothers and how they are affected by systemic sociological influences on their lives.

Narratives can also add to information *about* cultural universalities and specificities (Soin and Scheytt, 2006). As researchers above noted, quantitative methods may elucidate the trends, but qualitative methods can explain why someone's experience of something affects what they do or don't do. From a phenomenological perspective, the meaning that we make of our experience affects the way we act (Seidman, 2006).

Narratives have the added value of allowing empathy to disrupt established perspectives and oppression, enabling recipients to see through the other's perspective, helping them past ethnocentric stances. Historians, as exemplified in our quotes from David Carey Jr., have found oral histories a useful method in transecting, complicating, or verifying archival historical records. Furthermore, the collection of oral histories and other interview material has the added benefit of valuing participants as integral to the research process. The co-construction of narratives—a means of having the researcher tap narratives of participants and then having participants share in shaping them for dissemination—is a procedure that is often used in current qualitative research and is further discussed in chapters 7 and 9. Anthropologists are more and more involved in the co-production of ethnographic results in narratives and other texts. "There was a shift in emphasis from participant observation to the observation of participation," a "representational transformation" (Robben, 2007, p. 19 quoting Tedlock, 1991, p. 78). Culturally derived methods are a new and exciting development.

The last two chapters have been about getting started in research. I would like to summarize what most researchers said about getting started by leaving you with some of my own lived experience. Years ago, during hearings over the appointment of Clarence Thomas to the US Supreme Court, the University Budget Committee, for which I was the token woman, had just ended its meeting. At the time, Thomas's candidacy was being challenged by Anita Hill, who had declared some of his workplace behavior to be harassment. It was an interesting moment in US history, and the audiovisual staff at the university had rolled television cameras into the halls while clusters of students and faculty watched as stories of Thomas's bad behavior were aired. As the University Budget Committee moved toward the elevators, the chair started to get on the elevator, then backed up and offered me the first-on status as the only woman present, then he looked at me as if I was going to object to his deference, perhaps given my known feminist leanings. He said, in somewhat grumpy frustration, to all present: "I just don't know how to act anymore," and the other men surrounding the elevator were nodding in painful assent. I'm not generally good at brilliant lines that jolt home a point, but I did rather well on this occasion. As I got on the elevator first, I said, "Well, let me tell you, it is not about getting on elevators." The ride down was one of those face-forward silent ones. Drawing a parallel, respectful research across cultural borders is not just about methods, but it is most decidedly about power, care, flexibility, and good behavior. Researching well across cultures is as much about what comes before and after delivery of methods, about how the researcher engages in collaborations with those of different cultures.

5
Understanding Identity, Discourse, and Language to Inform Research

Having collaborated on an article in 1996, Tom Peacock and I were requested to write up "bios" before publication. Though it wasn't requested, he instinctively declared his Anishinabe heritage and his reservation home. I suggested that he put his Harvard doctorate and subsequent publications up front as that was the standard expected then in academic journals. He looked at me and said something like: "But my tribal identity is more important to me than the Harvard degree." I sighed, thinking: "But then, who am I?" I ended up writing just what academia expected of me: degree, tenure home, and publications. By 2008, when I was again writing a bio for the same journal, it actually requested me to declare my tribal identity. With more understanding, I lauded the editor for giving that importance to tribal identity, but I was still in a quandary. The concept of bundles of identity had helped me personally resolve my "But who am I?" dilemma, but I had difficulty declaring Maine as the heartfelt landed part of my identity. There was irony in the fact that my beloved tidal cove had been used seasonally by Abenaki less than a century before I arrived. Declaring my English, Irish, Scotch, Dutch, German, and French ancestry might have been perceived as sarcasm to the Indigenous reader base. Again in 2008 I just wrote up the academic component of my bundle, without aspects of my identity that might have been important to the reader's understanding of the text, what Lawrence-Lightfoot and Davis might call the "clarifying backdrop" (2002, p. 70).

This chapter looks at issues of identity, standpoint, discourse, and language as they inform cross-cultural research.

The danger of a simplistic take on identity

I am different persons in different "worlds" and can remember myself in both as I am in the other. I am a plurality of selves.

(Lugones, 1987)

Theories of identity proffered by post-structuralists as well as postcolonialists generally stress the fluid nature of identity, the notion of self as both multiple and resilient to the power factors informing a particular context. What we extend as the self is a response to the demands of a context, a specific performance and representation (Chaudhry, 1997, p. 451). Though the traditional research publication bio most often acknowledges only simplistic and academic parts of one's identity, in the research itself there is a danger in similarly simplistic takes on identity. Though one may declare parts of one's crowded self, there is a lessening of learning if the researchers haven't considered the complexity of their own identity and its effect on their standpoint in analysis.

Likewise, there is a danger of researchers' simplification of participant identities and consequent inaccuracies during access, data collection, analysis, and dissemination; there are inaccuracies and biases possible in narrowly defined identity. Consideration of participant identity can both complicate and expand the usefulness of research results. Complexities and contradictions beyond the binary conceptions of identity in the past (for instance, black/white, male/female, insider/outsider) exist, and there's a need to consider the issues of power inherent in those complexities. Furthermore, people's identity is always fluctuating, will not stand still. A researcher's job is often to unpack those complexities while considering that time- and place-focused research results only describe one moment in time and reflect only one context. Geographer Larry Knopp talked a bit about the history of thinking behind identity, complexity, and hybridity, and their application to research in diverse disciplines:

> Central to feminism is a foregrounding of gender identity issues because power dynamics and power differentials can be the source of some pretty incredible insights in the world. That is what queer theory is all about. Careful analysis of power in the context of sexuality can inform knowledge more broadly. Feminism has made us aware of home workplace issues, glass ceilings, and has caused us to sort of think differently about gender. But queer theory has caused us to think even more critically about sexuality, in more complicated terms, because the experiences of sexual minorities are so much about ambiguity, so much about hybridity, so much about indeterminacy. And so it is useful when we take some of the lessons of how identities are always in flux, for example, and apply them to other realms, like economics or politics.

We are past the essentialist notions that one is born with immutable identity. Postmodernity allows an understanding of "constructed" identities. Just by going into different worlds, seeing different ways of being, one is in the process of self-construction, trying different identities on in different contexts. Yet, as Stephen May, linguist at the University of Auckland in New Zealand, noted, "There's real tension with the post-modern take on identities that doesn't take much account of power relations." Grande (2008) adds,

"Moreover, the trenchant critique of postmodernism reframes the 'problem' of identity as a smokescreen that obfuscates the imperatives of Indigenous sovereignty and self-determination." This section will attempt to unpack the complicated interaction of identity and research, by looking at notions of identity, hybridity, intersectionality, power, and standpoint.

Hybridity, mixed-raciality, identity, and power

Hybridity has taken on meanings in research beyond the origin of the concept as it relates to the science of studying race or species origins. The term allows a more complicated view of identity in research and its applications. It was taken up by Homi Bhabha (1994) in talking about two cultures coming together, one group becoming dominant and imposing itself on another culture. Even when assimilation has taken place, there is a possibility of cultural adjustment. For instance, Maria Root (1998) identified changing aspects of the way that biracial individuals were identifying themselves in the baby-boom generation. Though many researchers talked about bi-raciality, multi-racial hybridity in relation to their cross-cultural research, two researchers I interviewed further complicated the notions. One, from a university in South Australia, talked about working with Aboriginal women:

> A woman once said something that stopped me in my tracks. She said, "I am a half-caste, that's what I was raised as, that's what I want to be known as. Why can't I be known as that?" How many lives are erased by suddenly saying that a term, as problematic as it is, must not be spoken. What does that mean in relation to the politics of gender studies? Why can't we have discussion or debate where we can actually say those things and explore what they are? Why can't the stories be heard? I was invited to Sydney to give a paper using that quote, to an Indigenous audience including Indigenous elders, and they really, really loved it because it resonated as an example of what happens when you cut out certain words, you actually close down certain kinds of histories. How is it that inside an institutional context that expressly says it is "anti-racist" the complexities of an issue are refused? Even inside contestation there are lines of affiliation and identifications, as well as disidentifications or separations.

The hybrid border crossers, be it with gender hybridity or racial hybridity, or even for economic class cross-overs, develop double consciousness and often double existence due to experience in both cultures. Tess Moeke-Maxwell, a mixed-race researcher from New Zealand, talked about the concept of hybridity in her research, and its acknowledgment, which created agency within ongoing colonization:

> We are not necessarily victims of ongoing forms of colonialism. We, as Māori women, are very creative, embracing that which we want and

rejecting that which we don't want. I interviewed over 20 women who talked about their experiences of cultural hybridity. I am a hybrid, trying to articulate where the boundaries lie for us as people who identify as Māori and Pākehā/other. The women were articulating themselves to me as having non-Māori ancestry as well, but their primary ethnic identity was Māori. Sometimes even that slips away when somebody says, "I am lesbian, and that's my primary identity." Women are saying they have some agency over their identity, using hybridity for their own purposes. Women talked about the psychological processes of preparing themselves to shift gears, so they could transition into, and out of, different cultural landscapes. For example, one Māori woman talked about wearing particular forms of clothing to associate in a Pākehā environment, a westernized workplace, in order to be a secretary administrator, taking the income back into her Māori cultural landscape, to sustain her family. But that workplace wasn't a comfortable place for her. And another example: someone, a fair-skinned (white Māori), was a victim of mistaken Pākehā identity and was abused by a brown Māori male relative. In diaspora, there is a sense of being dislocated; we hybrids often acquire multiple subject positions rather than just one (as a colonized person or an assimilated person). There are stories about people participating in traditional Māori customs during one part of the day and then going to their Pākehā family's place and participating in a similar but different cultural ritual at another time during the day. I illuminate the disjuncture and disparity around Māori identity being singular. I am using others' ideas about the third space to talk about hybridity—Homi Bhabha's work, for example. The third space speaks about a movement or vacillation between multiple homes and landscapes.

Moeke-Maxwell presents a means for researchers to work with hybridity in ways that affirm participants as having power in their dislocated lives. As suggested above, participants, indeed all human beings, deserve to determine and own their identity in all its complexity and to take agency on its basis instead of remaining "colonized." The researchers above affirm the power of narrative in the process. Agency in identity formation is at the heart of decolonization, the heart of postcolonial theory and practice. bell hooks (1989, pp. 42–43) talks about an oppressor/oppressed relationship:

> Those who dominate are seen as subjects and those who are dominated objects. As subjects, people have the right to define their own reality, establish their own identities, name their history. As objects, one's reality is defined by others, one's identity created by others, one's history named only in ways that define one's relationship to those who are subject.

Moeke-Maxwell gives her participants a chance to, as hooks says, "resist by identifying themselves as subjects ... naming their history, telling their story." As previously quoted in Chapter 1, Freire (in *Education for Critical Consciousness*, p. 67) says:

> Integration with one's context, as distinguished from adaptation, is a distinctly human activity. Integration results from the capacity to adapt oneself to reality plus the critical capacity to make choices and transform that reality...The integrated person is person as subject. In contrast, the adaptive person is person as object, adaptation representing at most a weak form of self-defense...If man is incapable of changing reality, he adjusts himself instead. Adaptation is behavior characteristic of the animal sphere; exhibited by man, it is symptomatic of his dehumanization.

Through participant narratives, Moeke-Maxwell has found a way to have her participants investigate their identity, to see the way they are in the "subject" position, the way they have found power in their worlds, and to lend stories to help others redefine themselves and their hybridity and to find the power within themselves to own that complicated identity. In some ways, Quinney (1970, p. 13) says, "Nonconformity may also be part of the process of finding self-identity. It is thus against something that the self can emerge."

Then how does this all affect research? We will talk about researcher identity and resultant standpoints in this chapter, but in thinking about methodology in relation to identity, the researcher must think through whether the complexity of identity adjusts the way people act in research, or about how a research method itself might affect a participant's view of him or herself. For instance, feminist sociological thought concerns itself with intersectionality of identity. For example, when studying oppressive marital violence, if a participant is first identified with an African female identity, that might not fully explain her response in research. However, her immigrant status may explain her vulnerability and behavior. It may explain why she may resist research or even social assistance, as she might legally be deported (see also McCall, 2005; Delva et al., 2010, pp. 140–141, and legal cases where aspects of this concept are raised). Multiple dimensions of identity fully attest to the way in which simplistic notions of identity in cross-cultural research can undercut its value.

Interdependence vs. independence in identity development

One aspect of identity that researchers in social settings attend to is identity development. Those from Western/Eurocentric cultures often develop identity through individuation, learning to become independent in relation to family and community, and valuing their own individualism. In comparison, those from Indigenous cultures may well view themselves as valuing dependent, collectivist, and relational attributes, focused on how their behavior might affect others (Markus and Kitayama, 1991; Bergstrom et al., 2003; Heine, 2011). This first came up in the work of my research team (Cleary and Peacock, 1997) when non-native teachers articulated their frustrations in working hard with native students, whom they saw as particularly "bright," to get them off to college and then to have them return home midway through their first semester. They talked about the "invisible umbilical cord" that drew them home. This was unlike the native teachers' response, who well understood the interdependent nature of their students because they had felt the stress of separation themselves in completing their own education. Related to this might be Kashima et al.'s (1995, 2004) finding that gender factors into relational identity development, women scoring higher in the survey prompt: "I feel like doing something for people in trouble because I can almost feel their pains" (reported in Heine, 2011, p. 210). Understanding differences in identity development, from either side of the independent or interdependent border, may help with cross-cultural research.

Researcher identity positionings

There is value, as Chaudhry (1997, p. 451) notes, in acknowledging "multiple subject positionings of the researcher" in research. As researchers we work to unpack our own identity and its subsequent biases and become conscious of their effect on our research. One aspect of the perspectives we bring to cross-cultural research originates in our disciplinary lens; we need to think through our disciplinary training and our methodological focus in relation to the data we collect. Susan Rodgers, said:

> Many Indonesian scholars tend to be pro-Indonesian and nationalist when they discuss the Dutch colonial period, but I interviewed a woman who was self-avowedly Dutch. She and her husband are a special version of Dutch people. Just to glance at her she certainly looks Indonesian, but she sees herself as a Nederlander, a Eurasian person who is culturally Dutch. I really had to think through some of the issues of that because if you're an Indonesia scholar, you tend to see the Dutch as the "bad guys" when you consider the colonial era in the Dutch East Indies. You have soaked up all this postcolonial theory about terrible European colonial powers and that unconsciously slops over onto my views of the Dutch, even though I realize how ridiculous that sounds when you're dealing with contemporary Dutch people. Still, emotionally it was there. So when I did this week-long interview with Gerdie Ungerer, the situation was ethically much more complicated because she was recalling a time during World War II when she was a Dutch-identified young girl who was only 12 years old when the Japanese forces threw her into internment camps for the Dutch or "Dutch sympathizers" caught in the Indies in 1942 when

the Japanese forces invaded after the fall of Singapore. So, that talk and her memories complexified the whole Indonesian personhood situation for me in a very transforming way. Interacting with a very likeable, intelligent, older person like Gerdie destabilized all the personhood categories for me. There's an internal dynamic in Indonesianist scholarship where we have bought into the glorious revolutionary rhetoric, and we fall into too easy condemnations of whole categories of people. I emerged a more sophisticated researcher after doing that.

Rodgers and I talked awhile about the simplicity of the postcolonial frameworks out of which our training had grown. She said: "I get a lot out of postcolonial work; I probably identify with that more than any of the other theoretical framework, but we have to work a little bit beyond it."

In the face-to-face contact that research in social settings often involves, one comes to empathetic insights listening to participants' stories about hybridity, permitting transformation and expansion of initial views. I remember my own initial sensitivity in response to the anger of a young Penobscot teacher who, at first, challenged my motivation in research ("Why are *you* doing this research?"), seeing me as only the "do-gooder" university person. When I told my story, he better recognized my bundle of identities and motivations and collaborations. And in my hearing his story, I saw beyond his teacher identity, hearing about his project of organizing a good portion of his tribe for the first of a number of modern sojourns to their sacred mountain, Mt Katahdin. He organized runners, walkers, canoeists, and community members in support vans who were bearing food and encouragement for those using only their muscles for the journey. At first I wasn't sure whether he was native or not, but then I saw the complexity of what he brought to teaching, his passion in restoring the native part of his and his students' identities and heritage. In face-to-face research there is the probability of the recognition and appreciation of each other's bundles of identity, which allows for better relationships and deeper understandings of the topic.

Application to research

Unpacking the effect of researcher and participant bundles of identity in research cannot be directed by a set of rules, but retaining a critical stance in all phases of the research process can. Wendy Holland, Aboriginal researcher from the University of Western Sydney, and I discussed this over dinner with the tape recorder running:

> Holland: We all have multiple identities. Identity is fluid, not fixed. I guess that is what I have been struggling with in relation to my own work. It concerns me when others persist on maintaining categories/'thinking in boxes'. Categorising/'boxing' people contains and maintains lives. Our lives/identities are just not that simple and we should never

assume anything of anyone. For example, people often see me as 'white' (whatever 'white' means) and are challenged when I acknowledge my so-called 'black' heritage. It is critical that we never assume anything of anyone and be mindful of the categories we, all too often use, which limits our thinking as well as relationships with others.

Holland found she couldn't superimpose her own young adult identity on the youth of the day. Two years and continents away, Angela Creese, researcher at the University of Birmingham in the UK, added to this discussion. She acknowledged what Trimble and Fisher (2006) term as the "ethnic glosses" and "simplistic panethnic labels" that no longer work in careful research:

> Cultural differences become really interesting and important in context. And the concepts of insiders and outsiders constantly shift. Otherwise, you end up constantly stereotyping, In EFL study, there's a kind of tendency to talk about the culture of India or English culture, national cultures, which I found problematic. And when you research something like a Gujarati complementary school, you realize that for the children those categories are just not helpful. That's not the way they see the world, and they live with all that kind of layering of who they are. And Arvind and I do too, as researchers. Certainly I have my histories and my backgrounds that I bring to it, and, on our team, Arvind has his. But in different places, they overlap, and other places they're separate. Identities don't stay still. Neither does language or culture, we know now. Children are in the complementary school because their parents want them to learn something about Gujarati heritage and language, but the children are bilingual, and they come from multilingual, multicultural Britain. And so they all become something very interesting, and so the Gujarati culture that's taught has to be made accessible to the children in ways that teachers make happen because they too have moved around. It's fascinating, but it doesn't stay still.

And again I hear Julian Cho's words: "Nothing stands still." In an introduction to Spivak's work (1993), MacCabe writes, "The force of Spivak's work lies in her absolute refusal to discount any of the multiplicity of subject-positions which she has been assigned, or to fully accept any of them" (xvi). Thus the hard job of the cross-cultural researcher: it's about unpacking identity, about unpacking hybridity, and about figuring out how to negotiate these with respect and insight, and still come out with something to say.

Complexities of "insider"/"outsider" identity

For years the terms and coinciding concepts of "insiders" and "outsiders" in research have been useful to describe the difference in perspective that might exist if the insider researcher were a member of the group being researched and intimately familiar with the surface and deep culture of the group being researched, so that nothing would seem particularly strange. The words depict a dichotomy of outsider vs. insider positions in relation to research, but further examination is important.

Anthropologists have long articulated the value of being an outsider to a culture. Sharon Kemp, anthropologist at the University of Minnesota Duluth, described the value that being from "away" lends to research: "You see things that members of the culture wouldn't basically see, and it calls into question things in your own culture." The deepest level of culture, that which is most deeply embedded and often unconscious, is sometimes more recognizable by an outsider than one who lives within the culture. Susan Rodgers said:

> I tell my students that it's actually easier when you're studying cultures that are manifestly different from yours because, if I were studying the American marriage system and I'm a part of American culture, it's hard for me to see the way the American marriage system works as an ideology with a hidden structure. That extra distance you get by living and studying in a very foreign culture actually makes traditional anthropology easier, though it's harder to learn the languages and to live in the village.

The inherent values of insider and outsider positions and perspectives are useful, but as issues of power in research have begun to be investigated, the insider/outsider dichotomy becomes more complicated. The binary opposition of outsider vs. insider which was at one time useful is sometimes a false dichotomy. Researchers have come to embrace the ambiguity resulting from the bundles of both researchers' and participants' identities and have found the need to unpack their implications. In interviewing researchers for the study that informs this book, I was both insider and outsider. I was an academic researcher who was interviewing those with similar academic credentials, with similar experience in research, sometimes with similar gender, age, and language, occasionally from similar regions, sometimes with similar white privilege, but often with different ethnicity and fascinatingly different cultural ways of being and perspectives. The common academic identity did not minimize my need to think through insider/outsider issues in my research, but it does make connections easier with participants.

Though the understandable outcry from communities, tired of having no power in research, has been clearly heard, there are also complications inherent in insider research. In support of insider research, many have noted that only members of a cultural group can look at subtle cultural phenomena with understandings and can understand the vulnerability of communities and participants in research. The relatively recent movement of "teachers as researchers," or in other areas "practitioners as researchers," has had an energizing effect on classroom teachers and practitioners, and also provides a way of gaining sorts of knowledge not available to a complete outsider.

Diversity, within what might seem to others as a distinct cultural group, further complicates the dichotomous concepts of insider/outsider. When doing cross-cultural research, you are by definition an outsider, but those who identify as Māori, for instance, can still be an outsider in certain ways within certain Māori communities, even though they have considerable "tacit cultural knowledge" (see also Lincoln and Gonzales y Gonzales, 2008, p. 795). Sarah Jane Tiakiwai explained:

> I belong to a number of tribes, and I have to understand that there are differences, and who I am in this context is not necessarily the same person in that context. So it's all those links that you have as a Māori person that have you "*ahi ka*," literally, to keep the fires burning. I go back as a person in the kitchen, working in the *marae*, doing the same things as everybody else because in that context that's my role. I might go back as a researcher, but it just won't cut it. The big criticism about some Māori researchers now is that they've become "authorities." As Māori, we don't look at the letters behind your name; it's how you live, and do you live with the Māori. It goes back to this whole assumption of authority. You have to prove constantly that you are worthy of the position given to you.

Linda Tuhiwai Smith talked of her recognition of the complexity of researcher identity when inside her own community:

> When I was a master's student, I interviewed these mothers who had obviously dressed up for the occasion, tidied up the house, and had their children wearing matching pajamas. It immediately struck me that these people who I saw everyday had changed their behavior because I was coming as a researcher. I went away thinking a lot more deeply. The mothers weren't engaging passively; they saw me not just as another mother. I had taken on a new role that required them to treat me more formally. When I saw what they did, a whole lot of things started to click into place about whether researchers really understand what a family might do to prepare for them, and you respect that because it required a lot of effort. That simple scene raised all those issues. I credit that with creating major work for me for the next couple of decades. It made me conscious that what I was doing was not an innocent activity and that the stories would have an impact on people who had gone out of their way to allow me to do it. I had a responsibility to them. I was a Māori woman, and a mother, and I was also not like them. I was a university student doing a master's program; I had a husband, a recognized marriage, all these other things which set me as an outsider. I became aware of the layers of insiderliness and outsiderliness.

Layers of insiderliness and outsiderliness are evident even when, in more traditional thinking, you are an insider. Angela Creese, an English-born researcher at the University of Birmingham, UK, said:

> We relied on the Gujarati-speaking researchers, both linguistically and culturally, for background information on festivals and histories and protocols in schools. But having said that, all of us were kind of inside and outside in different ways. Arvind had lots of experience both as a Gujarati speaker and as a teacher in complementary schools, so he was very much inside the community. But I was a woman and a family member, so those words, insider/outsider, don't capture the complicatedness of it.

The collaboration that Creese described in talking about her study allowed those with more cultural experience to discuss the collected data with those who were seeing it with a more outside perspective. As Lugones and Spelman (1983) said,

> The argument that only members of a community have access to the real meaning of events in that community, so outsiders' opinions should be discarded, runs into difficulty when one notes the great variations in opinions among members of a community and the difficulties in determining who is qualified to represent the group. In addition, members of a community often have difficulty noticing their own practices because they take their own ways for granted. (p. 571)

She articulates what Creese and her team practiced: "only when genuine and reciprocal dialogue takes place between 'outsiders' and 'insiders' can we trust the outsider's account" (p. 577).

Value in both researcher positions offers yet another rationale for research collaborations and multiple perspectives on research. Research has begun to fathom some simplifications that simply don't work on closer scrutiny. Identities, hybridity, insiderliness, outsiderliness: all these things shift. And, as we find below, relational connections can reconstruct these sometimes dichotomous concepts.

Finding an inside connection for collaboration and access

Research in social settings and the reality of bundles of identity open up connections with other people that one might not have realized were present when the research started. Renato Rosaldo (1993) says: "One hopes to achieve a balance between recognizing wide-ranging human differences and the modest truism that any two human groups must have certain things in common" (p. 10). Researchers found they were most comfortable when they and their participants started to find the identity overlaps. Bella Graham, Māori oral historian then at University of Waikato in New Zealand, talked of those connections:

Most of my research is done with people from my own Māori culture, so I tend to be an insider. But I have done research where I have researched Pākehās. I had similarities with them because I've been raised in an arts environment, and they were artists, and my mother is an artist, so I could actually cross their race and ethnic boundary into the arts culture and find similarities and things to talk about. I actually found it quite interesting and every time I found an affinity.

For many researchers, research became easier when those points of affinity were identified.

For those researchers who reach into other colonized groups, the connections beyond ethnicity are often through empathy with that common colonized experience, something James Banks (1998) calls the "Indigenous insider status." I saw this access in 2005 when Mary Hermes joined me in New Zealand. Because she was so dedicated to the Waadookodaading Ojibwe Language Immersion School that she was instrumental in starting, she wanted to talk to Māori people who had been quite successful in similar immersion school endeavors. On this trip she was eager to find answers to the pressing questions that she had. She knew intuitively how to be respectful in the communities we visited; she also knew how to be earnest but appropriate in seeking answers. At one Māori school, the students greeted us with ceremony, song, and dance on the steps of their school. Hermes responded with an Ojibwe song that echoed in the school courtyard. The students were smitten and followed her around the school, and she was down on her knees and interested in what they had to tell her. The Māori teacher talked eagerly to her of the premises behind his school's work. I witnessed that "Indigenous insider status."

Cross-cultural research by definition crosses into difference and respects difference; whereas colonization attempts to erase difference when it is focused on assimilation. As a researcher, finding commonalities while being interested in difference presents a stance more comfortable to both researcher and researched, and it layers the previously dichotomized concepts of insider/outsider.

Similarly, Stephen May, a sociolinguist from the University of Auckland, found that his outsider position when going to Wales to do research was softened by the solidarity created by the fact that his homeland, New Zealand, and Wales had been in a similarly colonized position:

In my research with the Welsh, in some ways being the New Zealand outsider was good. I wasn't English; I wasn't directly colonizing; I came from New Zealand where similar things had happened. What drove my research engagement was a fundamental sympathy for that context in which they had been dominated. That's a major change in the dynamics in terms of my prior research engagement. I suppose it also gave me the ability to look at both situations, I mean at a kind of meta-level. Key people in the Welsh language education context might not have been as open with me.

May had two contexts to juxtapose, hence a meta-level from which to gain new insights. His complex researcher identity and experience acted to position his perspective in research. If one looks at research participants in their contexts, it is one's own complex bundle of identities and past experience that, at first, informs what is perceived, until one's lens is widened by that juxtaposition. Through cross-cultural research, May was able to expand his view of the dynamics of colonization on language, and those with whom he worked were able to expand their focus as informed by their collaboration. How you see yourself, how you place yourself in relation to what you see and what you hold dear, all inform your perspective, your standpoint in relation to what you are researching. Connections, be they disciplinary skills, gender, sexual orientation, parenthood, age, and so on, become valuable in cross-cultural research for the understandings and relationships they enhance (see also Robben and Sluka, 2007, p. 63).

Identity, standpoints, and positionings

There is no one standpoint, no privileged way to view the world.

Çiğdem Üsekes, professor of English at Western Connecticut State University, USA, once resided with me as a graduate student, having come from Turkey to go to my university. When she visited me recently I hadn't intended to interview her but, as I asked her about her current work, I felt compelled to pull out the tape recorder and preserve what she said:

I've been looking at how African-American authors—August Wilson, James Baldwin and Lorraine Hansberry—talk about white liberals in their works, and what kind of critique it brought them. White liberals are challenged in their works, and the white liberals are used to thinking about themselves as the good guys. I once interviewed August Wilson, and my Turkish heritage was probably why he was willing to talk to me. He probably perceived me both as a liberal and as one who wasn't part of the white-American culture. I had a different vantage point. I told him that my dissertation was on Eugene O'Neil and blackness, and on August Wilson and whiteness, and he was actually angry with me because he felt his plays had nothing to do with white characters. He dealt only with the African-American world. He was not willing to talk to me about my research. I was quite upset, and he was quite upset too. He thought I was marginalizing the black characters in his work. The experience was tense. We talked about some other things. Why had I even gotten interested in this topic? It had to do with my personal interest in the underdog. I do have another perspective than that of a white liberal from the US.

Üsekes talked about vantage points. Other researchers, using different words, noted that their identities and experiences informed their perspectives, their positionings, and hence their standpoints in the research process. Coming from a bundle of identities, relating or not to the bundles of identities of your participants, and considering the way you understand and own your own identities affects your lens focus in all phases of research.

In the worst-case scenario, one is unconscious about one's standpoint, and one comes to research with bias or ethnocentrism. A contribution Emile Durkheim made to the field of social sciences was to urge that researchers eschew bias by striving to be value neutral. Since his admonishment, researchers have come a long way in realizing the potential of bias, the effect of standpoint, vantage point, and positioning on research, and the difficulties in maintaining an objective stance in research.

I first heard the word "standpoint" when reading feminist research years ago; then Thomas Peacock, with whom I was collaborating, talked about Ojibwe standpoint epistemology, and again Martin Nakata, thousands of miles away, talked about Indigenous standpoint epistemology. Of all the researchers who talked about identity, standpoints, and positionality, Nakata, a Torres Strait Islander, was perhaps the most impassioned. He constructed a grid on paper for me with the different identity positions that could be working simultaneously, showing how that matrix might be three-dimensional, a complex terrain in which one could be positioned in research in all kinds of ways. He talked at length about standpoint theory:

> We are at the intersection of complex terrains, and we negotiate a lot of different positions from day to day. We are mothers, sisters, parents; we're community members, we're academics, we're researchers. We're complex things, and complexity for us is our normal. Let me try to map it [as he constructed a grid from paper]. Whitefella researchers use a frame to simplify this: me black; you white, colonizer versus colonized, dominant/subordinate, either/or. This is how they reduced us to the subordinate other. The white colonist dropped the anchors here; they crossed over, but we still remain black, not only through our skins but through our long history with this land and through our epistemological traditions. This has not been erased as many would think.
>
> In history, and for the whitefella researchers, to understand us, they spent decades documenting and taxonomizing us into their sciences in these simplistic us/them ways, as they did everywhere else in the world. They measured people's brains; they charted territorial waters and lands. But as Torres Strait Islanders, we also have our own history, knowledge, spirituality, epistemology, etc. We have our own historical trajectories much longer than the coming of the whitefellas, and we know that, but not necessarily explicitly. We are guided by our parents and grandparents in

this down through the generations, through our peers, and we ascribe ourselves into space differently than these whitefellas have tried to position us. So there is thus an inherent tension, coming back to us, about who we can and cannot be. The tensions sit in our constellation as points of coherence for communicating our position. Foucault calls them "conditions of possibilities." On a complex, but not deterministic, terrain, I don't have to behave "black." I can actually stand up and say, "Fuck you, not on your terms." And we do stand up. So our agency is not simply one in reaction to a dominant ideological state. We can exercise a standpoint that is continuous with an Indigenous trajectory, and it can't be reduced to be seen simply as a point of resistance to the nation state.

Nakata's research (2007) shows how the place of Torres Strait Islanders had been constructed by colonizing powers. Consciously finding his own standpoint meant analyzing public texts to see how he had been positioned:

Knowing for the first time how I'd been positioned in history and how we continue to be positioned today was more powerful than giving me a gun. So this is about the "emancipation of the self," to use Freire's term. So this is very important to the cross-cultural research work because it now offers up a paradigm that sits in relationship to other paradigms. So, when you go out and collect data, whether it is ethnographic research or quantitative calculations or accumulation of numbers or stats, or the qualitative interviews that you may do, you bring the data back here, and then you have a particular standpoint from which you can deal with the data. Unfortunately, in today's world of doing Indigenous research, that standpoint is not necessarily named.

He went on to further describe his work with Indigenous standpoint epistemology:

We are in a different era of taking complexities as normal, rather than buying into acts of dumbing down things into neatly organized boxes, taxonomies, or either/or propositions. What I've been working on is Indigenous standpoint theory, to build methodologies that can actually deal with complexities. To get into the Indigenous standpoint, history needs to be really understood, not just on a chronological plane but on discursive, inter-discursive, intra-discursive levels, to get to the point where you better understand the intersection between different or competing kinds of positions. And once you can get there, you find another language for talking theory. I am still trying to develop a language for this because the English language limits what can be understood about it. One of the other things I've learned over the years in trying to move into this space for talking theory is that people find it very hard giving up what they know, and that's just a normal instinct. It also means for them the surrendering of a lot of understood positions, propositions, and histories, and knowledge, and [what seems for them abandoning a lot of established] common sense. And it's very difficult for people to do.

Nakata actually researched the way his people were positioned by Western researchers through the years, but he also used reflexivity, the "self-critical sympathetic introspection and the self-conscious analytical scrutiny of the self as researcher" (England, 1994, p. 82).

Reflexivity is critical to scrutiny of the self, understanding of the way the self has been constructed or positioned, movement toward self-construction, and the ownership of the standpoint from which one proceeds in research. If one takes the complexities of standpoints seriously, they are acknowledged in the research report itself. Patti Lather (1991, p. xx) says: "We are somewhere in the midst of a shift away from a view of knowledge as disinterested and toward a conceptualization of knowledge as constructed, contested, incessantly perspectival and polyphonic." In work with participants, this reflexivity involves acknowledging complexity, denying essentialist constructions of people in different cultural categories, recognizing their diversity, and gaining from those multiplicities of perspectives along the way (Kincheloe and Steinberg, 2008). We need to be "open to the inadequacies of our pet theories and to counterinterpretations" (Cram, 2001, p. 14).

Declaring your standpoints in research to yourself and seeking to understand the standpoints of your participants is an honest way to enter another culture/community. Though it may take more time, approaching data collection and analysis through the standpoints of participants and moving onto dissemination with consultation and collaboration will inform and enrich the results, and the relationships.

Consciousness of positionality in collaborative research

Learning how you and "others" have been positioned historically through power and language, breaking free to see things in their complexity, and even seeing the simplicity of the nature of complexities, enables one to do cross-cultural research with more care. Stephen May, who collaborated with the Welsh, talked about the necessity of recognizing one's own position in a cross-cultural context:

One of the fundamental problems in cross-cultural education contexts is the ongoing assumption that somehow European and dominant cultural researchers don't recognize their own ethnicity, their own dialect, as culturally embedded. Recognizing one's own cultural location, gender, and so on is important in establishing a cross-cultural dialogue that's ethically grounded where we can acknowledge our own positioning in relation to these issues and then start the research process.

Past cross-cultural research that has normalized European values has had detrimental effects. There is value in researchers of European heritage continuing to be involved in educational research, but within clear parameters and a framework of accountability, being clear about their own personal relations with research.

Barbara Comber, educational researcher at Queensland University of Technology in Australia, talked about how her consciousness of her own identity and resultant standpoint led her to be able to see things from the perspective of others in similar circumstances. Though motivated by her own standpoint, she is very conscious of it and its implications:

I came from a poor family. My father was an immigrant from Ireland. I'm interested in racism (including that which isn't color bound, more about ethnicity) and various forms of resultant harassment, and also the connections between immigrant status and poverty. So while I look like a mainstream white, middle-class researcher, I'm very much driven by my own history as a poor working-class kid. I research with some people with that shared history, and that's why part of our work is around poverty, which is what a lot of culturally different groups have in common. I want to be able to tell good news stories about these teachers and their kids, what they do against the odds, so I always go in with that standpoint of deliberately working against deficit notions. But, of course, I always go in sort of seeking to find out how advantage and disadvantage is constructed in the classroom, and also at the same time trying to get a better understanding of where things go wrong for particular groups of children and how it is that schools reproduce disadvantage. My own history is always there, but then I'm always looking to identify aspects of the pedagogical process and peer interactions that result in certain kids getting a bad deal from school. It's complex, and it always has to be locally negotiated, and you often uncover things you wish you hadn't.

Comber's recognition of the standpoint from which she negotiates her research and her reflexivity about that standpoint are heartening. As she implies, in phases of research, even standpoints don't stand still but are morphed through the thinking that the research evokes. As a researcher, using reflexivity to investigate both one's identities and one's standpoint in doing research opens one up to clearer understandings and better ways to represent those understandings to others.

Cultural discourse and standpoint

A politicized postmodernism shifts the debate to a questioning of what it means to know and be known, how and why discourse works to legitimize and contest power, and the limitations of totalizing systems and fixed boundaries.

(Lather, 1991, p. 88)

In 1998 I accompanied the University of Minnesota Duluth's first contingent of four student teachers to Toledo Community College in Belize. The prior year, in a conversation with the Toledo District Education Officer about his reading of Freire and about the need of his district to move on to a more dialogic form of education, he welcomed pedagogy that Minnesota student teachers might bring. Though Belize's colonizing country, England, had moved beyond the lecture and recitation mode of education at the primary and secondary levels, the remnants of that pedagogy were well entrenched in the local schools in Punta Gorda. In 1998, the kind people of Punta Gorda welcomed us with a day-long orientation. I had contracted one of those brutal colds just before departure and walked to the school that morning both fevered and snuffly. I should have been forewarned by Julian Cho's previous explanation of the place of praise in Belizian discourse as I was called on to use that same discourse: their conventions and their respect mechanisms. I did, however, recognize it as having political meanings that were beyond me. At the orientation, each speaker first praised each of the other 12 speakers-to-be, myself, and the student teachers as the "honored visitors," then acknowledged what the last speakers had said, shared what he or she had to offer about the community, then praised others again, though more selectively, and looked to me for some sort of comment. I was somewhat inadequate with this at first, uttering short thanks and minimal comments. Amongst the 12 contributors to our orientation were the mayor figure in the town, the District Education Officer (equivalent to the state minister or secretary of education), a district legislator, the public health nurse, the police chief, the principal, the vice-principal, the guidance counselor, and the head of the Advisory Board to Toledo Community College. Between coughing and observation, I became more and more accustomed to my role in this process: thanking again and again those who had turned out for this event, and acknowledging the contributions of the prior speaker about the health, safety, and educational wishes of the community in relation to the student teachers who were increasingly befuddled by the whole event. The discourse expectations became most interesting to me, especially given that community. Town leaders of Maya, Garifuna, Creole, Chinese, and East Indian heritage had managed to forge ways of living together.

The way that discourse evolved through, and in spite of, British colonization would make an interesting study, and I should not presume that this one event was representative of all Belizian discourse. After the student teachers were off to their home stays, Celia Mahung, who was to supervise them, prepared throat-soothing ginger tea for me. I articulated to her my fear that I might not have used the right respect mechanisms. She laughed and assured me that they were used to those who came from "the North." Nevertheless, I was aware that I had entered that world with a potentially impolite way of being, bound by my own social, political, and ideological tethers, struggling to understand the rules, perspectives, and motivations within that setting.

Foucault (1972, 1980) initiated some thinking about discourse, acknowledging the hidden power embedded and maintained in ways of speaking, the silencing or obscuring of some voices and ways of being, seeing privileged ways of being embedded in both textual and vocal language. Combined with my reading of James Gee, the orientation described above inspired some serious thought about the function of discourse when crossing cultural borders. As James Gee (1990) says,

> Discourses are ways of being in the world, or forms of life which integrate words, acts, values, beliefs, attitudes, and social identities, as well as gestures, glances, body positions, and clothes. A discourse is a sort of identity kit which comes complete with appropriate costume and instructions on how to act, talk, and often write, so as to take on a particular social role that others will recognize. (p. 127)

As one grows up in a discourse community, one learns to say the right things, using the right conventions for both written and oral expression, and to say them at the right time with the right gestures and in the right dress. Many cultures and nations use the same language, but the discourse structures and respect mechanisms may be quite different. The Belize orientation event contributed for me a moment of what Gee describes as meta-level knowledge about both my primary and this more foreign discourse.

Academics are conscious of working their way into the discipline-specific mode of communicating ideas. Quantitative researchers have different discourse conventions than do qualitative researchers. Different disciplines have different jargon, different presentation, and publication conventions than do others. The jargon that different disciplines use is perhaps minor compared with the different ways in which different disciplines have come to think and to report their thinking, perhaps as if they were cultures unto themselves. As Geertz (1983) says, "the various disciplines (or disciplinary matrices), humanistic, natural scientific, social scientific alike, that make up the scattered discourse of modern scholarship are more than just intellectual coins of vantage but are ways of being in the world" (p. 155). Individuals may be unconscious of their own conventions and just deem them as proper articulation of learning. Some researchers, in collaboration with researchers who haven't yet been socialized into the specific disciplinary discourse of power that gets articles published, talked of the rewriting they needed to do to replicate the target academic discourse. Geoff Munns, educational researcher at the University of Western Sydney in Australia, talked of collaborating with Aboriginal researchers who struggled with the academic discourse in their field:

> I agonized and agonized, and then I contacted others, and I just said, "Look, I think there's really good ideas in this, but I'm going to work on this, and if you don't like what I do, please tell me." And that's the only way I could do it; I virtually completely rewrote it as second author. So I still don't know if that was the right thing to do. I still don't know if whether doing that helps an Aboriginal person, but if that article had been submitted as it was, it would have been rejected, and here was an Aboriginal person that needed to be published in order to improve her career. There are tricky issues around writing.

An Indigenous researcher who wanted to remain anonymous articulated the difficulty that those, raised with very different modes of discourse, have in their apprenticeships into an academic discourse community:

> Academia, which doesn't exactly attract Indigenous people, is a very lonely pursuit. And the structures that are required, the linguistic requirements, scare people. These structures are almost a Western medieval tradition, like graduation caps and gowns. Our qualities come with speaking: our incredible teachers hold people through talking. I've never seen a relative of mine reading, oh, the Bible, but not just reading to inform, but they talked from sun up to sun down. I've heard some ridiculous papers read in academia. It's like looking through a thesaurus and trying to construct a sentence that looks like a piece of barbed wire. I think people are interested in discovering, but they're not interested in doing that expected and uninteresting writing with its tidy beginnings and endings. I see Western discourse as dishonest. The weight of it worries me. When you're the first generation of doing this, it's even heavier.

The researcher above and Geoff Munns give examples from different traditions. The irony is that the academic discourse of a discipline area perpetuates itself, and those who can replicate that discourse hold the power of publication, and the research of those who can replicate the discourse determines the knowledge that gets disseminated and acted upon. The order of things is locked through a dominant/elite discourse passed on most often in graduate school, most often an opportunity of the privileged with privilege perpetuating itself.

Recently, qualitative research journals have been resilient to alternative ways of articulating knowledge, making room for thick description and narrative, but often discourse conventions are reified. That said, Spivak (1993) acknowledges the above while articulating the value of written expression:

> The problem of human discourse is generally seen as articulating itself in the play of, in terms of, three shifting "concepts": language, world, and consciousness. We know no world that is not organized as a language, we operate with no other consciousness but one structured as a language—languages that we cannot possess, for we are operated by those languages as well. The category of language, then, embraces the categories of world and consciousness even as it is determined by them. Strictly speaking, since we are questioning the human being's control over the production of language, the future that will serve us better is writing, for there the absence of the producer and receiver is taken for granted. A safe future, seemingly outside of the language-(speech)-writing opposition, is the text—a weave of knowing and not-knowing which is what knowing is. (This organizing principle—language, writing, or text— might itself be a way of holding at bay a randomness incongruent with consciousness.)
>
> (pp. 77–78)

In considering gender and writing in years past, I have described comparisons of female rhetoric versus male rhetoric (again a simplistic binary). Female rhetoric: leaning toward the narrative, making points but acknowledging other points of view, making conclusions that encourage further thinking. Male rhetoric: centered on one thesis or argument, using refutation of other viewpoints as a mode of argumentation, ending with a restatement of the thesis (Miller Cleary, 1996). "Tidy beginnings and endings," as the researcher said above. This simplistic dichotomy of gendered discourses doesn't involve "words" but rather the conventions of writing. Women who manage the conventions of "male rhetoric" are more likely to be favored in publication of research. Many do very well.

In looking at Indigenous literacy, different narrative structures are interesting. I found it fascinating to attend native storytelling events with culturally mixed audiences. As Ojibwe storytellers shared their oral tradition, native people responded with nodding, laughing, and sometimes with contemplative expressions. They clearly followed the narrative line while white listeners looked pretty much puzzled throughout, and many stories ended without the mainstream denouement, to the consternation of these same Western listeners. In 1996, Ojibwe Amelia LeGarde ended a story I was listening to, seemingly mid-narrative, with "*Mii i'iw,*" meaning "That's all." A Hopi woman I interviewed (Cleary and Peacock, 1997) had a similar reflection on her childhood stories: "As children, we went away thinking." Thomas Peacock, the Ojibwe scholar with whom I collaborated, said: "This was the way some of these old Indians say things. They just say something, and then people have to think about it for a while."

Clearly cultures have different forms of discourse and narrative, and in research translations the intent and meaning can be distorted (see also Cleary and Peacock, 1998). Paula Gunn Allen (1986) in *The Sacred Hoop* shows ways in which white narrative structure can intrude in translations of stories or tales, "Language embodies the unspoken assumptions and orientations of the culture it belongs to. So while the problem is one of translation, it is not simply one of word equivalence. The differences are perceptual and contextual as much as verbal" (p. 225):

> Traditional American Indian stories work dynamically among clusters of loosely interconnected circles. The focus of the action shifts from one character to another as the story unfolds... But as the old tales are translated and rendered in English, the Western notion of proper fictional form takes over the tribal narrative.
>
> (pp. 241–242)

She illustrates this by fascinating juxtapositions of traditionally oral and newer translations of the "tale of yellow woman":

> The oral tradition is a living body. It is in continuous flux, which enables it to accommodate itself to the real circumstances of a people's lives. That is its strength, but it is also its weakness, for when a people finds itself living within a racist, classist, and sexist reality, the oral tradition will reflect those values and will thus shape the people's consciousness to include and accept racism, classism and sexism, and they will incorporate that change, hardly noticing the shift. If the oral tradition is altered in certain subtle, fundamental ways, if elements alien to it are introduced so that its internal coherence is disturbed, it becomes the major instrument of colonization and oppression.
>
> (pp. 224–225)

Julian Cho pointed out again how nothing stood still with his Maya oral tradition. He told how the original folklore in his village changed with Christian influences:

> The hootas, in the oral tradition, they did not listen, so they were turned into a snail. So when Jesus Christ talked to them about certain things, they did not listen, so Jesus Christ said, "Okay, you go ahead and live in the water." And that was how snails ended up living in the water.

He went on to tell how his Maya students had difficulty with a storytelling assignment and how narrative structures can change: "They have difficulty in telling the traditional folklores. They don't tell it just like their grandfather told it; they don't think the Garifuna and Creole students in our school would like it." Conception of audience and real purpose can change discourse. And so enters the tension between holding onto traditional culture and having its vestiges morph into new purposes that serve people in the present. For Cho, it was important for his people to hold onto important cultural values while still recognizing the needs of the people in the current world that would not stand still.

Recognizing discourse differences in all phases of research is important in representing cultures and their articulations of events, lived experiences, history, problems, and ideas. In a similar vein, historian David Carey Jr., from the University of Southern Maine said: "A problem with historians looking at multiple sources is that print technology was still controlled by colonizers." And as Gee (1990) says,

> To the extent that ideologies are tacit, removed or deferred and self-advantaging they are the root of human evil and leave us complicit with and thus responsible for the evil in the world. We cannot, perhaps, always remove the evil (though we must try), but we can remove our moral complicity. We do this, I believe, by doing a species of linguistics, namely discourse analysis, explicating our tacit and removed/deferred ideologies. That is why I think linguistics is a moral matter and why, in the end, to me, linguistics matters. (p. 21)

Martin Nakata's research (2007) looked at the hegemonic force that resides in words, the kind of discourse analysis that Gee (1990) was describing above:

> I wanted to understand knowledge systems and literature over a period of a century, and I tried to understand how it is that we have been inscribed into a Western order of things. How do all the disciplines play a role in that? How do they turn out subjectivities that look like they are based on science, whether it was in the memoirs of missionaries, government archives, or scientific research data, and how those subjectivities can inform us about our inscriptions. The 1850's was a time of understanding Islanders as "civilized/uncivilized," as "these uncivilized people." The talk is skewed on the relationship between these pairs, no matter which discipline. So when you read back into history, you see this sort of binary pair, the dominant principle for their mode of discourse between Indigenous people and Whitefellas. If you and I walked out the door now, and we saw a couple of dogs fighting, brutalizing each other, we'd say, "oooh savage," and that would have meaning in that context. But "savage" in this 1850's context rendered us as blood thirsty human beings. The next period in our history is around the 1870's, when missionaries first arrived, and they

started to produce written materials and bibles. If you look at all those descriptions, we are no longer "uncivilized" although they have the logic of that; the new binary was between "Christians" and "heathens."

In our interview, Nakata went on to describe the inscriptions made historically of Torres Strait Islanders, from decade to decade, from "heathens" on to "noble savages," whose lost souls needed rescuing. Then anthropologists declared after many years of research that Torres Strait Islanders were not animals but "inferior people" with a "scientized version of the savage mind," with capacities only at levels of young children, and as "childlike" (dirty, indolent, cheeky). For him this was the birth of the welfare state, evidenced by the many terms used for the government, legislation and their officers as protectors, in the sense of a father caring for his child. Nakata continued to tie the importance of discourse analysis to standpoint epistemology:

> Then the humanist period of the 1960's and 70's when Islanders are not inferior, just "different"...culturally. We're now living in the age of a people of difference. The hypothesis for me in my research work was that we were caught up in a knowledge system that we needed to understand in order to defend ourselves better. One of my reasons for seeking to establish an Indigenous standpoint is to depersonalize the arena, to lay grounds for open and mature discussion of ideas, to eliminate the patronization, defensiveness, and hostility, and to level the field for other conversations, so Indigenous research students can analyze their position as viewed by others. That will make it easier to develop the language needed to articulate their intellectual positions.

Nakata's analysis of discourse uncovered forces perpetuating oppression, and that analysis of discourse puts those inscribed through language in a position to defend themselves, enabling them to see the standpoints of those past and to encourage present Torres Strait Islanders and other oppressed groups to take on the agency of their own standpoints. Importantly, consciousness of discourse in cross-cultural arenas has become a sort of breakthrough in cross-cultural understandings.

The power of language issues in research

> Language is not a neutral medium that passes freely and easily into the private property of the speaker's intentions; it is populated-overpopulated-with the intentions of others. Expropriating it, forcing it to submit to one's own intentions and accents, is a difficult and complicated process.
>
> (Bakhtin, 1981, *The Dialogic Imagination*, 294)

In the fall of 1995 I learned just how offensive the misappropriation of a single word can be. I sat in on a session on Native American literature at the National Council of Teachers of English Conference. A speaker made the mistake of using the word "squaw" in her presentation, and a native attendee pointed out, very politely I might add, that "squaw" was indeed a native word popularized by white settlers to mean a native female, but in her language, from which it was drawn, it meant "cunt." Misused words can wound, however unintentional the wounding may be.

Whereas discourse involves the chosen language structure, conventions, and respect mechanisms for speaking and writing, this section will look at language at a more focal level and its complications in cross-cultural research. Through history the inextricable connections in language, culture, and reality have been studied. Of course, whole books have been written about language, but this section just gives a glimpse of language issues in cross-cultural research. There is an imperative to consider both the production of language and the reception of language between participant and researcher, and from data collection, to analysis, to audience in dissemination. By bringing forward the considerations of identity, positionality, standpoints, and discourse, as presented above, the links of language with all these concepts should increase our ability to do cross-cultural research with integrity. Language, as Sarah Jane Tiakiwai, a Māori researcher, noted, is a pivotal part of understanding the nuances of culture:

> Your cultural background has influenced your upbringing, and that influences your viewpoint and your perception. I would never say that I know everything about anything, and I don't speak the language fluently, though I can speak it. I think all of those things, including language, can influence who you are as a researcher and also how intimately you can understand the nuances of the culture.

Language, reality, and cross cultural research

For many years now, linguists have been trying to understand how and if language and culture can control perception and thought (linguistic relativity) because we use words primarily to articulate thought and because languages encode cultural and cognitive activity and intent. It has long been thought that language affects the way people think. Whorf and Sapir worked with these concepts in what is called the Sapir Whorf (1956) Hypothesis. Julian Cho gave me an example in talking about his Maya language, current culture, and conceptions of time:

> In terms of time: you can say a long time ago, last year, last month, yesterday, and now, but you can't break it down any more than that, the same with the future. Maya language doesn't go far in the future. For example, in Maya, people have not been used to planning for the next 20 years; it

has not been practical for them. It is not in our language. The concept of time is very different.

We do know that ancient Maya people had relatively sophisticated calendars, so this example may well be one of cultural loss as well as the way in which current Maya language can affect thinking (for more on conceptions of time, see Boroditsky, 2000).

Since the inception of the Sapir Whorf Hypothesis (Whorf, 1956), linguists continue to work with these concepts. Whereas a strong version of this hypothesis has been pretty consistently refuted because much thought does happen beyond language (Heine, 2011), a "weak" version of the hypothesis is recognized, acknowledging the influence of language and culture on thought and perception (Lucy, 1997; Geeraerts and Cuyckens, 2007). What linguists are still trying to discern is how much. Do multiple words for a concept that has only one word in another culture mean more semantic distinctions, or the ability to think in finer detail or complexity about something? While these debates proceed, what we do know is that language does in limited ways influence the way one thinks. For instance, there are culturally different perceptions of color, such as different numbers of words to describe the broad spectrum of color (Hardin and Maffi, 1997; Lucy, 1997; Davies, 1998; Heine, 2011). Furthermore, spatial descriptions can vary across cultures, from Western descriptions formulated as reading is done, from left to right, as opposed to descriptions by those who live in close proximity to nature, who describe a space based on directions related to the travel of the sun—descriptors such as east, west, north, and south (see Pederson, 2007, and Heine, 2011 for fuller summaries of these ways in which language influences cognition).

Language has been generated so that human beings can communicate information essential to survival and to relationships. Those in small communities need to say less to get across information than those who have to communicate regularly with those outside their immediate environment. The need to decontextualize information was rarely necessary in traditionally small, oral cultures that had little outside interaction (Gray, 1990; Cleary and Peacock, 1998) because "What binds people in a community is this shared recognition, this sense that 'I know that you know that I know what you mean'" (Bruner and Weisser, 1991).

When you come from outside of the small community, there is a danger in thinking that the participants are less adept at language, have fewer words, or, in the worst scenario, are less clever than those from your own culture. However, they may well be relying on shared information, eye contact, non-verbal communication, and tone of voice, all of which hold meaning that researchers might not recognize (Hall, 1973). Understanding the nature of language can obviate some of these misassumptions. Smaller vocabulary doesn't necessarily mean less cerebral activity, but it may mean that there is less need for an extensive vocabulary or a more abstract vocabulary in order to have a rich life in that community.

Further understandings of language and thinking are in the making. For instance, Kim's (2002) research notes that those of East Asian heritage are more apt to have their thinking impeded if they are simultaneously talking about what they are thinking; whereas thinking aloud has little effect on the performance of European Americans (see also Heine, 2011, p. 317). Furthermore, in some cultures, listening and learning are more accepted and practiced than active involvement in discussion. As Peacock says, silent native students may look as if they aren't attending but they are generally thinking all the time (Cleary and Peacock, 1997).

Language as power/status

Schooling and educated parentage have provided some people with what has been deemed "correct" speech, the standard dialect of a language. Those who do not speak the standard dialect may miss out on the privilege that accompanies it and bear one of the "hidden injuries of class" (Sennet and Cobb, 1973)—an acute awareness that their language is inadequate in some situations. For centuries, privileged discourses have legitimated the educated class (see Foucault, 1972, 1980). Although all languages and their dialects are linguistically complete (they have a consistent syntax), some hold more status and power than others. As many linguists have reiterated, "A language is a dialect with a Navy behind it." Dialects and discourse are fraught with political-economic factors (see Kroskrity, 2000, for a review of these issues). In interview, Shirley Brice Heath said: "People invariably link the language that you speak with the culture and degree of civility or possibility that you have within you." Dana McDaniel related an event that she experienced as a budding linguist when she wanted to better understand the dialect of her Tennessee relatives. She thought she would be an insider in her informal inquiry:

> I have relatives in Tennessee who I never see anymore, but we used to go there when I was younger, and I guess the last time I went I was already interested in linguistics, so I tried to ask them about their use of a certain structure. I wanted to know if they said it a certain way or another way. I couldn't get anything out of them. These were my relatives; they're supposed to be my culture. I tried to ask them and what they kept saying was, "We don't speak well, don't ask us, you need to ask someone else," but I was thinking, "I want to know how you speak."

This said, there can also be intense pride in dialect. Status for those with strong cultural pride may be speaking the dialect of those they respect, and resistance to standard dialect may be a way of feeling pride. It should be a human right to have pride in one's home language and to have others respect it, but, in past attempts at assimilation by dominant cultures, speaking one's own language or dialect has been both prohibited and, sometimes, punished.

As a researcher, unless one is an "insider," the dialect of a participant might be difficult to replicate; furthermore, it might be perceived as manipulative if a researcher were to try, instead of being interpreted as showing solidarity. Wandering between the "hidden injury" and cultural pride, there can be status language resistance. Renato Rosaldo (1993) talks about another aspect of this issue:

> In many cases, the oppressed fail to talk straight. Precisely because of their oppression, subordinate people often avoid unambiguous literal speech. They take up more oblique modes of address laced with double meanings, metaphor, irony and humor.... Wit and figurative language enable not only the articulation of grievances and aspirations under repressive conditions but also the analysis of conflicts and ironies produced by differences of class, race, gender, and sexual orientation. (p. 190)

Figuring out how to interact with people over language in a non-pejorative, non-patronizing, respectful way is important with people whose families or education hasn't enabled them to acquire what even they might deem to be the "proper" language and the language that they might well recognize as the language of power.

Culturally specific words, metaphor, and meanings

Paula Gunn Allen (as quoted above) and Archibald (2008) note that, as Archibald says, "The translations lose much of the original humour and meaning and are misinterpreted and/or appropriated by those who don't understand the story connections and cultural teachings" (p. 7). Hence, much can be lost in a translation. Yet, finding those who are positioned to do effective translations is imperative. Furthermore, we know that, even in the same language, the concepts behind a word shift from one culture to another. Even words won't stand still. For instance, several researchers were interested in the mutability of meaning of one text from one culture to another. Stephen Muecke, researcher from the University of Technology in Sydney, Australia, said:

> I'm fascinated by the way in which a text moves from one culture to another and takes on new meanings, a bit like the way in which the Bible gets picked up by other cultures and gets reinterpreted and integrated with their own traditions. I'm interested in the way new meanings attach, and what enables them to move around, and what kinds of theoretical apparatuses hang off a text that enable it to be read or used in one way or the other. A good piece of cross-cultural research will always have

funny words in it from other places, even if it's in their kind of Creole language, but then there are words you feel you have to include even in your English translation. You keep a word because it's conceptually important and, therefore, shifts understandings. But to just assume you can translate and present in English is not good enough. To take seriously the concepts from the other side is to allow your own conceptual schema to shift and change, and it reaches you as the subject's speaking because then you can talk to these other people now using their terms.

Permutations of meaning, when language moves from one culture to another, can be more complicated than interpretation. Though literal translation might be a necessary but problematic step, there are more subtle complexities that surface when one is trying to find common meanings as one translates one language and culture to another. I've repeated here some of what Chris Winch has said in researching the standardization of vocational qualifications across countries in the European Union:

> The word "skill" doesn't really have a ready equivalent in German. And also terms like "qualification" look the same but actually carry a very different cultural baggage and are substantially different concepts, even within the quite close western European countries... In Germany, social identity is constituted more by one's occupation than it is in the UK. And that is a significant issue in terms of what a qualification represents. The EU does want to develop an international way of recognizing vocation qualifications, but my research partners suspect that it's a great deal more difficult than it might seem—it's not just a paper exercise. The German concept of liberal education, a complex concept with elements of self-discovery, doesn't really map well onto the Anglo-Saxon one. The Germans distinguish between a rounded capacity usually committed to an occupation called a *Fähigkeit* and a knack of a specific skill called a *Fertigkeit*, both involved in preparation. And that simply does not map onto English at all. Superficially the conceptual issues in the way the two cultures think about education might look the same, but when you actually look what the competence is, it's a different beast.

Furthermore, in multicultural situations there can be complexities between different cultures even in the same country. Ines Sanchez at the University of Belize talked about his venture of studying history and its relation to the naming of places:

> I did research on the names of villages. The name that really started something was Sarteneja. Talk about that village name didn't stop, even when I left. One group said it was a Spanish word; another group said it was a Maya phrase: Sar-ten-eja, Yucatecan Maya. But the consensus was that the original people were from a Mestiso village, so would they use a Maya

phrase to name their village? They have a well in the center of a rock, a pool of fresh, clean water. It's claimed that this man came and built his house around this well. When other people came, they had to ask this Yucatecan Maya for water, and so they had to speak to him in Maya. "*...a...ten...ja.*" Give me some water. So that when the people ask you where you live, you live where you ask for water. But if the majority of the people were mestisos, would they ask in Maya? I like to think of it as an awakening of the people's historical sense.

As we know, words can change in their meaning depending on cultural standpoint. Taking things metaphorically, reinterpreting religious events, parables, or tales, all happens regularly. Taking things literally can also change initially intended metaphoric meaning. Unstable meaning at the word level is frustrating to researchers; even attempted direct translations of the words can hold different connotations and different conceptions. Metaphors add a complexity to communication. Once I was caught in a downpour with my French friend Christian. I had been practicing my mediocre French on him and said, "*Il pleut des chats et des chiens.*" Even though we were racing for cover from the deluge, he managed to give me a look of bemused astonishment at yet another weird thing I was saying in his language. For Christian, the image of cats and dogs tumbling from the sky did not describe our bedrenched situation. Metaphors, though, are often tied to images, and conceptually there may be connections between metaphors in one culture and those in another with the concrete image as a stabilizing force; nevertheless, metaphors rarely translate exactly between languages, and they don't always translate between cultures either. Interesting work by Lakoff and and Johnson (1991) indicates that cultural metaphors reveal something about how speakers of that culture's language think, just as language can influence thought and perception.

Metaphor was mentioned by many researchers as both a barrier and a vehicle for understanding. Language, in its metaphorical and even literal sense, is often misconstrued, which can complicate or even elucidate a researcher's understandings and subsequent dissemination. We return to Martin Nakata, who continued his discussion of standpoint, culture, and language in talking about metaphors. "People teach well, and when they get to difficult content, they resort to a lot of metaphors and analogies as aids to help students understand concepts that may not be readily understood. But as you know, metaphors and analogies are cultural, and for Islanders they have specificity somewhere else, and that is why they confuse us even more, not necessarily deliberately."

Dana McDaniel found it fascinating to figure out how words could morph between communities and situations in Eastern Europe:

I thought the word "gadjo" meant "non-Gypsies." They would say, "Is that a Gypsy or a Gadjo?" But they'd mean, "Is it a Gypsy, or is it a Serbian." And then for the Albanians who were living there, they would call them Albanians, so what ended up happening is a word that in other Gypsy [communities] means "non-Gypsy," they really were using it to mean "Serbian" because Serbians were the non-Gypsies they were used to; that's who they went to school with, that's who they dealt with if they had to go to the post office or the bank. It took me a long time to discover what "gadjo" meant. "You come from America?" It was as though I came from Mars, but they didn't call me "Gadjo." They had heard of America as this big, amazing place, so they didn't have those negative associations and that may have helped me. If I had been Serbian and had tried to do research, I might have had a problem because I would have been associated with the oppressor.

Ferreting out the nuances of a culture's language, metaphor, and meanings may take both extra time and extra advice from those of the culture. Cross-cultural research simply takes more time and care.

Further issues of translation and its funding

Data collected in one's native language allow for linguistic subtleties, including those from colloquialisms and idioms, but as soon as translation occurs, even when it is from one dialect to another, deeper meanings are jeopardized (Temple et al., 2006). The act of translation in cross-cultural research moves concepts, events, and opinions from one language to another, from one culture to another, and, in some projects, back again. Good translations, of both informed consent forms and of data, are dependent on the good cultural knowledge, good language knowledge, and good research skills of researchers and fluent field assistants. Although I interviewed Abenaki adolescents in French, when it came to the translation of recorded material, I finally depended on a French-speaking colleague, used to working with native youth, to make sure that I had translated French Canadian idioms correctly and to heighten my understanding of native nuances of the language the youth spoke. More recently I went to France to do research for this book. I gave up after my first interview, realizing that my language skills weren't commensurate to the task of talking about theory and research. I couldn't trust that I had made myself understood in theoretical realms, and I was unable to ask good follow-up questions based on initial responses. The best scenario would have been for me to be fluent enough in both languages and the academic idiom. I might have tapped rich and divergent, non-Anglo perspectives which were lost to me without funding and the linguistic expertise it could have purchased.

Dependence on those of the culture is essential, beyond translation, to discussion on the analytical level with those hired as translators or interpreters (Temple, 1997; see also Temple and Young, 2004; Lincoln and

Gonzalez y Gonzalez, 2008, for more thorough considerations of translation). As cultural assistants, they can help with words when there is no translatable equivalent, and they can assist with variations in wording that might be needed in surveys, for instance, or other instruments (Delva et al., 2010).

Though discussions of translation strategies are extended in the literature, Goldstein, extracting from Brislin et al. (1973), offered a summary of translation guidelines useful for consent forms, questionnaires, and other documents:

(1) Use short, simple sentences.
(2) Use active rather than passive words.
(3) Repeat nouns instead of using pronouns.
(4) Avoid metaphor and colloquialisms.
(5) Avoid the subjunctive tense (such as verb forms with could or would).
(6) Avoid adverbs and prepositions telling where or when (such as frequent, beyond, upper).
(7) Avoid possessive forms.
(8) Use specific rather than general terms (such as cow, chicken or pig rather than livestock).
(9) Avoid words indicating vagueness regarding some event or thing (such as probably or frequently).
(10) Avoid sentences with two different verbs if the verbs indicate two different actions. (Goldstein, 2000, p. 50)

Researchers find they need to be cognizant that important data could be lost and/or skewed without sufficient funding for adept and multiple translators. Many researchers, especially anthropologists, talked of the mandate of learning the language and the language nuances of a community. Those researching in multicultural settings, however, have a more difficult situation. Beyond financial concerns, both Brian Street, linguistic ethnographer from King's College London, and Aydın Durgunoğlu, psychologist from the University of Minnesota Duluth, noted how the word "literate," for instance, and its converse "illiterate" had different connotations in different cultures, and how those connotations carried potential disrespect for participants. Durgunoğlu, psychologist of Turkish heritage, said:

One of the things we always emphasize in adult literacy research is that though participants are not "literate," they are not little kids. They have survived, they have rich life experience. Actually in Turkey the word for "ignorant" is also the word for "illiterate." So instead of using the word "illiterate"/"ignorant," we use a word that literally means "not reading/writing." I sometimes think if I was put in that context, if I hadn't had the privilege my parents provided for me, I would not have survived as well as some of those women did.

When researchers use a translator or interpreter, inevitably that person can clarify, explicate, distort, or even delete information that is important to understanding during analysis. In addition, if the translator is from a different social class, generation, educational level, or even gender, unconscious biases can affect translations. Again we come back to the value of working and deliberating with a collaborative cross-cultural team. Working over an extended period of time helps all—the researchers, the bilingual field assistants, translators, and team members—to understand the research, its methods and methodologies, and to inform the intersect between language and culture. This participation can continue to be useful in analysis.

Beyond trust in translation, one must decide whether the participant will trust an interviewer/translator. Rachel Hodge, researcher from the University of Lancaster, UK, worked with asylum seekers who were from a range of linguistic backgrounds:

> My intuition told me that just because someone is from their language group doesn't mean that they're acceptable as a translator and interpreter. The teacher of these students said: "Why don't you have 15 minutes with each student to find what language they might want to be interviewed in. As a way of getting to know them, I had a big map, and they showed me where their country was, and then we talked about their language and what language to use in the interview. Some wanted to be able to speak fluently in their home language. Some people were going to struggle being interviewed in English but wanted to be because it was an opportunity to speak English. For others, being interviewed in English resolved the issue of fear of who else might be involved; they'd already come to trust me. These people are in very fragile, vulnerable positions. Just because it was somebody from their language group didn't necessarily mean trust. I went to a conference on language brokering, and somebody had done research about what makes an interpreter acceptable to people. And the findings were that it didn't matter how expert you were; it was the empathy with the person that mattered the most.

That translation of research instruments, questions, and data translation are dependent on the knowledge both of cultural norms and of the variability of language and its dialects. A few researchers talked about the value of surveys and transcripts being translated by one translator or group of translators, and then translated back by another to check for accuracy of meanings. This process identifies concepts or words that are not readily translatable. This "back translation" technique and others are further discussed at length in other sources (for instance, Brislin, 1970, 1980; Liamputtong, 2010; Heine, 2011).

Respectful language and discourse: a point of contact

As Steve Muecke, researcher at the University of Technology in Sydney, Australia, said:

> To take seriously the concepts from the other side [of a cross-cultural relationship] is to allow your own conceptual schema to shift and change. They reach you as the subject's speaking, and then you can talk to these other people now using their terms. That's why anthropologists would say how important it is to go into a field and spend the first year learning the language.

There is incalculable value in a researcher's knowing another language. Returning to Susan Rodgers, she said:

> I have a depth in the Batak language that I wish I had in my Minangkabau work. In Batak, the printed text which I was working with was published in 1941, written by this remarkable Angkola Batak folklorist. It's kind of a Batak *Beowulf*, the first formal version of a great epic. I was able to do the translation in a way that had some depth because I had a Fullbright and time to be able to sit in the village, work with a ritual orator, checking every word, and these words go far beyond the dictionary. I had the leisure of a year to finish the translation. I was able to go back and forth between a great text, and a culturally based translation, having the assistance of some really bright colleagues, so I could have a theoretical base. Many Batak living in Jakarta could not do this translation, even if they were very fluent in English. They just didn't have the resources to get up into the high registers of Batak used in this text. Batak has an everyday conversational register, then various forms of oratory registers, like orations that the chiefs would give, then they've got this extra level of turi-turian epic speech and lament speech, beyond the competence of most Batak speakers today except for the oratory experts, the rajas. The bards have died; I think I tape recorded one of the very last ones in the 1970s. In regular Batak you talk about "head" as "*ulu*," but if you're speaking lament speech it would be "head, the bearer of burdens," and "hand, the asker for favors." Most urban younger Bataks today know only enough of the ritual oratory Batak to mumble their way through their own wedding, but they speak mostly the national language, Indonesian. Batak orators have superb ritual speech range but some city-based Indonesian anthropologists studying Sumatran societies do their fieldwork in fewer speech registers. But, though my Minangkabau textile work gets a good reception, I don't speak fluent Minangkabau. I can treat textiles with some

fieldwork accuracy and some historical accuracy, and say some interesting things about them, but I don't have the long-term fieldwork with the weavers as I do with the orators.

Though Rodgers has spent a great deal of her career studying language, many who work with multiple cultures and, hence, multiple languages in doing cross-cultural work do not have that opportunity. That said, any competence in the language has its benefits, as Ted Glynn, a researcher from Waikato University who has taken the time to learn Māori language, said: "Even putting the other language in the English text, though challenging to some, I find is one little point of contact." As Dana McDaniel said: "I think I wouldn't feel comfortable studying a language from a linguistic point of view without knowing it first. I've always so enjoyed that process, and I think people actually see that as respect for their culture." Over and over I heard from researchers who talked about the respect that derives from showing eagerness to learn the participants' language, even if they chuckle at your attempts.

We have already learned from Eleanor Bourke of the sensitivity that some cultures have about what they sense as the misappropriation of their language when they themselves have lost it. Though some cultures would rather lose their language than have outsiders privy to it or its sacred connections, many cultures really appreciate collaborative research that assists in the reclamation of language.

As researchers, our learning shifts our viewpoints and perceptions. The more we learn, the better our potential is in getting close to what is important knowledge to give back and/or to disseminate. We must acknowledge the complexity of our identity as researchers and that of the participants in our inquiries, being conscious of the resultant viewpoints of those identities and being conscious of how language interacts with culture and identity. Working on all that affects all phases of research. Just as we think we have a good grasp on all that, we also need the resilience to be aware that all these things are fluid. And perhaps the simplicity in all that complexity is, again, that "nothing stands still."

6
Entering Another Culture

In 1997 I traveled to the Aleut community of King Cove, Alaska, where the Aleutian Island Chain begins. A student of mine from my early years of teaching had taken a job there and married an Aleut man. By the time I arrived in that port of clear waters, she was the mother of two children, and after I'd been there for a week interviewing King Cove teachers and enjoying what they were doing, I could see why she made King Cove her home. On the weekends, I was immersed in the lively life of the village. The crews of the fishing fleet were preparing for the salmon season and waiting until the time was just right to head to sea. In just one day I had gone clamming with a favorite family uncle; seen sea lions in the harbor when visiting the family boat that was preparing to get underway; seen the postcard view of the mother seal, with baby on belly, eating shell fish in a lagoon; and been to the dump in the family vehicle, seeing ravens and eagles sitting on fence posts while bears recycled the garbage. When back at the house, an aunt called up to tell me to look into the cove so I could see the whale she had spotted breeching a few moments before. I missed the whale, but I was in awe with the place that the Aleut family loved, and I felt welcome in that research site.

That night the whole extended family were together for a birthday gathering for one of the men going to sea, and they were joking about the residential schools they had to go to as children during World War II when families were forcefully "evacuated" from their homes. While sitting round the table, they joked about their pranks, about ways they had managed to use their Aleut language when nuns couldn't hear, laughing over long-told stories. I said (from the researcher part of my bundle of identities, always intent on finding explanations for discrepant events): "It almost sounds like it was fun." Before the words even got out of my mouth, I wished I could have shoved them back down my throat. Dead silence hit the room. I had poured over books about the history of Aleut communities enough to know why I had ruined the mood. I well knew about the distress that Aleut families had experienced during World War II. I apologized, saying I knew how horrible that time was for them. Then they talked in a more serious vein about the cold buildings, the deprivation of language, the severity of those who oversaw their schooling, and I apologized again, made a joke that I can't even remember now, and they were back to jovial tales of past salmon seasons. It was okay again. I had apologized and learned from it, learned to listen to humor in a new way, humor from whose soul wound needed a humorous skin. And, in interviewing local teachers, I was learning how these adults' perspectives on their past experience shaped the way they viewed the education of their children and grandchildren.

Renato Rosaldo (1993) says that for the researcher, "Eclectic book knowledge and a range of life experiences, along with edifying reading and self-awareness, supposedly vanquish the twin vices of ignorance and insensitivity." Thanks to the Aleut family's kindness and the reading I had done, my moment of insensitivity was brief and excused. I was comfortable in that community due to the welcome the family gave me, but it was also due to the preparation that I had done for the "world-traveling" and "cross-cultural loving" that Lugones (1987) suggests. In research, it pays to prepare in just the ways which Rosaldo describes, but the best preparation, I found, was being prepared to be surprised.

Preparation to Enter Another Culture

For cross-cultural research, the literature review on your topic is simply not enough. Celia Haig-Brown said:

> In a lovely article, "This Bridge Called My Back," Judith Moscovich, a Latin American Jewish feminist, basically says that she was tired of people coming and saying, "Teach me about your people." She said something like, "There are libraries filled with books, videos, CDs. Go out there and inform yourself, and when you know something then come and have a conversation with me." I tell my students they too should go and immerse themselves in resources, and then once they get a grasp of it, push it aside, bracket it. There is an equal danger going into a community thinking you already know it from the way others have presented it.

Learning about a culture before one enters it is important, but the concept of bracketing is essential so that your reading about the culture doesn't shape what you have the possibility of learning (also see Denzin 1998; Gearing 2004). Ian Anderson talked about the parallel difficulty for researchers—unconscious assumptions:

> You carry a whole set of assumptions that you will unlearn through time. Understand, in the social sense, who you are about to engage with. Not your stereotypes. Find out a bit, ask some people, read a bit of history

to get a context, not about your research project but about the community. Be critical of taking for granted assumptions of words we glide over, like community identity. Ask: What are the institutional structures in the community? What are the systems of governance? Don't look for your model. It's probably not a parliamentary democracy. Secondly, is there a community leadership? Can you understand who represents whom? Never assume anyone represents everybody. Who are the agencies you need to engage with?

Below you will find the areas for which Anderson and other researchers urged preparation: politics, history, literature, language, religion/spirituality, time and patience, surface vs. deep culture, respect mechanisms, and humor.

Politics

The political structures of a culture may be easier to discern than the more subtle aspects of political interactions. At the more national level, are there political parties and what are they? Do people feel free to talk politically no matter what their political leanings? What parties represent what sort of people? What are the past and present driving issues of the day? How might these issues affect the way people line up on the problem you are studying?

   Multiple sources of information are safer than depending only on available print information. Before I went to Belize, I had studied what was available about the political situation, both of the prior British governance, which had left its mark, and of the country's present governance. I was surprised that many were appreciative of the traditions that colonization had left on education, but there were others who were both skeptical and frustrated. In the section in Chapter 5 on discourse, I related my experience in trying to get through a simple orientation meeting by figuring out the mode of discourse that was respectful in that meeting. I was also trying to understand politics in the community. Innes Sanchez added to my understandings:

> When I became the chief superintendent of education in Belize, I found that if someone is thinking and begins to criticize the government, it immediately becomes hard party politics. People have lost their jobs because they questioned. When you serve the government, you are to defend its policies and implement them. The day you can't keep from criticizing, you resign. Now I'm at the university. I'm enjoying independence and can use critical freedom.

Had I been working within a Maya village, I might have had to better understand political tensions within that particular community, or doing another study I might have needed to understand the tensions between the Maya communities and the federal government over land rights, or between that Maya community and the Garifuna, Creole, or East Indian communities, or between Belize and other Caribbean countries. For me the politics in the region were important in understanding the literacy issues. Anderson says: "Don't look for your model." But seeing other working models might enable you to see malfunctions in your own. Your research probably hasn't been designed to challenge the political system, but you do need to understand how that system might affect your area of inquiry.

History

Learning about the history of a community can give you much information to bracket. Billings and Donnor (2008, p. 74) note that even scholars of color must learn the intellectual antecedents of their cultural, ethnic, or racial group. Julie Canniff, who looked at notions of success in both Cambodian and Maine Island cultures, talked of the value of multiple sources for information:

> You absolutely have to know the historical context, the religious, the social, the political context from which the people come; for me, that was knowing about what happened during the Pol Pot regime, but also knowing about Cambodia prior to that time, knowing about the years that it had been colonized. There's preparation you need to do before you start conversations. Most likely, you're initially going to be talking to people in the community who are the best educated and have the best understanding of the nuances of the English language, but if you depend on them to be your sole informants or even the sole generation of participants then you're going to have very skewed ideas.

Preparation requires good start-up time in a library while realizing that colonizers often had control of the presses when much of history was being written. Time with other available informants will also give you different perspectives on the history of a region, or group within a region. Brian Street addressed another reason to study history that others shied from: "What do you do when you find things to dislike in other cultures? Develop some historical understanding of how behaviors came into being, find the reason for them. A certain situation may not be okay with you, but if you know why, you can still be respectful."

Literature

As one who prepares prospective teachers for working with literacy, it is perhaps natural for me to turn to literature in preparing myself to go into a new culture, if the literature is written by the people of that culture. My reading of *In the Castle of My Skin* by George Lamming was useful before I began research in Caribbean regions, and in arriving in Belize I found the secondary students reading this same book about Barbados. Critical reading of literature can allow one to see through multiple perspectives, to discern world views different than your own, to make sense of many facets of cultural life, to lessen the surprises that you get when you are within that culture. As Toni Morrison says (1993), "Cultural identities are formed and informed by a nation's literature" (p. 39). Of particular interest may be the literature of postcolonial critique and also literature that conveys "the function of indigenous origins in modern thought" (Cook-Lynn, 2008, p. 330), often contemporized use of myths and, hence, implied ethics of the community to be entered. Many cultures have their own indigenous folklore, as well as ethno-ethnographies and vernacular journalism. As I was winding up my interview with Chris Winch, I was glad to hear him talk about the value of literature:

> I want to mention that literary sources can be quite useful in terms of the European cross-cultural work. I've found it's useful to go back to this concept of *Bildungsroman*. It sheds an awful lot of light on what Germans understand, and what vocational education is thought to have. Reading people like Goethe and Gottfried Keller is a way of opening and clarifying a lot of issues. And for various complicated reasons, a lot of Germans are not as acquainted with their national literature as you would expect them to be, even people in the academic world.

I found that people were surprised and pleased when I alluded to their literature, letting them know that I valued the understandings that it leant to me or querying them about my confusions. In conversations, participants often gave me unexpected views on the literature, allowing me adjustments of interpretation and new perspectives. In talking with researchers in Australia and in New Zealand, I was astounded that many asked me whether I had read Toni Morrison's *Playing in the Dark: Whiteness and the Literary Imagination*. I was embarrassed to say that I hadn't, though I must have read every novel that she had written. I listened to what they had gotten from that nonfiction, and went home to read it and compared notes, better understanding where they came from.

Language

Since a good part of Chapter 5 is about language and its connections with identity and positionality, it hardly needs to be repeated that the more you know of a culture's language, even if it is a little, the more you might understand of their culture, and the better you might be accepted during your inquiry. As Michael Rosberg, economic anthropologist, said:

> When you go to Paris and try to speak French, and when you go into the Spanish-speaking world and try to speak Spanish, you simply get a better reception for your trying. People think you are very funny, and they'll help you, and in the Caribbean there is a modicum of respect because

you make the assumption that the other people are smarter than you are, and then a lot is tolerated. That was the lesson I had to learn, to throw back my head and talk.

Religion/spirituality

Religion, as described by Saroglou and Cohen (2011, p. 1309), "may be part of culture, constitute culture, include and transcend culture, be influenced by culture, shape culture, or interact with culture in influencing cognitions, emotions, and actions." In colonized lands, it is sometimes hard knowing what traditional religion was originally practiced and sometimes even harder to discern its residual effects. Ken Ralph at Yalbalinga Aboriginal Centre at Australia Catholic University said:

> Though many Aboriginal people put themselves down as Christian, of course the real question is: What are the others? We don't know. You have Aboriginal spirituality and you have Christian spirituality. In some communities we have different traditions, depending on what missionaries were there in the '20s or '30s, or even further back. When there has to be a ritual, the only rituals that are in place and ready to go are Christian; the other cultural rituals that might have been there are mostly undermined or lost. On the edges there are Aboriginal additions, but someone not sensitive to the past might see it as Christian.

Knowledge from books about the basic tenants of spirituality or religion in a region may be different than seeing it embedded in the ways of a community. Furthermore, it is important to learn how private a community is about sacred knowledge before beginning to ask questions. In trying to squeeze in a final interview with a gifted Hopi teacher before my departure, I tentatively asked her whether she would have time on the weekend. She explained to me that she needed to prepare food for a ritual for her son. I asked her if I might help her to prepare food and talk to her at the same time. That was a mistake. She abashedly, politely, but firmly explained to me that preparation of food was a part of the ritual and asked if we might go on after school hours and finish. Ted Glynn gave another example of how interwoven the spirituality of Māori is within the routines of daily life:

> I have found that Māori people can often switch mood, from formal to informal, almost like the ways the weather can change in this part of the world. They can have an extremely informal and joking kind of interaction going, and then remember someone who has died recently. Mid-sentence someone might say something directly to that [deceased] person: tell him off for forgetting to do something before he left this world or laugh over something hilarious the person did. Then suddenly

you are sensing deep, intense sadness, and then the mood of the inter-action may switch back again, and you can't predict those shifts from an agenda. For them, the spiritual world is real, and they are always present within it. So you just need to know that that can happen. And then they'll go on with the meeting, or revert to the previous interaction. While in my experience, Māori are fully task oriented, working with them can be a bit like being on an emotional roller coaster. At any time one or other of them might say, "We'd better say the *karakia*." Any Māori meeting, even quite formal ones, start and finish with a *karakia* (prayer or chant), usually, though not always, by the oldest person.

Spiritual events or even vestiges of traditional spirituality may be deeply embedded in the present and in the way of looking at the world, the ways of acting in the world, and even in agenda-led meetings, as above.

Time and patience: waiting at the well

You are asking us to make ourselves more vulnerable to you than we already are before we have any reason to trust that you will not take advantage of this vulnerability. So you need to learn to become unin-trusive, unimportant, patient to the point of tears, while at the same time open to learning any possible lessons. You will also have to come to terms with the sense of alienation, of not belonging, of having your world thor-oughly disrupted, having it criticized and scrutinized from the point of view of those who have been harmed by it, having important concepts central to it dismissed, being viewed with mistrust, being seen as of no consequence except as an object of mistrust.

(Lugones and Spelman, 1983, p. 580)

So many researchers had stories to tell about the need to have more time than they first considered for research. Wariness is a human attribute born from the defense mechanisms that accumulate from what Lugones and Spelman rightly identify as past harm. Of course, the more preparation you do, the faster things might move along, but if you think that you can enter a community and wade right into research, you are often mistaken. I found that having that patience was sometimes one of the hardest parts of research. Others were better at it. Sharon Kemp said:

I had planned to do research in a setting where there was a well-known sociologist, but he was out of the country when I arrived. I was there, but they didn't know what to do with me. In India the division of labor is such that sociologists study villages, and anthropologists study tribal people, so I was an anomaly. I had to explain why I was an anthropol-ogist studying in a village. They were doing a village study on health, so I followed a health worker so people could see me, and then I would sit at the well when the women would come. It seemed like I wasted and wasted time. Here I was, I only had so much time, and I had to get into my research. Finally, one day I went to the well, and someone said, "We've decided that you're here," and after that other women started talking to me and inviting me to their homes. It [my waiting] was almost like magic.

Though it is hard to relax and wait after finding as many connections as possible before locating yourself at your research site, time and patience are needed if research is to begin well. Steven Muecke from the University of Technology in Sydney said:

In relation to indigenous communities, the question should be: How much time are you prepared to put in as a researcher? Because you can go to an indigenous community and say, "I'm here to do such and such," and they might say, "Go talk to the old person over there." In other words: we don't have time for you at the moment, and we're only going to be prepared to work with you if you're prepared to spend time and do it gradually and go from the very superficial accounts we'll give you initially, through to the deeper accounts later...if you prove yourself worthy of receiving this.

Relative insiders too found they needed patience. Ken Ralph talked of approaching research having community connections:

Being Aboriginal doesn't necessarily give you an entree into every community. You have to take the time to be known. Even if you were introduced to someone, they might be suspicious of you. However, if you were going to a place where you had an entree, family connections or knew other people, that would help enormously. You just come around for a while, and people would notice how you react and how you deal with them, and eventually someone would say, "Are you Koori, and you would say, "Yes," and then it gets out. You can't push yourself onto a community. You just be yourself. If you try to be something you're not, then you will come unstuck somewhere along the line.

Being oneself while not offending local sensitivities has been repeated by many researchers as a value. This is quite distinct from wanting to be of the other culture, a form of escapism from what you didn't value in your own culture, wanting to be of a culture because of its desired facets, to be a "wannabe" in indigenous cultures or to "go native" in anthropology (Sluka and Robben, 2007).

Time itself is differently conceived and lived in different cultures. Robert Levine (1997, in Goldstein, p. 337) "suggests that one of the most profound adjustments a sojourner must make is to cultural differences in the pace of life." Those in cultural studies often distinguish between "clock time," monochromic, sequentially scheduled events, and "event time," polychromic time, often experienced in non-Western cultures when relationships matter more than a schedule or calendar. The latter is termed polychromic because multiple events might be happening simultaneously, so a schedule doesn't work. A good conversation wouldn't end because one is out of time (Hall and Hall, 1990). Even in Western cultures I've noticed differences: In England, I noticed, academics actually take time for tea, often twice during the academic day; whereas, American scholars race from meeting, to class, to office hours, back to meetings, often eating lunch at their desk. In the United States, native people often tease themselves about being on "Indian time," yet my Ojibwe colleagues sometimes teased me about running more on "Indian time" than they did, as I often ran in the door a few minutes late to our collaborations. In Chapter 5, Julian Cho noted that some languages do not even acknowledge the time constructs of Western culture. Mere Berryman, a Māori educator and researcher at the University of Waikato, said:

> Absolutely, it's a matter of time. Mason Durie, a really esteemed Māori academic, talks about the concept of time as being a period in which particular events have to unfold and be addressed, suggesting 'the domain of time' in Māori as being quite separate from how it is understood in Western society. Things will follow a cycle where certain things have to be done, and it may take a lot longer, but in the end of the time you will be sure that what needs to happen has happened. I think that's hugely sensible.

Beyond time, some research questions just demand more solid relationships. As anthropologist Louis-Jacques Dorais said,

> Once people are confident that you will keep confidentiality, then they generally speak, but of course it all depends on the topics you are to do. I know some people doing research on suicide; things like that are more difficult to do. You have to have longer contact with the community. They have to know you, to trust you, and to know you full-on.

In most cases, the more invasive the research questions, the more solid the relationship between the researcher and the community must be. Yet, in some cases, in some cultures, your closeness to a community might make troubling things harder for participants to talk about, might make participants feel more vulnerable because of that very closeness. Hence the friendly bartender phenomenon: when it is easier to talk to a stranger than to someone who has connections to you.

Entering a community may be considerably easier if research questions are initiated by the community members; then finding the connections for access may follow logically. That was the case for Rachel Hodge, researcher at Lancaster University, UK. Her path to a research setting was paved by the concern of those running a program for asylum seekers, though that still didn't obviate the time and patience needed to approach the collaborating teacher and the asylum seekers:

> At first the collaborating teacher was protective; she had rotten research done in her class before where people had parachuted in and thrown questionnaires at the students. I'd decided early on that absolutely every aspect of the research would be negotiated with the teacher, paying her for a meeting a week so that we could both bring our expertise into it. So rather than me explaining methodology, we discussed methodology, roles, how to acknowledge students' time, what to do about analysis, and to what degree she wanted to be involved in different stages of the research. So she became totally committed and excited. Time was the key to working with her and her students: time to build rapport, being around before doing any interviews, explaining the benefits of the research.

Because funding for research is often a necessity and because tenure clocks run unabated, time is an issue. Until funding agencies have the money and see the need for lead time and on-the-ground time in communities, this will always be an aspect of cross-cultural research that will be problematic. Until university tenure committees see the value in collaboration, time will be an issue, hence the reason why many experienced researchers return to the same community once trust is gained, collaboration forged, and partnerships nurtured.

Surface/deep culture/world view/taboos

In 1985 at the University of Massachusetts, I felt honored to be included in a seminar with Paulo Freire. His stories given within the seminar meetings were fascinating. One week he told of an experience saying something like this:

> When I was in Africa, talking with an African scholar, I was walking along, and he took my hand and held it. I was so uncomfortable that I had to remove my hand, hoping that I wasn't looking shocked. Then some time later, I was walking with a Scandinavian scholar, and without thinking about it, I put my hand on his shoulder. I could see him squirm, and I thought again of my walk with the African scholar.

Proxemics and other ways of being are often different in different cultures. Edward T. Hall (1966) explained Freire's discomfort above using the labels of low contact vs. high contact cultures (see Goldstein, 2000, p. 177, for more on appropriate display of emotions). What is comfortable in one might be deeply uncomfortable or misinterpreted in another. Though surface culture is relatively easy to fathom, knowing how to react to it can be confusing. Recently, I had discussions with student teachers who felt that they should be able to dress in the inland Maya villages in Belize as they dress at home: tank tops with exposed shoulders and short shorts. Our discussion ranged from whether you should feel free to live your own culture no matter where you are, to what is respectful to those who might feel offended by what they perceive as provocative dress, even to whether any of those reactions might be a form of racism. They ended up saving their beachwear for Belizian resorts.

What is often called deep culture is harder to discern and its understandings harder to articulate, and yet that deep culture is often the well spring of human motivation and behavior. Other words researchers used for deep culture were "cultural norms," "ways of being," and "world view," or what Shein (2012) terms the "third level of culture." Whereas cultural artifacts (modes of dress and eating, for instance) are the first level, and espoused values and beliefs the second, the third level (unconscious and embedded ways of being) is difficult to recognize. Knowing something about all three levels before entering a culture will get a researcher on the way to being culturally competent and sensitive, but again brackets are advised. As Howard Groome, retired professor from the University of South Australia, said: "I think to be a successful cross-cultural researcher, you have to be very aware of the world view of the people. That sounds very obvious, but so many people aren't." Groome went on to talk about the shame/honor society in which he worked:

> Many Australians still don't understand how deeply "shame" is ingrained in the Aboriginal psyche. Shame can be inculcated by the simple act of being spotlighted [praised], not necessarily for antisocial behavior. Some sensitive schools refrain from spotlighting. Instead of saying, "Johnny won a competition," they'd say, "Ah, you know Johnny Alberts had a great time over the weekend." He was recognized, but he didn't have to come out and be praised in the front of the whole school. Other schools embarrass and shame Aboriginal children by following their accepted patterns of praise and reward. This is not limited to younger Aboriginal people. Some indigenous researchers can struggle when they come to publish their results. How do they achieve this without drawing too much attention to themselves?

I immediately remembered what I observed at Tuba City High School in Arizona, USA, where they had developed ways of acknowledging Navajo students for success that were quite private. White children would have quite liked the public praise, but Navajo children were shamed by being praised in public. And shortly thereafter I was in New Zealand where Joan Metge, who writes extensively about non-verbal language and behavior, told me about what her book (*In and Out of Touch,* 1986; see also Metge, 2010) had said about shame:

> *In and Out of Touch* is about a phenomenon that causes a lot of misunderstanding between the Māori and Pākehā. [For instance,] the way Māoris behave when they feel shy, embarrassed, or ashamed covers a wide spectrum. And they behave in ways which often Pākehās interpret as either sulky or guilty. And a lot of the very painful stories are about situations in which teachers have misjudged their behavior and punished them for something which certainly did not warrant punishment.

I use the issue of "shame" as just one example of the deeper culture that the eye can't always see. Shame can evidence itself differently in different cultures and show itself through different non-verbal behavior. Finding books like the well respected one that Metge wrote can be a boon to a researcher, offering understandings that can be bracketed. However, as soon as that is said, we must be conscious that our ability to know the ways of being in another culture through written material or images, is, as Said (1985) noted earlier, plagued by those very sources of information. Information through media narrows one to the perceptions and expertise of the source (see also Stonebanks, 2008; Heinle, 2011). Images given to us in media or in book literature may have their biases that we must scrutinize through lived experience, observation, and reports by "others." Again: "Be prepared to be surprised."

Being observant about non-verbal behavior may also be useful in discerning deep culture. Several researchers have mentioned that in interviewing in cultures where eye contact might be considered disrespectful, they (and I include myself here) found that sitting next to a participant was less discomfiting to the interviewee than sitting across from them. Cho talked to me about Maya adolescents who were expected to be able to address audiences in the multicultural Toledo Community College curriculum. Being from his culture, he knew why the Maya secondary students had so much difficulty. Yet, being the spokesperson for the Maya people in land-rights disputes, he also understood their need to have such skills. He said:

> Sometimes the Maya students even put their face to the board and their back to the audience, and I can relate to their experience because I went through that, too. That would be very strange for your American teachers. It takes time for young Mayas to have the confidence to project to the entire class. In the Mayan tradition, you don't look at the person when you are talking to the person. Especially when the elders meet, they don't

look at each other. You don't get very close to a person when you talk to them. When you visit people, the visitor might be at the door, and the other person might be very far away. I think it's from oral tradition, but you might translate that into shyness.

Ways of showing respect were also seen by Flynn Ross, researcher at the University of Southern Maine. She reiterated something that Clifford Geertz (1983) said, calling research as much "unlearning" as "learning." Ross said:

We've been researching students who used to be teachers in their home countries—Indonesia, Somalia, Sudan, Serbia, Iran. Pretty universally, American schools are different for them. I've been learning about cultural response to clinical supervision from my students rather than always my students learning from me. For instance, a mentor teacher thought that his student teacher from Somalia was being "lazy." I was trying to understand this because when I worked with the student, he did show initiative. I asked, and he said that he respected his mentor so much that he was waiting to be asked. What was perceived by the mentor as laziness was behavior of respect in his culture. His mentor teacher was accustomed to self-driven student teachers from the United States. For supervisors, cross-cultural interpretations of specific behaviors can result in misinterpretation of intentions.

Martin Nakata prompts an important caution:

Work that I have done critiques the cultural difference model. This is because often people use the term culture as "static," assuming a single entity that is unchangeable, and that it is the same for males and females and the children, and that it is the same for all the different language groups. What's amiss in all this is the concept that culture is always about changing. I understand truly why people have latched onto this anthropological concept. There are now decades of positive benefits that have come from the efforts to identify as an indigenous culture, and I think that is healthy. But is this acceptance of the apolitical forms that suit and benefit the colonial regimes?

And we come full circle, yet again, to Julian Cho's "Nothing stands still."

Respect mechanisms

Closely related to issues of discourse and other deep culture are the respect mechanisms that fieldworkers should consider. Susan Rodgers said: "In Muslim Sumatra, I do have to take care that my unruly curly hair is stuffed primly into a neat ponytail so as not to insult the more conservative Muslim men; we need to be ultra-respectful as unveiled hair is a big issue in parts of Muslim Southeast Asia." Shirley Brice Heath described respect mechanisms as particularly important in the research that brought about her seminal text *Ways with Words:*

> I grew up bi-dimensionally, and you might even say multiculturally. I was able to learn to identify across situations because of my foster parents: my mother worked in a factory and my father as a milkman. And those various identities had a lot to do with my being very observant and quite able to pass, wherever I was, as something else. So it was a case of my being multi-selved. In a way I was an anthropologist from day one if what this means is that you observe and remain the fly on the wall and not try to interfere with whatever the environment is. I could move comfortably between the white working class and the black working class. It was ease with the language, the ease with the respect mechanisms, the ease with the cross gender, the cross age. In Trackton, I never called anyone who was older than I by their first name, ever. They were either called Aunt Berta, Uncle Freja, or if they were between sixty and forty, and I would've been in my thirties, I would call them Mrs So-and-so or Mayor or Reverend or Pastor. You have to know and abide by the politeness terms.

Humor

> One of the best ways to understand a people is to know what makes them laugh. Laughter encompasses the limits of the soul. In humor life is redefined and accepted. Irony and satire provide much keener insights into a group's collective psyche and values than do years of research.
>
> Vine Deloria (1969, p. 146)

When you figure out the humor of a community different than your own, you are on your way to entering with a deeper respect and with more comfort as a researcher (Goldstein, 2000, 323). As Tom Ketron, a participant in a past study of mine, said about his work in native settings in the southwest of the US,

> Finding their sense of humor helps. Humor works, but not to insult or to degrade. And I'll poke fun at myself. So you can't be wrapped too tight. In this setting, you joke with them, but you have to let them laugh and joke at you, too. In this setting it has to go both ways.
>
> (Cleary and Peacock, 1998, pp. 39–40)

As a researcher, I have learned to listen carefully to humor. In some cases I have found messages ensconced in humor that are calculated to tell me something. Sometimes the messages come straight to me, but I have learned to listen and try not to take offense when others attempt to tell me something circuitously through humor. It is intended to be gentler than anger.

This takes concentration. I can give the immediate response that humor often elicits, laughter, even if it is at myself; one must come up with some immediate response. But, I also need to distinguish between the kind of teasing that lessens social distance from the kind of teasing that has a serious message about the topic I am researching or my method of gathering information. Tom Peacock, my colleague in research past, taught me a lot about humor. At first I bristled when his humor was directed at me, and then I settled in and laughed and learned. He said (Cleary and Peacock, 1998, p. 40):

> Laughter is often prescribed as the best medicine for all that ails us. That laughter is good for all parts of the self is an assertion that has proven itself through medical research. Humor is a way of coping with hardship and sorrow. But humor isn't solely a way of survival; it's a way of teaching, and it's part of humility and leveling. Think about it that way.

In summary, preparing as much as possible through library resources and contacts with people, cognizant of the culture in which you want to enter, offers a preliminary resource for the researcher, but skills of observation, resilience, and responsiveness while one figures things out in situ are essential to the researcher. "Bracket" what you have learned while waiting to confirm it or to vary your initial understanding with your own experience, but, again, prepare to be surprised.

Value of a long-term commitment

Commitment to the community also indicates that the primary allegiance is to the community and not to other entities. David Carey Jr. said:

> The longer I was there [in Guatemala], people really saw me as independent. A couple of people started to identify me as a local historian. So, there was a sense that people could come and tell their stories, that I wasn't connected politically with the alcalde or other leaders in that way.

Geoff Munns talked about the willingness to wait until the time was right:

> There were times where I turned up for interviews, and I could tell that the time was wrong. They didn't want to ring me up to say, "Don't come," but when I turned up, I could just sense that the time was not right. So I just said, "Look, what if I come later, in two weeks' time?" When I came back, I could sense then that the interview was ready to go, so then it became a lot richer.

In some areas with some purposes, researchers might want to collect information from multiple cultures, but anthropologists and historians, for instance, might want to have a long-term continual presence in one place. Susan Rodgers said:

> It's just like Malinowski said, that you have to cut your ties with your home society for a sufficiently long period of time so that in the nature of social relationships you begin to depend on the local people for your everyday friendship relations. And you do all of your work in whatever language they're using, so you are no longer dealing with a translator. I have the extra benefit of living with a Batak family. That just gives you access like nothing else; you're plugged into a friendship network, people know who you are because the family introduces you, but you have to select the right family first or you make big mistakes.

Long-term commitments can allow you to wrap back on your research with residual or evolving questions, and allow you to follow up on local needs that you might not have been fully conscious of in your first round of research.

Arriving as a respectful learner/collaborator

I asked all 70 researchers: "What advice can you give to others about crossing into a new culture?" Although they had many suggestions for sensitive and effective methods of presenting themselves and talked about problems that arose in both initial and prolonged contacts, most used the words "respect" and "learn." Joan Metge summed up what respect meant succinctly: "Develop friendly respectful relations; and respect means not manipulating, not pushing them into doing anything, not intruding." The trick, of course, is learning what is "pushing" or "intruding" because what is, for instance, intruding in one culture isn't necessarily so in another. When interviewing teachers on the Navajo reservation, I wanted to go to some of the events and open ceremonies in nearby villages. Navajo people told me often that events would be happening, but they didn't expressly invite me. Another academic explained to me that just their telling me of events was equal to an invitation; more than that would have been trying to influence my decision whether or not to come. As a non-native person, I would have be invited, even urged to come, to feel like I was not being intrusive. In a similar way, I also learned that outsiders intervening to "help" can be irritating to many Native Americans, even perceived as meddling; advice was only appropriate when requested. In contrast, when my Turkish friend first came to the USA to do graduate work, I learned to ask her three times if she wanted more to eat at dinner. On the third offer, she had seconds; whereas, in some regions, Americans might say, "Mind if I have seconds," and then I would feel flattered by their appreciation of what I was serving. In a similar vein, I appreciated what Mere Berryman, Māori researcher, said about entering another culture: "You are a guest. Observe. Children learn their own culture by observing. Wait, watch, wait some more. Your unconscious mind may be making sense of the culture faster than you are able to in your conscious mind." She continued:

> It's about being able to step outside one's comfort zone in order to do that learning and in order to participate, with humility, realizing that we can learn from the other. It takes a huge amount of humility to come to that positioning, and it helps to learn interactional patterns.

Some researchers noted that it was important to drop assumptions in order to be able to learn. Celia Haig-Brown said:

> I understand a lot about the problematic relations colonialism has left, but once I go into a new community situation I need to listen carefully, not assuming to know. Once you've actually listened you can begin to try to figure out how you can be useful, but you absolutely can't go assuming anything. If you know how to be in one Aboriginal community, you know quite a lot about being in another Aboriginal community, but not everything. You just have to assume you know nothing; be quiet and listen.

Michael Rosberg also talked about the humbling process of learning. His sage advice:

> Saying, "What is going on here?" as opposed to seeing it as wrong. What is the logic behind it? In what way does it make sense? Everything that a person does, there is some kind of logic to it. I had to figure out about not making assumptions over and over again because I was raised with people making assumptions all around me, about inferiority: "If they were smart, they wouldn't be poor, would they?" It turns out it isn't like that. So you have to have those embarrassing situations when you say, "Oh, I was just behaving like an ass." After awhile, you get smartened up by the constant reminder that you are dealing with people who are bright. The critical factors aren't education, color, location, third world versus first world; it's the experience of the individual, the breadth and depth of their vision, and their ability to articulate something or to keep something to themselves.

Entering a community as a learner also means looking past some things that distress you, to the system that created those things. As Shirley Brice Heath said,

You are a learner, you are a know-nothing, and what they know will have strong elements that will enrich you and that you can respect. That's not to say that you come away saying, "I love everything they do." No, I didn't love the fact that the people were taking much more alcohol into their lives than quote "I thought they should" and that people were getting ripped off in the local system. But I looked at the system as it was interacting with them.

Opening yourself to understand another

This is one of the unresolvable problems of anthropology...A process by which each of us confronts our respective inability to comprehend the experience of others even as we recognize the absolute necessity of continuing the effort to do so.

(Edward Said, 1985)

When we come to another person with the genuine impetus to learn and understand, we have to do that by coming away from our initially myopic views and ways of being, resultant from our inextricable embodiment in our home culture. Enculturation is powerful, and researchers often have to endeavor to work beyond it. Going into research settings as respectful learners is essential in this endeavor; Lugones and Spelman (1983) summarize its difficulties:

This learning calls for circumspection, for questioning of yourselves and your roles in your own culture...; it demands recognition that you do not have the authority of knowledge; it requires coming to the task without ready-made theories to frame our lives. This learning is then extremely hard because it requires openness (including openness to severe criticism of the white/Anglo world), sensitivity, concentration, self-questioning, circumspection. (p. 581)

Quoting from my interviews with Michael Rosberg,

Alfred Shutz, the phenomenologist, starts off in the direction that we are pretty much locked in our own selves. There is cotton batting between ourselves and everything else of our own awareness. Alfred Shutz suggests that you would have to imagine what it would be like, you cannot know what it would be like. A lot of the trouble is to get past ourselves. We keep on tripping over our world views; it is very hard to acknowledge another world view. We mouth it, but there has been a lot of imagining for me, like the taxi driver and the nun who told him: "God will pay." I wonder what it is like to be her, to be him. How would one experience the world like that? And for him, what is it to be deferential? You can learn about the factors that are influencing a behavior, but ultimately you are going to fail to experience that position, you can just see the logic of it. One-on-one formal experience helps you at least find the space to understand that there could be another perspective.

Schutz (1967) also notes that by interpreting outward behavior in terms of what lies beneath it, we can come to better understand others, but we must acknowledge that the meaning that drives a participant's behavior might not be the meaning that we attach to that same behavior. In research, one attempts to interpret the actions and words of others as others intend them. Schutz points to the phenomenon of attention, of thought and reflection beyond simple observation of others, moving toward understanding another; and, at the same time, he talks of the rediscovery of the "I" in the "Thou." In simple observation, one observes another without trying to affect the other, but in a social relationship both observe each other and both affect the other, not only, "mutually sensitive to each other's responses" but "sensitively aware of the nuances of each other's subjective experiences" (Schutz, 1967, p. 202). In face-to-face interactions, not only can I, the researcher, constantly correct my own responses and understandings ("Have I understood you correctly?" "Don't you mean something else?" "What do you mean by such and such an action?" (p. 140)) but also the participants can change their interpretation of me.

Beth Bartlett, researcher in women's studies at the University of Minnesota Duluth, says in *Rebellious Feminism: Camus's Ethic of Rebellion and Feminist Thought (2004)*:

> The point raised here by Camus has also been picked up on by feminists grappling with the issue of enlarged thought—the problem of how we attain knowledge of perspectives other than our own, how we know the voice of the concrete other. Specifically, feminists have raised questions about the possibilities of imaginative knowing. (p. 92)

Bartlett quotes Spelman (1988) as saying:

> If I only rely on my imagination to think about you and your world, I'll never come to know you and it. And because imagining who you are is really a much easier thing for me to do than find out who you are, ... I may persist in making you an object simply of my imagination, even though you are sitting right next to me.
>
> (pp. 179–180)

Bartlett continues:

> Even with the best of intentions, we cannot assume we can imagine the perspective of another. We must actively seek out and incorporate the standpoints of others. When we cannot, solidarity requires at the very

least recognizing that all are not included and that our knowledge is at best limited.

(pp. 92–93) (see also Geertz, 1973; Black, 2010, for more on imagining)

Whereas objectivists are apt to urge the researcher to construct a purposeful distance from the participant to eliminate bias, others believe that such elimination of bias is impossible. Those who consider "participatory consciousness" would rather believe that eliminating distance is a way to understand the other. Stemming from the work of Goethe, participatory consciousness allows a holistic mode of knowing another. Some of our senses, like sight and hearing and taste, are rather developed at birth and other higher-order perceptions, like empathy, develop more gradually. Bishop and Glynn (1999) cite Heshusius (1994) as noting that this involves having a "somatic, non-verbal quality of attention that necessitates letting go of the focus of self" (p. 15).

Lugones (1987) recommends traveling to each other's worlds to recognize one's plurality of selves. She also values "openness to surprise":

A particular metaphysical attitude that does not expect the world to be neatly packaged, ruly...We are not wedded to a particular way of doing things. While playful we have not abandoned ourselves to, nor are we stuck in, any particular "world," We are *there creatively*. We are not passive...The reason why I think that traveling to someone's "world" is a way of identifying with them is because by traveling to their "world" we can understand what it is to be them and what it is to be ourselves in their eyes. Only when we have traveled to each other's "worlds" are we fully subjects to each other. (p. 401)

The best we can probably do is to bring together all our faculties to understand another:

- our ability to juxtapose our world against others, to explore our own world view, the assumptions it carries, its limitations, using all our senses to take in information;
- our ability to explore our own similar experience and compare it with that of our participants, to find the commonalities that we share in our "crowded selves" and to project from that experience to others' reactions to issues and events;
- hence, our ability to imagine, to place ourselves in the position of others;
- our ability to use our logical thought to follow the reasons behind the circumstances, reactions, and motivations of another;
- our ability to develop our "participatory consciousness" and its sense that allows for empathy;

- our reflexivity and humility to critique our own initial reactions to another, and, as Bartlett notes, "to recognize that our knowledge is at best limited."

Then there is the issue of responding negatively to what you see in another culture. Ever since going to Mexico in the mid-1960s, I have been alarmed at how thin dogs are in Central America, assuming their health was of low priority. Much more recently, in Belize, I went west from Punta Gorda with Julian Cho's widow and his two young children to a small Maya village. I wanted to buy some baskets, and she wanted to go there to get some advice from the elder who made them. Just outside the village, we sat down for a picnic. We spread some food out and then noticed three dogs coming down the hill from the village. Normally a very gentle woman, she told me to pick up the baby, and she reached for stones and threw one at the nearest dog, then another at one further back. She looked at my shocked face and said something like: "Either we and the children eat or the dogs eat." I had an attitude adjustment. My view of the treatment of Central American dogs shifted. The scrawny dogs kept their distance but were close enough to take advantage of a lapse in our attention. We picked up the picnic and went on for the baskets and advice. By US standards the dogs were emaciated, ravenous. By Belize standards, due to more limited resources and village poverty, they were hungry and, therefore, aggressive. As Brian Street said, "What do you do about what you dislike in other cultures? Develop some historical understanding of how behaviors came into being, find the reason for them. A certain situation may not be okay with you, but if you know why, you can still be respectful."

Understanding seeming differences in thought

For years researchers have told us that there are no differences in the thought processes of humans. Clifford Geertz (1983) did an interesting review of the complications of discerning thought in other cultures, noting that thought is inevitably contextualized in cultural living space. We don't necessarily understand easily the thought of others because we are out of their space. Geertz notes that the actual processes of thought are invariable across culture, but the product of thought is highly contextualized in the culture from which it emanates. It is the products of thought that we, as researchers, consider. Denny (1991) stated that all humans use rationality, logic, generalizing abstraction, insubstantial abstraction, theorizing, intentionality, causal thinking, classification, explanation, and originality. He summarized research to state that "Cross-cultural differences in thought concern habits of thinking, not capacities for thought.... Different cultures make some of these thought patterns fluent and automatic, whereas the opposite patterns remain unusual and cumbersome" (p. 66). The complication for researchers, then, is not only discerning how meaning in one culture might be expressed to another (as introduced in Chapter 5) but also in understanding the products of thought in other cultures. Phenomenologist Alfred Schutz (1967), in considering J.S. Mill, questioned whether anything could be free of value assumptions. Lived experience, cultural surroundings, and modes of expressing thought both inform our assumptions and cause our initial, less reflective, stumbles in understanding others. We need to be continually aware that thought expressed by others, though initially confusing to us, is based on differences between its cultural contexts and ours. Thought may be logical to those doing the expressing, and we must strive to understand those other-cultured meanings.

Identifying and respecting resistance

> Researchers and community partners who spent less time in identifying and processing participant resistance in the first year of their project reported more major barriers to implementing the research methods in subsequent years and significantly less successful research projects than those who made the community participants' *no's* their first priority.
>
> (Fantuzzo, McWayne, and Childs, as cited
> in Trimble and Fisher, 2006, p. 32)

Being able to read "resistance" may not be as easy as it might seem because signals for resistance in one culture might not be the same as those in others. Çiğdem Üsekes, researcher of African-American drama, currently at Western Connecticut State University in Danbury, told a story about her difficulty in recognizing resistance even in her original homeland of Turkey:

> Turkish people see me as a hybrid now, positioning me in interesting ways. Talk about cultural borders! James Baldwin was invited to Turkey by a Turkish actor who had worked in New York City. Turkey became a second home for Baldwin. Though he just spoke a few words of Turkish, he hired a Turkish assistant and directed a play written by a Canadian playwright, relying on his friends' translation. I researched how it was perceived by Turkish critics and public. His closest friend in Turkey shared some of his documents with me, but I think he was more willing to share things with me that he hadn't shared with others because I was Turkish. Then I met with the Turkish assistant, and she gave me some documents. Baldwin wanted to shake up things in Turkey, and the Turkish public loved it even though it dealt with the most scandalous things at the time, like homosexuality. Some tried to shut the [production] down many times, but the theater managed ways around it. Most interesting was my experience with Baldwin's closest friend. He had Baldwin's notes that had never been published. I had called him several times, and he said he was going to share them with me, but he said he was sick and hadn't time to find the notes. We were friendly. He said he would get back to me.

A couple of days later I was walking with a friend of mine, and I saw him walking up a high hill. As a Turkish person, I had to ask another Turkish person what this meant. I had a suspicion, but I couldn't be sure. Turks don't feel comfortable saying "No" to a request. I finally understood. By then I had lived out of the country 13–14 years, and I expected a straight American "yes" or "no" answer.

As researchers we, again, need time to learn to recognize resistance and to recognize its source. Resistance can even be taken as discrepant data in a study, that which adds to understanding when examined. Roy Young talked about cross-cultural research in Belize, a country with many different ethnic cultures. He identified some strategies by which to overcome resistance:

Let's say you are doing some investigation about developing a health clinic in the area. You might get 200–300 percent more response if you called a meeting to present this. "We might want to build a health center; we want to get some information." They have a concept of community, *fahina*, working together as a group, say, to clean up, patch a house, help a neighbor; they work as a group to do that. Another thing is how you approach people. You should go in a mannerly way, say good morning, how are you, you seem to be working hard, and you ease them into a questionnaire. If it takes half an hour or hour—they may not be comfortable, and they may try to get rid of you, so build up some rapport. Another thing we have observed: you don't want to go with shined shoes if you are in the rural area, but you want to be presentable. And say I'm going to interview some of the kids to see why they are working at the terminal, their circumstances, whether they have gone to school. They might perceive me as an authority. Maybe if I go there in just short sleeves, with jeans and sneakers, it might make a difference. Other advice would be the timing of your research. In the rural area, you need to find out when people are at home—don't go at five o'clock when people are at their supper. And you have to know who is the best person in the house; it doesn't have to be the head of the household. For example, you need to know the dynamics within the household. In the Maya families, the female is not supposed to talk to anyone unless the male is around. What other advice? Word gets around too. If you start here in this community, by the time you get over there, they will know what you did over here. So if it was a poor exchange here, your reception over there might not be the best. Be open, honest to people, and be consistent in doing it. You don't want to interview and leave vegetables with one family, and then you go over and interview Sanchez and not leave vegetables. Some may want to give mangoes to you and your mouth is watering, but don't take advantage of your participants.

Although contextualized in Belize, Young's advice and well-considered respect will lessen resistance in other areas. In the USA, Peacock and I found, in interviewing native and non-native teachers of native adolescents, that we encountered little resistance if we let participants know the purpose and possible product of our research, gave them a choice of when and where they might want to be interviewed, and let them know the variety of people we were interviewing and the anonymity with which we would accord them. Though all this was in the consent form, we found discussing it helped with lowering resistance.

Russell Bishop, the researcher who had investigated his Māori heritage, warned that the researcher needs to respect resistance based on generation and oppression:

> My Māori family had undergone a big dispersal, almost a diaspora, the whole family being flung to the four corners of New Zealand in the 1870s. And I wanted to know why this had happened. I found an analysis of this from Jim Ritchie, an eminent psychologist in this country, and he told me that the first generation who undergo a very unpleasant experience don't want to talk about it, and the second generation quite often know about it, but they don't want to talk about it either. It is the third generation who are far enough removed from the hurt. I am a member of the third generation, and what was interesting was that when I finally tracked down the descendants of my grandfather's siblings, in most families there was at least one other third-generation person who was, like myself, very interested in the family story, even had been researching the family story.

Christine Sleeter, educational researcher originally interviewed at California State University at Monterey Bay, even changed her research agenda to examine good examples to limit resistance:

> My research actually has shifted over time from looking at how to get resistant teachers to change their practice to looking at what teachers who are really interested in multicultural teaching *can* do. Then I am not beating my head against some of these folks. And it is really fun then to go into classrooms in which you see some really brilliant teaching, and then to have conversations with the teachers and have them collaboratively put together their portrait: a totally different way of engaging and researching.

As Joan Metge said above, "Respect means not manipulating, not pushing them into doing anything, not intruding." For an interesting examination of the "art of resistance" in its many guises, see Scott (1990), who states: "Every subordinate group creates, out of its ordeal, a 'hidden transcript' that represents a critique of power spoken behind the back of the dominant"

(p. xii). Resistance is a form of power. If you sense resistance, you will need to seek to understand it, maybe even revise your team's plans and purposes, but you also may need to remove yourself, recognizing that your position of privilege/dominance and its historical antecedents may undermine the success of your research. You may need to graciously accept your failed attempt in that one site and to learn from it.

The way to be

Ian Anderson said:

> In a non-indigenous context the professional relationship is the most important thing, but in an indigenous context it's more important that you be known as a good person, reliable and trusted, than that you have the reputation that you are the sharpest analyst around the tracks. They care about personal values and about the nature of the reciprocity.

Susan Rodgers complicated these issues when I asked her: "Are you the same person in the field as you would be in your home environment?" She said:

> Sometimes, if you're working in a very distant culture like the Batak, you can't be totally honest. For instance, if Batak friends ask how much money I make as a college professor, I either make something up or don't tell them. There are certain things that would be just so mind-blowing, like an American-style faculty salary. So there's some dissembling in fieldwork just because you're in other people's world. Anthropologists try not to live in our fieldwork as, say, a consultant would. I've never had a car in the field; I always take buses. You try not to be the richest person in the village, and that allows you to get more accurate information about the social world than if you had a fancy house and Land Rover. People can't understand the economics of the American level of luxury.

You need to be yourself even when your participants may not fully understand your other life. As I became more and more interested in the question of "how to be" in another "world," I asked researchers for examples. Sarah Jane Tiakiwai gave both good and bad extremes of researchers she had known; the juxtaposition makes "the way to be" clearer. Good example:

> She has always presented herself as an outsider who had skills that we might want to use and that there might be mutual benefit. She's always stood back on issues until being asked to come forward for her opinion. She's always made it clear that she doesn't speak with authority about things, but because she's worked so intimately with the people, she could do that.

Bad example:

> The community gave all the information for his doctoral thesis, and when he went back to his own country and wrote it all up, it was actually quite derogatory, not what the community had anticipated, and the community hadn't anticipated it would be published. He made the community look very "native" in a negative sense. It really reinforced the suspicion of research and really hurt because they had taken so much time to help and support him, feeding his body as well as his mind. It's still talked about today.

A summary of researchers' advice seems to be as follows. Be yourself. If sincere, other people will sense it and forgive mistakes. When you have built trust, you will not be alone and will have advice from elders and/or assistants from the community. Don't necessarily say everything you are thinking. Be honest, but hold judgment. Hold true to your values, but remain silent until you fully understand the motives and history behind what others are doing, behind the values they hold. Rely on intuition and be honest with yourself about your internal reactions, but don't react overtly. Be respectful, in the way that others would understand respect, with tempered honesty, humility, friendly two-way communication, and reciprocity. In many cultures you will need to self-disclose and answer personal questions in a natural and friendly way. Perhaps all that has already been said in this book.

Types of collaborative relationships: "shared puzzle quests"

Collaboration is a way to build success into research, using researcher and local expertise in mutual respect and reciprocity. Chapter 2 talks about collaboration with communities in setting up research questions and agreements, but this section concerns itself more particularly with collaborative relationships. Though the best scenario would be one in which there were completely shared goals between the community and researcher with interactive and shared decisions during all phases of the research, there is a continuum in the completeness of collaboration. The section will start below with researcher collaboration with "assistants" and then move to an example of a complete collaboration.

"Insider" research assistants

Many researchers work with what are variously termed cultural brokers, field assistants, insiders, or research assistants. With agreements forged, the researcher participates in what Delva et al. (2010, p. 86) labels as "strategic collaboration." Though some researchers collaborate from research initiation through to dissemination, others seek assistance for certain phases of the research or certain combinations of the skills: collecting data, and/or for their facility with the language and potential translation, and/or their knowledge of cultural norms, values, and behaviors (see also Lincoln and G y G, 2008, p. 792).

The assistants specifically termed "cultural brokers" become an interface between two cultures because they are familiar and comfortable in both, often "bridging, linking, or mediating between groups or persons of different cultural backgrounds for the purpose of reducing conflict or producing change" (Delva et al., 2010; see also Jezewski, 1990). Research or field assistants normally own the same language as those being researched and are paid for their contributions in answering the research question(s). In my recent interviews, researchers rarely refer to "cultural brokers," though Sharon Kemp, anthropologist, used the term, interestingly enough, for a child she met while doing ethnography in a fourth-grade class. She laughed as she said:

> I sat in one of those little chairs as a fourth grader in the classroom. A troublemaker sat next to me. He was most delighted when I got an 80 on a fourth-grade math test. He was a sort of cultural broker who would talk to me about what was happening.

I've used the term "insider research assistants" in the title here, but even the notion of "insider" in this context is complicated.

Though assistants are often distinguished from researchers in that they have not had equal weight in the inquiry, often hired after research questions have been decided and having less involvement in data analysis or publication, this is not always the case, and in researchers' descriptions of assistants' contributions, much greater collaboration was going on. Almost always, researchers had furthered their understandings from assistants in ways they hadn't initially expected. Sharon Kemp told me of her quandary as a young anthropologist when she realized that some of her participants in India didn't necessarily know how old they were: "Then an assistant would simply ask about the first thing they remembered and calculate their approximate age." This may seem like a simple solution, but it's just the kind of thing that can stump the researcher. Kemp also had to learn to assess the strengths and the class issues that her research assistants might have:

> I wasn't particularly good at Murahti, but I could do pretty well. I had an assistant, and sometimes there was a disconnection between what she translated and what I would hear. And sometimes the assistant would say that the participant had said such and such, but then add: "but it was not right." The assistant disagreed with the participant. Then you knew there was something going on. I thought it might be a caste difference. I would work with different translators. I began to use the assistants in different ways, according to their strengths. I had a untouchable

woman. She told women that she was Murato, the dominant caste, but the interviewees knew. I worked with a Brahmin woman as a translator. Caste was having another layer that I had to work through to know what I was getting.

Having different skills, assistants can fill many different roles. Geoff Munns was working with a research team that included assistants who were involved in finetuning methods: He said:

> The assistant I'm working with now is older, maybe late 30s, early 40s. He's confident and understands quite clearly what he has to do, and we've looked at the aim of the project, and we've worked out the questions. He's strong in saying: "Look, I'm going to put it this way." I'm quite keen for him to use Aboriginal English and to speak in a way that works well with the kids. So we have a process where he's going to take 10 or 15 minutes before he even turns on the tape to find out what dialect the kids are happiest working in. So that process and the relationship is working quite well. I've got a role to play in analysis of data and theoretical input into the project, and he understands that, but he's really important in bringing forward a strong interview.

Though researchers talked often about having great respect for their assistant's strengths and presence in the research, sometimes circumstances kept the process from being seamless. For instance, differences between assistants and participants in terms of age, gender, and status might make the research more complicated than initially expected. Aydın Durgunoğlu, psychologist at the University of Minnesota Duluth, had given one assistant time to work her way through her own discomfort:

> We were doing some studies with Hmong speakers, and I had this 20-year-old research assistant who was talking with older men and women. She was born in this country, and those she talked with were natives of Thailand and Laos, and they came to this country pretty recently. Others had been here for 20 years, but all born in that other culture. So instead of being a traditional woman, she's a college student, and I think at the beginning she felt uncomfortable asking her elders to talk about their literacy background, especially when they were saying, "No, I didn't go to school." She gained more confidence, and people started respecting her and realized she wasn't judging them or dismissing their concerns. At first she was uncomfortable in talking to an older man as a young woman, maybe a role her parents wouldn't want her in.

Finally, Barbara Rogoff honored the dialogic collaboration with assistants in its best sense as a "shared puzzle quest":

I have been fortunate for a number of years in having graduate students and long-time collaborators who have helped inform the projects in that Mayan town in Guatemala where I have been working. Joining them is a privilege, and I also realize that I have something to say even if my knowledge isn't complete. Recognizing that everybody that I am talking to also has something to offer, and that is also incomplete, is part of the process. So that it becomes a sort of shared puzzle quest.

In Rogoff's process, all contributors in the research collaborate.

Cross-cultural research collaborations: recognizing the strength in each other

In recent years, collaborative teams with those from dominant and marginalized groups have become prevalent and have exhibited liberating, empowering, equitable, and democratic qualities, variously termed research collaborations, research teams, co-learning groups, participatory community research, participatory action research, inter-collaboration, indigene/-colonizer research. The names for collaborations have proliferated to express the unique methodologies of particular teams. In these collaborations, researchers with formal training and with particular areas of expertise team with a community, or people within a community, who may or may not have research expertise but who have both certain ways of knowing and knowledge essential to the inquiry. There are no assistants. Knowledge and efforts are contributed by all team members, and team members learn from one another. The community has research questions that interest the researcher so that they work toward mutual goals and outcomes. In an equitable collaboration, partners share power and dialogic conversations in defining and finding questions and funding for the research; they share credit for the findings; and they acknowledge and reflexively examine the problems in the research, the relationship, and the collaboration throughout (see also Fine, 1992; Jones and Jenkins, 2008). Certainly, there is ongoing debate about the appropriateness of anyone outside of a culture doing research in another culture, to be further addressed in Chapter 10. In this section, however, I will have two members of a successful collaboration elaborate on phases of their shared puzzle quest.

While in New Zealand, I heard, from a number of sources about a team that seemed to be "doing it right." I interviewed Ted Glynn, the Pākehā researcher on the team at the University of Waikato. I also wanted to meet Mere Berryman, then a Māori educator and team member, but my return flight and funding wouldn't permit it. A few years later I found out that Berryman was going to be at a national conference at which we were both presenting. I have taken quotes from both their interviews to show how a team can work with both reciprocity and equalized power relations. Throughout my interview with Berryman, she compared research partnerships with personal relationships. She said: "Living with a more powerful, dominating and controlling partner can lead to the destruction of the personal identity, self-esteem, and power of the non-dominant partner." Below you will see how Berryman and Glynn forged an equitable and respectful partnership. Again, they were not interviewed together in the same room, as it might appear in what stands below. I've juxtaposed their comments, however, to elaborate what others had described to me as their carefully wrought collaboration, one variation on many that are possible.

The invitation: the researcher offers skills

Mere Berryman: Basically what Ted did is he laid down the *koha* [gift] of a reading program for a Māori medium educational facility, and Aunty Nan [now an elder on the team] laid it before the elders. Basically, it was about his being able to say, "Well this is a resource; do you want to do something with this for children who are in Māori medium?"

Ted Glynn: I didn't want to begin with a research question. I wanted to work with them and figure out how they saw the problem, and what they thought needed to happen. Could I bring some skills or experience to the resources that are in the community? But I put that in as a *koha*, that's like a gift, something that I am freely giving, no strings attached. They could decide to include me or not. I had a tutoring program in English language, and had done several research studies with it, and at the time the Māori were getting their heads together around what they wanted to do. I was invited to a national gathering of Māori staff to come along and talk about this. I took my daughter, and we said: "Let us show how this works." And so my daughter role-played a reader and I role-played a tutor. And we tried to do it in Māori. Our Māori wasn't that great, but it got the message across. I put the program down on the floor and walked away from it, explaining: "There's a videotape in that package." And the symbolism of that was "There it is." But I left it up to them whether any of them wanted to pick it up. They could have let it lie. And when I explained the tutoring project, they gifted me a name for it. One of the older women connected with another tribe in the region said, "It's called Iti Rearea," and the rearea is New Zealand's smallest bird, a tiny little bit called a rifle. And it is at the beginning of a proverb, "*Iti rearea, tietei kahikatea, ka taea,*" the smallest of the birds can easily reach the top of the tallest of the trees. It's the little things that count in learning to read, but together they will add up to something big and important. One group picked up the koha from the floor and said: "We would like to take this back to our elders, and we will work with it, and that was the beginning of a long journey." They actually redesigned and reconstructed it, and came out with a Māori language video and training resource, which we have used and share it, and we run training workshops.

Mere Berryman: I guess one of the things I want to highlight was Ted's place in the *whānau* [family-like group, in this case centered around educational concerns of Māori children]. He seemed to be an important researcher already, and none of the group who had formed the *whānau* had ever worked in research. So its reconstruction into a Māori medium resource drove us into this whole field of research. I came as a teacher with more than 20 years of experience wanting to ask teacher questions. I think we also came, all of us, into it as parents and grandparents. That experience has been really huge in identifying what we're still calling the *kaupapa* (agenda) of raising the achievement of Māori children. With the New Zealand foundational document, the *Treaty of Waitangi*, we've got the grounding for working collaboratively and in partnership.

Researcher and community members forge a relationship: maintaining dignity and identity

Mere Berryman: The relationships within our research *whānau* are such that we engage, relate, and interact in ways families would. When I talk about relationships, it's researchers being prepared to meet with each other's families, knowing each other on a personal level as well as the professional level. Ted has been to family funerals, has been to family celebrations that are quite outside the professional role that we also have. In fact, there has been a merging between the professional roles we have and the personal roles, and that requires a lot of a person to say: "Mere needs me because of a family crisis or death, so I have to go there." He's prepared to go the extra distance that relationships require. We all know we both have to work at making those connections. I talked to my father about resigning my permanent position to work in a contracted position with a professor. So I said: "Look, Dad, you're just going to have to come and meet him." I am sure Ted didn't realize how important the meeting was. I never talked to Ted about what they talked about that night, and my dad has since passed away, but I know if my dad had given Ted the thumbs down, I never would have resigned my position. That was the respect I had for my dad. Dad didn't trust hearing about the relationship, he had to have a relationship with Ted himself. So on the way home, Dad said: "So what does he do?" I said: "He's a professor." And I can remember my dad saying: "Is that sort of like a headmaster?" "Well, sort of, Dad." And he said: "He's a good man; you can work with him." That sums up Ted: he's a good man. I think Aunty Nan refers to him as having a Māori heart.

Ted Glynn: You have to take the relationship seriously and constantly be aware of having different identities: an identity as a researcher and an identity with the group. At first I found this challenging. You enjoy the privileges of the group: they'll support you, they'll back you, and they'll make you lunch if you are too busy to get to it. But with the privileges go responsibilities, which means you have to fix them lunch if they are busy. They'll share stories, and they'll tell you more about the culture as you need to know it. If you are going to talk about it, you talk about it with respect. The notion of a *whānau* is behaving as an extended family with the commitment being to the well-being of the *whānau*. If there's anybody in the group who is not in the state of well-being, the approach is: this is interfering with the work of the whole group so that has to be dealt with. The need may be purely physical: "Send your kids to me for the night; I'll look after them." Or is the *whānau* member worried because she doesn't have any money, and they'll deal with that. Or it might be: her role in the group has suddenly gotten too complex, and it's all beyond her. So it's the elders' responsibility to deal with that.

Mere Berryman: And basically the *Powhiri* rituals of engagement that Māori do is to know who you are and where you come from, before we know what you are. That's what Dad wanted with Ted, and once he had done that then he might have been interested in what Glynn did, which is a total flip again from the Western paradigm, which is if you're a banker or a lawyer or a doctor you're pretty important. For Māori, it's about saying: "Where are your roots? Where is your ancestry?"

Importance of elders and all team members

Mere Berryman: In our *whānau* the elders are absolutely critical to decision making. That is why we have Aunty Nan with us now at this conference. And, we must never do to non-Māori what has been done to us, so we respect that other person for their own cultural background rather than think they're like us. I look at Paul who works with us, and I've got to remember he's not Māori, and I've got to remember that in a respectful way. Ted, and I, and the research *whānau* presented a paper, which really looked at what we can learn from elders about life relationships in relation to research partnerships.

Ted Glynn: When we first go as researchers, there is always a suspicion: Who is this person? But we work through it with elders in the *whānau*. They will take the position in a *powhiri* [formal Māori welcoming ceremony to the community], and they will make the connections. They will say a little bit about what we've come for, and refer to me, and then if I am to speak, I say a little bit. Some Māori question if a Pākehā should speak at such formal occasions. I am not saying I am great, but I can speak the language, and there is so much respect that comes from that, and the difference it makes is that they will talk after the formalities. Elders and others will sit and talk and use both languages; they'll slip from one to the other as appropriate, and so you get a better understanding of the concepts and metaphors that show where the values are. You stick with your mentors, the elders and *whānau*. Even if you are not actively doing projects with them all the time, keep including them, keep visiting and being interested in them, keep seeing them and telling them things that have happened to you.

Team comes together to develop research questions, materials, and research methodology

Ted Glynn: So, in a research project, we are all committed to seeing this project finished: we want to get some data that will stand up, and we want to get something that will impress the school board, etc. Keeping a relationship is to maintain the goals. What I find to be the big cultural difference is when we interpret the outcomes. I am able to feel good in the empirical sense that we've got some data that show that kids have made progress. But what they take out of it is that these kids are now standing tall in their culture with a really good range of first-class reading material in Māori, little books for children, series of greater books, and actually employing indigenous artists to illustrate them and indigenous writers.

Mere Berryman: The research methodologies that we were [initially] applying were very mainstream. The outcomes were that we were measuring progress, pretesting and mid-testing and staggered baselines. But we then moved to working with other Māori researchers and within a Māori worldview. I guess it's about learning what we can in order to improve the research from a wisdom paradigm. And then we went back into Māori epistemology because we didn't necessarily know it. I mean, Aunty Nan has understandings that I still don't have. It was about recapturing that kind of knowledge. And I suddenly saw the power of using both methodologies.

Researcher and community members learn from each other

Ted Glynn: The first and most important step in this process is to learn and to listen to your research partners. I think being aware, having some background, getting a good person to be a sounding board, that's the whole point about collaborating with people from the other culture. They will tell you how to go and what you can't do as well. We are visitors in someone else's cultural space. Good visitors do not tell their hosts what to do.

Mere Berryman: I remember a conversation Ted and I had that was about something I wanted to do. We were gathering [data about] reading accuracy; we were gauging how many words children could read per minute. We had concentrated in the first study on how much reading was being done and how accurately it was being done. I wanted to look at how much understanding was also going on, and I wanted to really push that whole connect between children reading in Māori and how we could identify it as comprehension. I remember Ted saying, "We have no tools ready for that," and I can remember how very arrogantly I must have sounded at the time, saying to Ted, "Well, nobody's going to tell me what I can and can't do because that surely has to be the very reason why we have got to do this. If we have no tools to measure by, don't we go out and figure out how to develop those tools." It set a precedent, and I feel safe to say what I actually think. Teachers are always trying to push those boundaries to do a better job as the teacher. I think it was about building a different level of relationship, and we did it with respect. And he talked me through it when I needed it, many times, always there and able to share his ideas. We learned from each other, and I found, a little bit stunning at first, that I could actually teach him something. I had expected all the learning to come one way.

Research is reported; relationships are maintained

Ted Glynn: Sometimes I still get caught thinking in the old ways. Somebody would ring up from one of the educational newspapers: "We hear there's this study going on. Would you like to say something about it?" My first reaction is, "OK, I'll give you five minutes about it." And then I start thinking and saying, "I can't give you that. I have to go back to the group, and if they are willing for me to talk about it, that's fine." It's collective ownership. And it is fascinating, isn't it! And then with publications it's the same thing. If you get driven by APA style guides, you are not allowed to have eight authors. And so we've had to fight our way through that.

The research proceeds

Mere Berryman: The work that we're doing at Māori Medium, which we started with Ted, continues because we've learned a lot, and some of the things we will never do again. But that's part of research, too, isn't it? The things that we would do again, that's the important stuff. One of the things I feel very comfortable about [in the collaboration] is now we take whatever is going to be the best method or the best way to meet our ends. That gives us huge freedom. Now we are in a space where we can say, "What do you know about this? And shall we try a bit of this? Well, I've thought about this; let's bring that into the mix." We grow in terms of our own knowledge and reflect on its application. I think it's hugely empowering.

Ted Glynn: For instance, in the meetings with the school, they use their own control devices. They respect everybody that's there—the principal, the parents—but they don't always end up supporting the specific outcome that the school wants, which in one case was for the school to get rid of this kid as fast as possible. So that works with research, too; the ownership is collective, collaborative.

The powhiri model of collaborations: honoring the strengths in the other

We know that collaborating with people in a different culture will be different depending on the values and ways of being in the two different cultures. Different collaborations will be informed by the cultures involved in the collaboration, but I was impressed by this Pākehā/Māori collaboration, as you can see by the space that it receives in this chapter. Before I even interviewed Ted Glynn and later Mere Berryman, I talked to their colleague, Russell Bishop. He talked about the kind of respect that went beyond equality, the kind that is represented in the collaboration above and the kind that is represented in a formal Māori meeting, the *powhiri*:

> Somebody might have expertise in one area, another in other areas. We recognize each other's strengths, and you can explain that again in terms of Māori metaphors, because that goes back to that p*owhiri* again. In a *powhiri* what you do is you get up and you say, "I recognize you": "*tena koe,*" a formal way of saying hello that literally means: "There you are. I recognize you, I acknowledge you." And everything else that's done in a *hui* [meeting] is all about that: I recognize your particular strengths, and your particular power. So we are really doing research in a way that is fundamentally Māori. The most fundamental everyday expressions are based upon the notion of self-determination. You are an individual, you have strengths; you are able to explain who you are—the discursive practice that is Māori. I am not saying I empower; empowering is not an activity I am interested in. I am saying you don't have to give them power; they already have the power. You are just going to recognize and implement it.

Originally I was thinking of cross-cultural research as being a mutually empowering sort of activity, but when leaving the University of Waikato, I reflected on my own research collaboration. I thought about the strengths that Peacock and I recognized in each other and how that fed our research. I feel grateful for those recognized strengths and for Berryman's, Glynn's, and Bishop's pointing out a model that might work for any cross-cultural collaboration.

Complications to overcome in research partnerships

Eleanor Bourke talked about the possibility of all parties in a team benefiting from another, but she also acknowledged the resistance to collaboration: "A lot of non-indigenous researchers will work in collaboration with an indigenous person. Sometimes it works and sometimes it doesn't work too well. But a lot of people have said: 'I want a whole Aboriginal team.' "

Clearly cultures that have not traditionally had power in the research setting want to have power and autonomy in the research that concerns their communities. Resistance to academic researchers is understandable, so it is important to talk about the collaborative difficulties.

Funding for collaborations and resultant senior faculty preference

At most universities there is pressure on faculty to receive grants which act to enhance the university's reputation and replenish coffers from the overhead gleaned from the grants. Fiona Cram talked about the shortcomings of funding agencies in understanding the nature of collaboration:

> I think the research agencies don't appreciate the time and cost of collaboration. My experience is that to get to the stage of community partnerships or community collaborations you would need to be talking to a community for six, twelve months, but the funding agency has a firm date. It's possible that communities will generate ideas, and some communities have the capacity to take those further and engage with researchers, but not many.

As noted in Chapter 3, granting agencies also want accountability to rest with senior faculty, who have track records. This does not acknowledge the value of newer faculty and often the non-mainstream faculty new to academia. Sarah Jane Tiakiwai, a Māori researcher, gave an example:

> We had a committee with a mixture of the old people [elders], and younger researchers, and senior academics. The decisions were collective decisions, but one particular occasion a decision was made which went against that collective responsibility. I could handle feeling humiliated as junior academic, but they had done that to the old people as well. My colleagues and I talked to the old people and then expressed that we were really uncomfortable with the process, and they were happy for us to make their point. I am not sure whether it was a positive thing in terms of the relationship between the senior and junior academics, but I think it was really important to make a stand if it was something that was culturally not right. There are notions of respect.

The power differential in collaborations is likely changing. We all need to learn from each other and to have patience in the process. Wendy Holland brings us back full circle to time and patience:

> It is often challenging for many 'non-indigenous' Australians to 'stay on the journey' with 'Aboriginal' people. Working with others who may

be culturally different from one-self might mean that plans may be disrupted. It is important to have patience, to 'stay on the journey', even when it might get a little tough. There needs to be a preparedness on the part of the researcher to be open to new ways of thinking about and 'doing' research particularly with those culturally different from oneself. It must be a respectful and negotiated process.

Publishing in collaboration

In reflecting on publication in team collaborations, I know that teams benefit from talking over issues of property and ownership and authorship while setting up the research, but sometimes you can't predict all the issues until the research is well underway. Do those from the community take a stronger role in analysis and oversee the dissemination of research findings to the community? Is it the researcher who deals with academic publications? Or is that minimizing the possibility of each party learning from the other? A number of academic researchers felt they took on an inequitable weight in the writing and the publishing process because they knew that their community partners didn't always feel comfortable with the academic discourse (as in Chapter 5) and conventions. One party in the partnership might know the right discourse formulas for publication; the other might know its way round the culture, local report back, and the culture's further goals for dissemination. In most collaborations, partners want equal authorship and equal acknowledgement, and they feel undervalued if contributions are not fully acknowledged in dissemination. In addition, motives for research will differ amongst members of a research team. Angela Creese talked of her team study of complementary schooling:

> Arvind and I wrote the initial bid for external funding together, so he was always the named researcher. Arvind was key and continues to be. But we're all under different pressures because he really felt that the research was very much about increasing the profile of complementary schooling, and he's been less interested in publications.

Academic researchers and their teams generally do have sensitivities about authorship, and just as funding agencies are not necessarily cognizant of the time that collaboration and flexibility take, academic departments don't necessarily know the time that collaborative publication takes, nor do they understand the richness possible in the cross-cultural results. I have had my own consternation in this area. Though the book that resulted from my collaboration with Thomas Peacock and Amy Bergstrom took three national awards, my own English Department decided that collaborative work should receive half the merit credit of a single-author book. I was grumping about this to a department colleague who took on multicultural scholarship. He said to me, "You have to look at the Zen of it. It's just the gift that you give."

I was probably more distressed at the lack of value accorded to collaboration, but, in the end, I didn't contest, deciding to take my colleague's advice and to let it pass as a gift, a *koha* the Māori would term it. It was giving a part of myself.

Two-way bridge

Members from all cultures have to put themselves in uncomfortable positions in cross-cultural experiences, but some are more used to that discomfort than others. As Renato Rosaldo (1993) said, "Indeed, the dominated usually understand the dominant better than the reverse. In coping with their daily lives, they simply must" (p. 189). When my research partner, Thomas Peacock, and I began research, we talked about the "bridge" over which native students trod to enter mainstream schools, and we talked about their need to have a strong enough anchor in their culture to feel grounded and whole when entering the school culture. Then a colleague of ours, Priscilla Day, pointed out to us that that was just a one-way bridge. Berryman, the Māori educator in the partnership described above, added: "Mainstream partners are more used to the indigenous partner adapting to their continuing requirements, but partnerships for indigenous peoples must not come at the cost of their own language and culture."

Constructing a two-way bridge in collaborations seems a worthy, equitable endeavor. As I began to realize that Tom Peacock had to "switch codes" (as linguists might say) or take on what W.E.B. Du Bois (1903) termed as a "double consciousness" every time he entered his place of work, I better understood the strain he felt—daily. With the discomfort, this "double consciousness" can bring the wealth of multiple perspectives to data, a gift Peacock offered to our collaboration. Though Ted Glynn talked about what he had learned and gained from entering into the Māori culture, he also talked a bit about what it had cost him in terms of ongoing engagement in the academic world:

When we had completed presentations at a big conference, sometimes I need some time to myself to just think about what comes next. But because you are living the conference with your research *whānau*, it means that after the paper, there's sort of a communal debriefing, replaying it and talking it through. And then, when they go to hear other people's papers, they prefer to go as a group, to show their *tautoko* (support) for the work of the other presenters; the collective identity shows itself. We sit down and decide collectively what paper(s) do we want to go to? And it's not that we all have to go to the same things, but we have to discuss it. I'd feel a little strange if I said, "Well, thank goodness we've got our paper over; that went well, didn't it, see you guys tomorrow; I am going to dash and hear this paper." They might see that as my forgetting my identity as a member of the group. And my own colleagues won't approach me because it means their having to break into a very animated group. It's all about people learning to do things differently, and sometimes the most eloquent thing you can do is to be present.

I feel that my best research has been in collaborations. The act of entering another culture, though often uncomfortable, is an act that makes me grow in richer understandings. Working to learn, listening to others, and debating issues—all these actions expand my perspectives and my knowledge and my patience. But disorientation upon entering another culture is inevitable. When I haven't been well prepared to cross the bridge into another culture, I have felt more disorientation than if I have done my homework. I urge the preparation described above, but the surprises are rich as well. The disorientation is part of the learning process. I understand now that the giving up of my comfort is part of the gift, that *koha* of collaboration, and a gift of the other's discomfort is one to me because I am enriched, able to see things in new, sometimes more complicated, sometimes more simple ways. You give and you are gifted.

7
Gathering Data while Respecting Participants

In 1997 I interviewed Julian Cho, the teacher from Belize to whom this book is dedicated. Our interviews were about the literacy of the Maya people and about his entwined views on education and politics; the interviews were long and intense. On my bus ride back to Belize City, I learned from an amiable seat mate that the humble teacher Cho was the official spokesperson for all the Maya people in Belize and was involved in charged discussions over land-rights issues with the Belizian government. In 1998 I organized a session at the Bordeaux International Literacy Conference, in part so that I might introduce Cho to other Indigenous educational leaders and advocates for their people from Australia, the USA, Nepal, and Canada. In the fall of 1999, Cho asked me to review his application to a prestigious US graduate school. He was finishing a land-rights initiative that was to meet with an initial success and wanted to put some temporary distance between himself and his tense homeland. Several weeks later, on November 11, 1999, a teacher at his school contacted me to let me know that the perfectly healthy Cho had died in "mysterious circumstances."

This event catapulted me from research collaborations on Indigenous literacy to, what was to me at that moment, the more compelling topic of the complications in research when it crosses cultural borders. I was devastated and Cho's death left me with some heavy questions. Should I have gone beyond my original research purposes with Cho to encourage subsequent conversations and conference sessions with other Indigenous leaders? Had I nudged him into precipitous directions that he might otherwise never have taken? What should I have done differently in the research that touched the life of Julian Cho? Had I not been reflexive enough in my stance with research participants? Soon after that I was interviewing researchers about cross-cultural research. Later, in front of a palatial fireplace at Australia Catholic University near Sydney, Ken Ralph helped move the emotion-driven beginnings of my research into a genuine and more complex inquiry. In talking about protecting research participants, he said:

> Aboriginal people are entitled to be treated as thinking and knowledge-able people in the area that you are asking them to be. There is a fine line between being concerned and being patronizing. You have to respect them to make informed, evaluated decisions. They are aware of risks, and they usually have elders around them to say something like, "Listen John-o, it's a bit dangerous. That mining company isn't going to be too happy with you." There is not an Indigenous people in the world that is not in a state of struggle, and there has never been a struggle when there hasn't been some blood on the ground. We all know that and have to accept that as one of the consequences.

Ken Ralph and the other 70 researchers have pushed me into thinking beyond my initial impetus for this research and into a serious interest in the topic itself, but I still have asked the question of when researcher actions are patronizing and, with respect, what researcher's actions further a participant's self-protection.

Collecting data is perhaps the most engaging part of research in social settings. In this phase, researchers are gathering insights that others have about the topic and trying to make sense of the surprises that further complicate, simplify, and/or enrich initial understandings. The more care that the researcher has taken in gathering preliminary knowledge and in negotiating permissions, the less potential there is for doing harm. Frontloading the research process, especially considering and negotiating questions and benefits, allows participants to build their own self-protections when data collection begins and when dissemination follows. As a researcher, taking your own curiosity across cultural borders is important to your motivation and to your future understandings, but adding an addendum to your own curiosity—mantras in question form ("Am I doing no harm?" "Am I using an ethic of care?") —is essential.

In spending time with participants, in focus groups, in surveying participants, or in any other research event that requires face-to-face interaction, the researcher is acutely aware of the participants' humanity and most often empathizes with their positions, whether privileged or powerless. If one hears participants' stories, if one senses their trust, one feels respect for their well-being; however, researchers still wanted to talk about their concerns. This chapter is about respecting participants in the process of collecting data. Respecting participants during dissemination follows in Chapter 9.

Doing no harm can be complicated: being aware of cultural assumptions and misassumptions

Back in the front of that same fireplace in an administration building of Australian Catholic University, Ken Ralph said:

> We had researchers who went into communities in the 1940s and '50s and observed life at an Aboriginal mission. They made comments [describing the community] like: "Ah, this person is married. There were six illegitimate children here." A person coming along 20 years later might recognize Grandma in the text, or Auntie. There are variations in morality even in Aboriginal communities. To some it doesn't matter; to others it's a shame job. The most important thing to know in Aboriginal matters is that there is diversity. There is diversity. There is diversity.

Researchers on four continents were contemplating the mistakes of past researchers that had engendered understandable mistrust. As Russell Bishop said, "I don't think you need to tell some stories." Past researchers have left scars that today's researchers must heal. In part, what has been seen as moral in one generation is not necessarily what is considered moral in subsequent generations. "Nothing stands still." Colonial arrogance and ethics allowed past researchers to grab research data and leave nothing behind, offending those living in foreign lands and stepping on cultural mores of communities near and far. In recent decades the maxim of "Do no harm" has been in place, but even well-intentioned researchers can still make erroneous judgments in discerning what might be harmful across cultures, generations, and time. Furthermore, even in small communities, researchers have been taken unaware by the "diversity" of what is hurtful in the research process.

Time and time again, generational difference in what is appropriate has taken researchers by surprise. For instance, Wendy Holland, Aboriginal Australian researcher noted that even within her own family/community, there was a generational/cultural difference of which she hadn't been aware:

> My maternal great-grandfather had Aboriginal, Irish, and African heritage. His exotic-ness was a part of his circus performance. My inquiry was about his circus experience, and I agreed to do a radio interview for the 150-year celebration of circus in Australia. It happened that one of my elderly family members had heard the interview and reprimanded me. It was made clear to me that: "You don't raise things; it is none of your business, it's all in the past." It was devastating to me. I tried to reassure my elder that we have every reason to be proud of this heritage, but it became clear to me that many of the older 'Aboriginal' generation lived through very different and often tougher times.

Beyond the different views of what is acceptable within the same community across time, a number of researchers talked about troubling situations in which blowing the proverbial whistle meant harming others. Australian researcher Howard Groome spoke of these dilemmas:

> One researcher compared successful and unsuccessful teachers, and I'm still not sure she understands that the way she portrayed the unsuccessful teacher was so damning that the poor woman never recovered. The researcher was dead right, the teacher picked unfairly on Aboriginal kids. If a child was borrowing a pencil, she'd say, "Sit down. Don't steal the pencil," a very authoritarian teacher. Readers all knew what school the researcher had been working in. I think research should not create harm for anybody. Remedial action might have been taken; the researcher might have just said: "Look I really don't think you are handling this class well, and I think I need to absent myself." And then again, in one school there was an Aboriginal girl who had been really lauded to us. She was vice-captain, a great model student, but in talking to her, she was obviously distressed with the system and felt exploited. So what do you do in that situation? You listen sympathetically, but it's hard to write out what she said to you because she herself would be identifiable with her criticism. We pulled back from going too far and in doing so distorted our research.

Doing no harm is complicated. Does one blow the whistle on a system seen as harmful, unavoidably identifying and harming participants or others along the way? Does one protect participants at any cost? How does one situate oneself, as a researcher, when two groups are involved (for instance, in the above case, mainstream administration and Indigenous students)? Do you owe your allegiance to those who have approved your research, to having a "deliverable result"? Does Bentham and Mill's utilitarian stance ("greatest good to the greatest number of people") come into play here? These are all questions that researchers need to ask themselves. Of course, foreseeing problems or collaborating with community members who might have a better idea of local consequences is the best route; nevertheless, if a problem is discerned, then flexibility—changing research procedures or protections, even requesting permissions anew or opting out of a particular research setting while, as Groom suggested, making objections known—may go a long way in solving research dilemmas.

The researcher–researched relationship

> Knowledge derived from ethnographic studies is rooted in relationships, and as relationships change, what we know also changes.
>
> (Timothy Black, 2009, p. xxiii)

Over the years, researchers have evolved in their ideas of how to work respectfully with what the participant–researcher relationship entails. In the traditional Western model, the only research relationship that was ethical was one that ended when the research was over. The basic advice when I was in graduate school was: "Stay around to honor your commitments, give back information, but don't get involved with your participants, don't encourage their dependence on you." When I was interviewing high-school students for my dissertation, I was tempted to intervene, to advocate for several students (and I guiltily helped a few), but I dutifully steered clear of the participants' lives after my dissertation passed the eagle eyes of my committee. In later research, we, as researchers, have complicated the "Don't get involved" maxim.

Research often relies on understanding another's position in relation to a topic. Bartlett, writing about a feminist approach to relationships in conjunction with Albert Camus's work, talked about coming into a relationship with that intent to understand. "Responsibility toward relationship also entails a willingness to engage and persist in the relationship... In this respect, we come to the importance of dialogue for Camus in breaking down human isolation. For Camus, genuine speaking and listening enable mutual understanding" (Bartlett, 2004, p. 94). The attempt at genuine understanding is implicit in good research in the social sciences, but this introduces the question of how the responsible researcher should act when the research is complete. Stacey (1991) talked about the human relationship in ethnographic research:

> Because ethnographic research depends upon human relationship, engagement, and attachment, it places research subjects at grave risk of manipulation and betrayal by the ethnographer... The greater the intimacy—the greater the apparent mutuality of the researcher/researched relationship—the greater is the danger. Critical ethnographers tear the veil from scientific pretensions of neutral observation or description. They attempt to bring to their research an awareness that ethnographic writing is not cultural reportage, but cultural construction, and always a construction of self as well as of the other.
>
> (Stacey, pp. 113–115)

Researchers of the 21st century recognize that the more genuine the speaking and listening, the greater the understanding of the position of the researched, the less the social distance, the greater the empathy and responsibility the researcher might feel and, hence, the less likelihood of the researcher's inadvertent harm.

Nevertheless, a disconnect in the relationships and life experience between the researcher and the researched can make researchers uncomfortable. Henry Amoroso from the University of Southern Maine told of how he came to rethink his approach to participants from prisons in his projects:

> This prisoner's stories had moved me and others. The prisoner was real; he was a person; he wasn't just a drug addict. His tutor and I moved to Canada. He was sent to another maximum security prison in west Tennessee, and for a long time he wrote to us begging us for help. But I couldn't get him out of that prison. That bothered me a lot: the fact that you listen and if they open up, then there's an obligation to be more than "Well, see you later!" As soon as a person trusts you, there's got to be some form of reciprocation or otherwise it's not genuine. I try to be faithful to that in my work now; otherwise it's hypocrisy.

Mary Hermes (1998) described how she buffered the complicated power differential in the relationships she had with the Ojibwe community in which she lived. The "cross-cultural" in this situation had to do with her complex bundle of identities, academic/community member, as she sought to study language revitalization and start a native language elementary school.

> I challenged the idea of a rigid hierarchy of power by building relationships that had multiple dimensions or, perhaps, just in recognizing this multiplicity. For example, in elders' meetings, at moments I was the organizer or facilitator and could control the agenda, but when it was time to eat, I was just as easily a waitress or, at the meeting's end, a driver. In many social contexts with the elders, I was simply a young person or a helper. So, although I set the meeting dates or held the tape recorder in an interview, these positions of "power" could quickly vanish in a different setting. I believe this interpretation of power relations is a different one than a power-blind approach to research ... I continually tried to involve community members in all levels of the project, to recognize my position as "not the expert," and to problematize the positions of power I did occupy. However, at some point I had to recognize that I did occupy them, even if I tried not to reinscribe them. (p. 16)

As Hermes had, Māori researchers continents away expected to have some kind of collaborative and personal relationship with participants (Bishop, 1996; Smith, 1999; Pipi et al., 2002). This focus on relationships and connectedness is diametrically opposed to former Western practices where the researcher worked within a guise of objectivity. An important value in Māori society is that people meet face to face so that trust and the relationship can be built. Linda Tuhiwai Smith said:

> When you enter a research relationship, you're entering a human relationship, not just a technical relationship that finishes. You can't walk

away from it. Building the relationship is regarded as a third of the task. Then there's the interview, which is like a moment, and then there's this long-term relationship. Many people still stroll in here to say hello, or email me, or ask me to do things. Just before you came in here I had an invitation, and "No" was not an option. If you're building relationships on respect; it's mutual and it's reciprocal. They're not knocking at your house and coming to stay because they are respectful also. It's not like reciprocity where there's a sense of obligation. It's relationship building, relationship maintenance.

Impact on participants' thinking and realizations

Certainly both benefit and harm can come from researcher interactions with participants. I'd like to believe that the interviewing that I have done has had mostly positive outcomes for participants, sometimes positive effects that I hadn't counted on. I interviewed Zac, a 16-year-old African-American (Cleary, 1991), who talked about writing, about classroom contexts and school struggles, about his hopes. He was a bright young student who, though in a "remedial" class and vocational school, wanted a "desk job" for his future. I was so surprised when his teacher approached me at the end of the research cycle and said: "I don't know what you have been doing with Zac, but I wish you would do it with all my students. He is writing up a storm." We know of the metacognitive benefit that occurs when humans reflect on the processes that they bring to some skill. The "thinking-it-through" can improve the skill, the motivation, and a deeper view of its purposes. Jean Mills (2001) acknowledged the dialogic nature of the interviewer's role in the performance and construction of the self. A participant's consideration of and response to a researcher's questions and the researcher's consideration of the participant's responses can bring on powerful interchange and changes to both the researcher's and the participant's viewpoints. She said:

> They [participants] have power of disclosure of what they are going to pass on, and they also have the power of hanging on to certain things and not disclosing them. Leslie Milroy uses this phrase "tokens of exchange," i.e. the interviewer clearly gets something out of the interview, but so does the interviewee. So there is a reciprocal relationship, and a much closer relationship than you would get, say, from a supposed scientific-type interview.

Interviews can cause a disequilibrium or dissonance, adjusting the way the participants see themselves or their possibilities. But even though I like to imagine Zac behind the desk he wished for, I know there are other possible results. Right now he could be on an assembly line because his interest in education and his view of its purposes came so late. To get his desk, he would also have had to combat the possible prejudice of employers toward young African-American males who do not speak standard English. I cringe as I remember that I gave Zac a blank journal and a two-inch-wide button to wear saying, "The Meek Shall Not Inherit the Earth." He was puzzled. I told him that it was something I had found in a store near the university and that I thought he might want to think about it, even write about it in the journal. We can do things with such good intentions and think years later about possible consequences. Is Zac behind his desk? Or does he feel diminished because he didn't inherit the desk, feeling what Sennet and Cobb (1973) called the "hidden injuries of class"?

Celia Haig-Brown also talked about the benefits and discomforts that listening carefully to a participant can engender:

> Of course, there's that thing with the interviewer—it's like the bartender in the airport who listens intently, and suddenly you're telling things you have never said out loud before. A lot of people might not want to talk about a painful [topic], "I am never going there again." But the people that I encountered were ready to talk and wanted to talk; for some reason the time was right to talk.

There is power in listening and there are metacognitive benefits from reflecting and telling, but researchers, myself included, articulated concern over how to deal with these "voicings." While some researchers wondered whether the voicing of those who usually go unvoiced or the nudging of participants to more evolved understandings was always the best thing; others were strong in their thinking that such an endeavor should not be an explicit goal in research. Patai (1988, p. 35) uses a phrase of Marie-Francoise Chanfrault-Duchet in questioning this process as "savage social therapy." Research participants might examine inequities in power, something Zac might well have been doing. Does paying attention to circumstances that underlie powerlessness have the potential of making a person feel more powerless, without necessarily exploring possibilities of agency in the face of powerlessness? Should I have prolonged my relationship with Zac, showing him how to close the distance between his desk wish and his then existing skills, perhaps leaving him even more vulnerable if he never achieved it?

Ines Sanchez, a Belizian educator whose first language was Spanish, was both perceptive and thoughtful about the positive aspects of metacognition in research.

> Reflection is an integral part of research. You visit and ask the questions and ask people to think. You can count that as a positive aspect of research, where you, the researcher, are contributing. You came here [to Belize], and you are contributing to my thinking. And I pass this... [on], and then you are contributing to other groups. But, like everything, there

is danger. If I misuse that or naively use that, there are consequences that might not be good for me, but those are the risks we [as researchers] have to take. Growth is painful. When I think about your question, I might think: "Well, I have been doing this stupid thing all my life, and then now let's look at it." So I don't get offended. In Belize, we have been too intellectually passive. That's why foreigners could come into a community and exploit a community easily.

Some researchers talked about the intrusive nature of research. Karin Tusting, educational researcher at the University of Lancaster, UK, said:

We are excited because we are trying to understand education while looking at the realities of people's lives. But there were moments, particularly towards the end, when I started to feel actually prurient. One woman told me she had an abortion in her teens, and she put a lot of her subsequent difficulties down to how that had been dealt with. She had never told anyone this. Do I even have the right to put it in our public research report when people could potentially work out who she was? Does she understand what might happen to this information? I have explained, but she is not a researcher. And how is that going to help us really with informing policy. I took it back to her; she was fine with it, but when I did public things, I took it out. In interviewing you don't actually know what sorts of bombs might be going off in people's heads.

As Howard Groome and Karin Tusting noted above, material that gets out to the public can be for the public good, yet, as soon as it becomes public, it's really hard to keep people anonymous. It's one of those quandaries. Tusting's solution was to allow the information to inform the research project itself but to remove it for public audiences. Her working for the public good was yet another part of what researchers deemed to be their ethical responsibility.

Many researchers talked about the obligations that we have to participants who offer their reflections and voices when they might otherwise not have access to an audience. That requires the researcher to disseminate the contribution only if participants fully understand the power of their voices and want the results that their reflections might bring.

Rachel Hodge, researcher at Lancaster University, UK, and I had a conversation about researcher responsibility in her university office, about her work with asylum workers:

Probing into people's pasts with the young asylum seekers can get into counseling territory…where angels fear to tread. It may be unturning stones. I had an interesting dialogue with another researcher. She found out about one of our participants who had ended up taking his own life. And she said something like: "Why don't you get this group together, critically reflect on it, and see what political action they might take, like writing to newspapers." She didn't quite understand the context, how they were desperately trying to settle in a new country and how the death had affected them and their learning. They were positioned at a very difficult time politically, both locally and nationally, if you've ever seen the way our newspapers go on about asylum issues. It would have attracted attention to them as a group, and there were some nasty right-wing politics going on in the area.

"Bombs going off in people's heads," "unturning stones," and below Linda Tuhiwai Smith talked of "light bulb flickers" and their potential ramifications:

> I think what we've come to understand is, if you're naive about the power of that tool [interviewing], you can hurt yourself and others. It's a particular kind of tool that requires a process and one that can privilege the researcher over the researched. So you need to understand the dynamics of the real community and real people. I would be irresponsible if I lit a fire and walked away. Sometimes you can sort of see a light bulb flicker on, and you're going: "Okay, something's happening here." Through the interview and after the interview it's maintaining the relationship.

Furthermore, there are complications in the way in which participant identity or hybridity factors into research, as introduced in Chapter 5. For example, Tess Moeke-Maxwell's research participants identified as Māori or Pākehā depending on what best served them at the time:

> Many of us recognize our bi-multi-raciality, and many of us actually live across multiple landscapes. We strategically align ourselves as Māori when we need to, and we strategically align ourselves in non-Māori landscapes to achieve a particular agenda. Often it is the Māori woman that gets located as a bridge between two patriarchal alliances, and she is the one that often gets burned there (suffers physical, psychological and/or spiritual harm). Stories were told by women who were harassed, undermined, underpaid, overlooked, invisibilized; getting it from the Māori side, getting it from the Pākehā side as well. I would definitely not tell her story in any way that she could be identified in the place where she works, but having these narratives out there can actually help people in their dislocatedness. We allow people to get in touch with what they initially hadn't had the words for and [give them] a safe space to share that information with other people who could not find the words.

Moeke-Maxwell knew intuitively how to respect the anonymity of participants and their way of moving across multiple landscapes, in part because she was in the same position. A researcher who had not experienced that hybridity might not be aware of how important it is to proceed carefully. The gift Moeke-Maxwell gives to her participants is both emancipatory thinking and a realization that they are not alone, as she said: "for reconfiguring their identities and creating new subject positions of themselves." The gift that she gives to the readers of her research is an understanding of the positioning that those of mixed blood need.

In summary, there are simply unforeseen consequences when you, as the researcher, are not at home in the culture and cannot judge the effect of participants' articulations and realizations. Some 43 out of the 70 researchers I interviewed talked about participants developing critical consciousness, and though they appreciated their participants learning to value or critique their own experience, many worried about what they couldn't fathom, as researchers. Simply stated, perhaps too simply, when a participant has a change in thinking about the world and their place in that world, there is, at best, an uncertainty of consequences from what Paulo Freire termed "conscientization." The outcomes may be positive for the person who has been nudged into thinking in a more nuanced way or who has been nudged into resolving issues that he/she may have avoided for years. On other occasions, the disequilibrium or dissonance might adjust what the participant saw of themselves in a way that could hold discomfort. As a researcher in social settings, you are going to be asking questions, but you must look as much as possible toward risk management, toward the short- and long-term consequences of your presence in others' lives.

Unintended disrespect

When the maxim "Do no harm" was broadened to include "Do care; do respect," figuring out what was respectful had its own complexities. Zac (the student whose life goal was to work behind a desk) was identified by his teacher as a student who was doing quite well in his remedial class. Did he realize he was selected as a "remedial student"? There is the danger of participants feeling marginalized simply because of the categories they fill that are of interest to the interviewer. Daphne Patai (1991) talked about "interviewing down," which involves recognizing the dynamics of researching groups that have less economic, political, or social power than the researcher. This section deals with some of those complexities.

Disrespecting and diminishing through pity: To Po-Ting-Fy

Pity includes its own form of disrespect. As Daryle Rigney said, "Indigenist research rejects the oppressively dehumanizing characterization of Indigenous peoples as oppressed 'victims' in need of charity and saving." Daphni Patai (1992) wrote that "Feminist critics of feminist cross-cultural research charge that US feminists who study other societies project their own experiences instead of understanding the other society on its own terms...Critics argue that women who seemingly are subordinated in the researcher's eyes are not necessarily subordinated in their own" (p. 119). Michael Rosberg, Canadian-born economic anthropologist, recognized this in his, then, Belizian context:

> Raising consciousness implies a hierarchy of consciousness with, of course, mine on top. And if there is an unequal playing field, what are the ways in which the nature of the transaction can be adjusted so it is in the interests of both sides to be doing it? Well, Marx could tell you a violent revolution could do it, but he is not looking at why it's not going to play out the way he predicts. So instead of looking at the "oppressed," it's a question of game players. Even that is simplifying it because research ain't no game. I'm afraid of the arrogance that comes along with thinking in terms of who's the oppressed and who's the oppressor. As soon as you allow yourself to feel sorry for the oppressed, you've moved them into a position of, as they say locally, as being "potingfy" which is to say "poor-thing-a-fied," objectified, reduced to a thing of pity.

How does one adequately respect participants without "potingfy"-ing them yet still get action on some very distressing social problems? Some years ago, Brian Street found this diminishment in funding agencies as he set out to do ethnographic work in Iran on existing forms of literacy:

> "Falling standards, dreadful illiteracy," [officials] said. "Glad you foreigners are coming to teach them." We get a lot of that in anthropology, "Oh, we have backward native people up there in the hills." Somebody tried to put on my visiting card (you had to have [one] for getting around in Iran), "researching bisavod," meaning those without knowledge. And that's generally true of international agencies and in local agencies. If you say you're interested in literacy, then they recode it to say you're interested in illiteracy. Most languages don't have a word for literacy/illiteracy; they will have "knowledge" and "ignorance." So it's seen as studying ignorance, backwardness.

There are ways in which consciousness raising, as David Carey Jr., historian from the University of Southern Maine, says below, is patronizing:

> I find the concept of consciousness raising condescending because Maya already have a keen sense of their reality and have developed strategies to assert themselves against hegemonic forces. Moreover, past attempts to "educate" Mayas about their oppression and encourage them to take action often fueled increased violence during the civil war in Guatemala.

The danger of condescension, paternalism, pitying, sympathy, or the urge to solve others' problems is that they assume that one group has the answers about reality or can advise about living in the reality of the "other" and that the other group must be given answers. Possibly implicit in even compassion is that one culture is superior to another, another form of Eurocentrism, ethnocentrism. The distinction between sympathy and empathy becomes important. For instance, the Christian ethic of the "Golden Rule": "Do unto others as you would have them do unto you" doesn't necessarily work cross-culturally. What might work would be: "Do unto others as they might want you to do unto them." Discerning what is respectful means immersing oneself in the culture long enough to get at least the beginning of an understanding of what someone from that culture would want. Doing your own form of caring may not be the form of caring those of another culture might want or need.

Diminishment through stereotypes, broad generalizations, or romantization

Another form of disrespect is the stereotyping of participants. In order to analyze data, we often look for themes, for commonalities, for patterns, yet in the very process of analysis, we often deemphasize the individual characteristics of the participant, seeing individuals as inhabiting only boundaried places. This overlooks the crowded selves, the multiple identities from which individuals operate. Though we also look for discrepancies in data and seek to complicate our reporting as a result, the emphasis is often on the commonalities. Do we, thus, diminish individuals, and then groups of participants, or even the communities that they live in? John Arthur gave an example of immigrant African participants' response to being lumped in a group with which they did not identify:

> With reference to the Black African immigrant experience, most of them find themselves being racialized for the first time. Before moving here, race was not an issue. If anything, class or tribal or clannish issues were the issue. The American preoccupation with race was overwhelming to them. They didn't like the pressure put on them to identify with Black America and for others to lump them with Black America. They would take time to point out to me the separateness, stressing the difference in values and educational background. Immigrants might distance themselves linguistically, but society as a whole doesn't see the differences. In England, too, they find themselves separated from the British born black.

Jean Mills, a mainstream researcher from the University of Birmingham, UK, talked of the kind of participant stereotyping that she had learned to resist as she interviewed those from another culture:

> They did start to talk about their upbringing, education, and families as it related to their feelings about their languages as well. You can get on

these sensitive topics, and, I did get the sense, with the women I talked to, that in at least one case, the husband would actually be aggressive towards them. And yet in other cases, the husband was very supportive. So there's a range of experience there: there are all these different relationships, different marriages. So this is an issue to do with stereotyping different groups. There are different experiences, even within a group you would want to think of as holding common cultural assumptions.

Foley et al. (2002) notes that "Ethnographers of color are also replacing negative stereotypic portraits of ethnic minorities with positive, complex, humanizing ethnographic portraits" (p. 51). As John Arthur and Jean Mills have, many researchers are attempting to avoid the perpetuation or initiation of stereotypes.

Mary Hermes has alerted me to another form of stereotyping that diminishes the diversity of native people by "romanticizing" them. These expectations interfere with seeing people as they are. Vine Deloria (1969, p. 82) notes that this even affects those who are romanticized: "Not even Indians can relate themselves to this type of creature who, to anthropologists, is the 'real' Indian. Indian people begin to feel that they are merely shadows of a mythical super-Indian." When researchers sense this glorification of a culture happening, they might really need to reflect on their reactions to their own culture that might be making them so attracted to the romanticized version of those in another. James Clifton (1990) uses the term "cultural fiction" either for focusing on deficiencies measured against Western standards or to describe a people positively using Western ideals.

This form of stereotyping can play into the research situation in several ways. If readers of research expect the romanticized or even dysfunctional stereotypes that might have been portrayed in literature or media, they may not be able to open their minds to reality or diversity in preparing or carrying out research. And there are other ways that this can undermine research. As reported in Chapter 2 when talking about representation and access, my research team depended on guidance counselors to identify student participants for us (Bergstrom et al., 2003). They did identify them for us in the academic categories we requested, but chose those who were mostly traditional, either because they wanted to make their schools seem responsive to cultural issues or because they were smitten with these students. In either case, we needed to declare it as a weakness in our research because, though we tried to remedy this during the research, we probably did not reach culturally removed native students across all research sites.

Respecting participants: the essence of good research

Originally this chapter was entitled "Protecting and Respecting Participants." However, I realized early on in this writing that the concept of "protecting" could be seen as paternalistic, heralding the assumption that I, as a researcher, might know more about the means that would protect participants from harmful effects of my research than the participants would themselves. As a researcher I have come to understand that mature participants have an uncanny sense of how to protect themselves. They know their own culture better than the researcher and know how to protect themselves within that context; many also have dealt with those from other cultures enough to know how to protect themselves in the wider context. This does not absolve the researcher from working to "do no harm," and there will be a "nevertheless" section to follow about protections that researchers found to be important, but first we will hear from some who realized that they shouldn't underestimate their research participants' ability to protect themselves.

Respecting participants to make their own choices

On a few occasions in interviewing for this study, when it only seemed respectful to the researcher I was interviewing to do so, I talked of Julian Cho and my anxiety about whether some of my actions that extended my relationship with him might have nudged him to act in a way that led to his death. I was surprised at the response. Mainstream researchers empathized with my concerns and told me their own stories about times when they had concern over vulnerable participants.

Joan Metge had worked successfully for years with communities in New Zealand's North Island. The depth of her experience was valuable. On this topic she said:

> Māori have learned their own strategies for protecting themselves, and if they don't want you to intrude into their lives, they have their own ways of keeping you out. Sometimes it's by being terribly polite, sometimes it's by being very rude, sometimes it is just putting up a facade, diverting you. In my experience, they will take from you what they want, will reject what they don't want. You do have to hold back from encouraging people in a certain direction, but, ultimately, you can't live their lives. The people, who are for various reasons angry, feel they have been denied part of their birthright. Uncertain of their own identity, [they can] become aggressively protective of it. If you approach people with respect, that's partly something you give them, but something also that you learn to give them because they are worthy if it.

Over and over again, Indigenous researchers had similar points to make that I found to be both interesting and comforting in connection with my concerns about Julian Cho that started me on this research: don't underestimate participants who are fully able to be savvy of their own circumstances; to do so is a form of patronization. Ines Sanchez said:

> When you research, you ask questions, set people thinking, and people could take action, and it might be good for their community, but it might be bad for the person. That person has grown up and can think for himself and be able to influence his community for action. Maybe there is a need to warn people that these are dangerous ways of thinking, [but] they have freedom of expression and freedom to act. To feel guilty is not to respect the person for his own free will. I believe in free will; freedom of thought comes with taking responsibility for your thought and the actions that come from it.

Rachel Hodge worried about her more mature age in working with the young homeless, but she learned that they too were able to make their own choices: "The manager and other people said: 'Age absolutely isn't the issue. They will vote with their feet; they are so volatile and so resistant to any kind of being organized, controlled, being told what to do, they'll soon see you to the door if you're not the person they want to speak to.' " The voluntariness of participant participation also allows for self-determination.

Nevertheless: methods to increase safeguards

Despite the respect that a researcher accords to participants by allowing them to protect themselves, there are "nevertheless" measures that researchers can take to decrease the chances of harmful research. The most common method that researchers reported was attempting to insure anonymity for participants and their communities.

Cross-cultural complications in the use of pseudonyms

Most researchers talked about the difficulty of insuring anonymity, and though no one had discovered infallible guidelines, many researchers had devised means of respecting participants in their wishes in terms of anonymity. Many warned that, as a researcher, it was difficult to know how to insure anonymity in a culture that wasn't one's own, and many feared that their participants might not fully understand the audiences and purposes for which their data might be destined. Rhonda Craven talked about methods to keep participants from feeling vulnerable:

> We are doing a study, and it actually asked students to report whether they have ever been bulimic, whether they've had suicidal thoughts. Now if a teacher was collecting those questionnaires, the students would be worried that the teacher, principal, or a member of the community might

see them. So you do have to be very careful, so they don't feel vulnerable. We are having them hand it in in a sealed envelope.

Aydın Durgunoğlu, a Turkish-born psychologist who studies literacy in the USA and Turkey, described ways in which she deals with anonymity and pseudonyms:

> I know anonymity is an issue some researchers struggle with; some say if you want to give voice to a person you don't want to hide them. Most of the people I talk about are far away in Turkey, so I don't think people will recognize individuals because it's a far, distant culture. In the psychology end of things, though, we do group tests; aggregate data are presented rather than individual cases, so keeping the anonymity and protecting individual participants is easier. However, we have instances when people ask how their child, class, school did on the tests. There I have diagnostic information only on the average patterns of the group. But, also, you have to check with the school: does it want to be identifiable? They may not want shortcomings announced to the whole world. And if the schools say, "No," then you can't thank them either. People sometimes say things that are personal, especially when you're asking, "When did you come to the US?" and "Why did you come to the US?" I was told by the IRB [University of Minnesota's Institutional Review Board] that you can get subpoenaed to make the records available. Confidentiality becomes a big issue because some of them volunteer the information, for instance, that they have been in camps in Thailand. I don't want people's names to be on the records so that information can be used to deport them. It's not a likely scenario, but given the current climate, why have something that can be used against the person? I don't use names.

Recognizing and dealing sensitively with political situations is often something that an outsider has difficulty doing, but even insiders found their difficulties. Māori researcher Bella Graham, oral historian from the University of Waikato, New Zealand, talked about the benefits of anonymity even when doing research in a small Māori community that she knew well. For her, the end purpose of research (fair land-rights decisions for the community) determined the means (gathering narratives for those determinations); yet her research decisions about anonymity had to do with internal community concerns and the integrity of research material entrusted to her, valuable cultural knowledge that only an "insider" might have.

> I am working very hard to minimize the deductive disclosure of identity. I was actually most worried about the tribal audience. I just didn't want some [viewpoints] to be dismissed just because of the person, because of intertribal, intra-tribal personal differences. I wanted one informant

valued in the same way as another informant, although I do say "one person who is an elder" or a "young person." I tried to put together a narrative so that people [would] listen to what was said. It's being able to recognize the politics, my background, and it's more dangerous if you don't notice. That's quite different, actually, than what I've done before as an oral historian.

Though many researchers decided they would never use real names, many others left partial or complete decision making about the issue of pseudonyms to the participants themselves. Rachel Hodge, researcher at the University of Lancaster, UK, recognized the age factor in making determinations about the use of pseudonyms:

> She was quite happy to tell her story and was delighted with how I wrote it up. She said, "Yeah, that's spot on. That's top. The only thing is, I don't want you to use my name because I wouldn't want my daughter to read it in a few years' time." She, as an older volunteer worker *recalling* her turbulent adolescence, had a sense of how she might feel later, but I don't think most of the homeless younger participants *living* their turbulent adolescence, even though I talked this over with them and suggested they chose pseudonyms, had that same sense of how they might feel about these accounts later.

Continents away, Tess Moeke-Maxwell, cited above, talked about similar age-related concerns:

> A famous Māori musician actually wanted to be identified. For women like that who have *kaha* and the *mana* (the strength and the integrity) to actually stand behind their diaspora and their cultural hybridity and their bi-multi-raciality, anonymity is not a problem. But then there are women who are situated in a vulnerable place, or in a young place. I interviewed some women who were 16 or 17 at the time. One wanted to be identified by her name; it meant something for her. I wanted to respect the fact that when she grows and develops new subject positions, the story may not serve her well. I do believe that I have a responsibility in caring for Māori women and not being an interlocutor in them being exploited in some way for my own gain.

Jean Mills from Birmingham University, UK, found wide variance in her student participants' pseudonym preferences, though they lived in the same region and were from a similar culture. Pseudonyms were especially important to some because they had to convince their husbands to let them enroll in the university program by telling them that they would still have time to prepare meals and were taking courses on Islam.

Publishing in an international journal, I was more careful. Not that they seemed to have these sensitivities, but I just thought it's fairer to them to be more reticent by not using their surnames. I did ask them if I could use their first names in the thesis itself, and, on the whole, they were all okay about that, except for one person because she talked quite a lot about her family and didn't want to be readily identified. In later academic articles I changed the names.

As Mills pointed out, "In order to finish the thesis, her material was open to faculty scrutiny, so the research group was potentially identifiable, but, whereas dissertations are on library shelves and less available to the public, articles that have more public readership open participants to broader identifiability."

The university edict of "publish or perish" puts an ongoing pressure on researchers to disseminate research to a large audience. Celia Haig-Brown talked about the use of pseudonym and the limit of biographical detail as a way to avoid the loss of a publication:

> I did life history interviews, and the interview of one public figure was phenomenal though I only used bits of it. I literally felt like the interview transcripts, sitting in my filing cabinet, were glowing, saying, "This is too important to leave in the drawer." After a few years, I got a hold of one woman and said: "This is an amazing interview, and I would really like to publish it." She said that sounded fine. I asked her if she wanted a pseudonym, and she said: "No." She didn't think it would be necessary. I sent it to her, and I didn't hear from her, so I called her one day, and she said,: "Oh, I gave this to my children to read, and I told you stuff I never told them. They don't want me to publish it. And I said: "We don't need to publish it. The last thing you need is pain out of this process." But I was thinking, "Oh my God, I am a doctoral student, and I really want to publish this article!" Then I said: "What if it was published with the pseudonym?" So she thought about it for a while, and then she said: "I am going to do it, using a pseudonym."

When I was interviewing in the Four Corners area of the US southwest, a 14-year-old girl, who wanted the pseudonym "Sunshine," told us a story that probably has made a big difference to young native students who have read *The Seventh Generation* (Bergstrom et al., 2003). We did a profile of her using her own words:

> You think it's just a game, but it's hard. Live one day with me, and you'll see what I go through just to try to make my child safe, make sure he's not sick, and make sure he's fed, make sure he's clean, loved. You're going to be there by yourself, and some people just run out on you. (p. 10)

On Sunshine went, talking about family dysfunction and her struggles to stay in school. She was courageous. Even though both she and her mother had signed the consent form, I worried that she might be identifiable if her tribe were named, but my native research partners were stalwart in their insistence that Sunshine and the other native students would see it as a matter of loyalty and pride to be identified by their tribal name. My research group let me know that there would not be the same shame that I, as a white researcher, might connect with Sunshine's 14-year-old single-parent status. I respected their judgment, of course, but I still felt discomfort because of the assumptions that come from my culture. Had I been working alone, I might have played it safe but wrong.

Nevertheless, many researchers insist on pseudonym use. Fiona Cram noted that the need for pseudonyms often arises: "The Māori community is a small place, and people seek a lot of help before they'll tell their relations, and the last thing you want to do is out them."

Use of pseudonyms becomes an issue that all researchers must fathom, both by thinking through the complexities of anonymity and by taking participants' wishes into consideration. Susan Rodgers made her decisions about protecting participants by weighing the pride they might feel against their ability or inability to fend for themselves. She showed me a beautiful book she had written and turned to a particular page:

> The Barbier-Mueller Museum in Geneva holds a collection of Indonesian ritual gold jewelry, and the museum sent me to various parts of the outer islands for fieldwork. In the Eastern Indonesian islands many of the old aristocratic families have a lot of gold jewelry in their house treasury, and many were gracious enough to allow me to do a family history of the jewelry. I was really worried about publishing pictures. This beautiful piece of gold chickens and water buffaloes, all of 24 carat gold, had never before been published via a photograph. I was afraid that some rapacious art dealer in Bali could send one of his runners out to this farm family, cash-poor old aristocrats, and offer 500 dollars when the auction house price would be thousands and thousands. But we went ahead and did it because I had the sense that that particular couple was self-possessed, and they could defend themselves. When you're dealing with ethical issues about publishing pictures in the international collectors' circuit, it's different to have people proudly wearing their jewelry rather than having the jewelry laid out, in terms of anonymity.

Respecting participants' decisions about anonymity and accuracy of data

Many researchers find ways for participants to have power over the data that interviews generate by respecting their self-determination, allowing them to act as editors of their own words. Sue Middleton from Waikato University in New Zealand devised a two-phased consent form:

> In a bigger project, most of the 150 teachers wanted their names used, especially the older ones. They went, "I want to be in the book," but then one would say, "I don't want you to use this information," because they'd started talking about an alcoholic principal. I worked out a second consent form. The first consent form [protected] anonymity; then if I wanted to use [their] names, I'd come back to them. I said, "Here is your transcript. You already agreed that I can use a false name, but here are some options: use your real name or use a false name, one you choose or let me choose it; or use a real name and then, in certain matters of sensitivity, use a false name."

With such choices, participants are nudged into making careful decisions that help them protect themselves. Tess Moeke-Maxwell, as cited above, talked about a woman who felt power over the interview process and who had a good sense of what she did and didn't want made public:

> I am talking about a woman who occupied a particular position of status within her *iwi* [Indigenous tribal community]. She had control during the interview process. Throughout the interview she would say: "Now, look, I am not going to tell you this because...," or "Turn off the tape recorder." I felt really humbled to be a scribe and an advocate in helping her to record and tell her story.

Years of lived experience endow research participants with the means to make informed decisions about what they want made public and what should remain disguised. And, as Seidman (2006) says, "Each participant or interviewer may have different boundaries for what he or she considers public, personal, and private" (p. 107).

A number of researchers had their participants edit transcripts or material to be quoted. This research method allowed the participants to give second thought to what they wanted to go public, and it allowed the researcher to benefit from the participants' second tier of reflection, thus deepening the researchers' analysis. Jean Mills used a process by which she interviewed parents, and then had them read the interviews and comment on them. Then after interviewing their children, the parents had their children's interviews to comment on, forming a third phase of her process. Mills' intentions in this design were twofold (2001): "To acknowledge issues of power and control in giving the interviewees some ownership of the research process and the power of veto, if necessary, over their own contributions," and "To have the opportunity to ask follow-up questions, to clarify, possibly to expand, certain areas of enquiry" (p. 288).

Karin Tusting questioned whether going back to participants in literacy classes with full transcripts was too much for them. She said:

> And in this project I decided to use summaries based on the interview, including some quotes, because a lot of the people I was working with were in literacy classes; it just wouldn't have been appropriate to give them a 15-page interview to work through. But I was nervous because I felt like I should be taking full transcripts back. I found that people, in the main, were thrilled with having these summaries because we were doing kind of life history-type interviews.

Liz McKinley, Māori researcher, was curious about how women would respond to her analysis after they had already approved the transcripts:

> Educated Māori women are not silenced at all; they are published. I'm trying to do what these women with PhDs in the sciences had already done. In interviews they talked about their *whakapapa*, the ancestry stuff, cultural information. I did send it to them to make sure it was accurate. They haven't seen anything written up yet. I will give them a copy, a *koha*, a present, giving back. But in terms of postcolonial theory, you start to look at the unconscious moments. So I've probably written things that they hadn't even thought about, and it will be very interesting to see what sort of reactions I get, apart from the ones I already had, which were positive.

This brings up a consideration that researchers did not talk much about. Is it necessary to give participants editing privileges over the material within its final context, when the search for patterns and theory is complete?

Participants do not always take advantage of the opportunity to review transcripts that are sent out. Lack of response in the past has left me uncomfortable. Were the participants intimidated by the white university envelope that appeared at their door? Or were they too busy, unconcerned, or simply approving, feeling an answer to the request as unnecessary? I am not alone in feeling the discomfort of not hearing. Julie Carniff sought such response and said: "At each stage the young people received copies of the transcripts, and they were able to comment on them or add to them or elaborate on them, though none of them ever did."

I mailed off Sunshine's profile for her final permission and mailed profiles to other students as well, but only one student responded. I tracked down others who said things like: "Oh, sorry. Yes, it was fine, exciting." But Sunshine and two others had moved, contact information unknown by their past schools. As Haig-Brown also found, without feedback, there is a discomfort. Should one seek out the reason for the silence to a request for feedback? Or is that, in and of itself, intrusive?

When researchers have been open to feedback along the way, they have sometimes got more than they wanted and had to wade through how to deal with it. Celia Haig-Brown said:

> I was the main writer, and I eventually had all the field notes and all the transcripts, and I went to my house in British Columbia and wrote the draft, and then I said to the research team: "Okay, we have to take the full draft back to the school, divide the chapters out (because there were chapters related to different groups of people in the school) and get their response." So we set up this whole day at the school where they went through the chapters with a fine-tooth comb, and, oh, they gave us feedback! I managed not to cry until the end of the day. They even criticized the style of a piece that was very interesting to me.

Vicki Crowley was honest in her discussion of the snags she ran into in research, and the kind of decision that is especially hard on an academic:

> I sent people a transcript, and some people sent them back to me, and then I didn't hear anything [from others], and so then I sent them a letter to say, "If you haven't written back to me to say no by such and such a date, I'll take it as being approval." Some people withdrew their stuff. Someone even thought I was doing something else altogether, that I was just going to write a book with a photo with them and do a life history instead of actually doing the [analysis]. So you can actually go and personally track people down and sit down with them again. You make choices, and they're not ideal in some ways, and research does make people vulnerable, and I suppose that's one of the reasons I never published it.

In many forms of qualitative research, we want to establish dialogic and non-threatening relationships with participants, but if participants feel listened to and respond, we may elicit material that the interviewee wouldn't want public. When I sense that this is happening, I remind participants of the presence of the tape recorder or video recorder. Sometimes they still want to continue their story with the recorder turned off. On other occasions, they don't mind if the recorder keeps rolling, either because they feel comfortable with the content going public or because they know the consent forms give them the right to edit at a later date. As a researcher, I lost several compelling stories when the tape recorder was turned off or when they were edited out. I would have liked to use those stories; nevertheless, they still sit in my mind and inform my analysis, even though they can't play out on the page.

Intervention/referral when harm is possible

Participants do not seek researchers for therapy and it is rare for researchers to be trained as therapists (deLaine, 2000; Seidman, 2013). As an important contingency in research plans, researchers are trained to go into research settings with possible referrals in mind (see Graham Smith, cited in Swadener and Mutua, 2008, p. 41). Many ethics protocols obligate the researcher to develop a plan for situations when harm is observed or divulged; a plan, for instance, to refer participants to therapists, social workers, health workers, guidance counselors, or lawyers. This is particularly important in cross-cultural research in which the researcher is unlikely to know all the circumstances that might surround what arises in research. Barbara Comber gave an example of such a time when intervention needed to occur:

> One of the case-study children was being harassed by one of her peers, partly due to gender and partly to culture, and the teacher couldn't see it. I would make sure that he [the teacher] found that out as soon as possible. I explained what I had seen and how I had seen it. There's a question of harm. So then you know you want to intervene. As a researcher, I would always want to act if there was potential harm.

In this case the researcher referred harassment to the teacher, who could go through the routine of referral designated by the educational institution, termed "mandatory reporting" in the US. Sue Middleton, a New Zealand researcher, knew she needed to act in a less formal manner when the participant was not under the umbrella of an institution:

> In my PhD research, a woman in her 40s talked to me about her schooling. She'd run away from home at 15 and lived with boys and survived. Then it came to why at the end of the interview: she'd been sexually abused by her father, but her mother had found her diary and started calling her a slut. She had never told anybody else why she ran away. By the time she was interviewed she was ready to do something about it, so I suggested a friend, and she went into counseling, a kind of a referral.

John Arthur referred African immigrant participants to immigration lawyers when needed: "I know a couple of immigration lawyers in the Twin Cities. When immigration issues came up with people I interviewed, I would give them the card of the lawyer who knew how to handle it. 'They can help you on a pro-bono basis.'" One researcher made the distinction between "observers" and "fixers." Though trauma cannot be erased, certainly researchers need to be caring observers, and often they need to refer participants to qualified "fixers" when they observe harm happening or hear of harm that has happened to the participants in the past.

Protecting communities as well as individuals

Keeping individuals anonymous is complicated, as is anonymity for institutions and communities. In 1997 I asked Julian Cho about real purposes for literacy in the Creole, Garifuna, West Indian, Mennonite, and Maya communities in southern Belize. "I think the best learning is what you can associate with your everyday life," he said. Wondering about literacy for real audiences and purposes, I asked: "Could the students write letters to the government about the problems with the election that just occurred?" He tried to explain how things were different in Belize than in the US: "The school, community, and certain teachers would be seen as political. You can write your political leaders, but write them to compliment them. If you write them to constantly challenge them or their ideas, it would not be taken well." The next day, his lesson was to have the students write letters to the minister of elections. He explained to the students the form the letters should take: first compliment the minister on his good character in two or three different ways, then tell him of the well-run election in Punta Gorda, tell of some little incident that they witnessed that may have undermined the fair election, then again congratulate the minister on the well-run election, thus ending with admiration. I asked whether the students would be able to send the letters that he had collected. He told me that he daren't chance it because the school might then be vulnerable to loss of funding.

My initial misassumption might seem relatively harmless because Cho was patient in explaining it to me (indeed, he crafted a lesson to demonstrate Belizian political rhetoric), but the interaction was poignant to me because if I hadn't pursued beyond my initial research questions, I might have missed something important about Belizian literacy. Furthermore, I was about to prepare student teachers from Minnesota to work in his school, and they would need to understand the political implications of possible assignments—assignments that might be perfectly acceptable in the US. The long arm of research can reach beyond the data-collection moment, deep into the well-being of communities. I needed a better understanding of the politics and power behind criticism and compliment in a rhetoric other than my own.

Communities can be vulnerable. Barbara Rogoff warned:

> The APA ethics rules don't say much about communities; they protect individuals but not communities. Anthropology's ethics document does attend to the impact on communities, but I have met other social scientists, and I don't know what their ethics statements are, but the impression I have is that it's much easier to think about protecting individuals from negative side effects of research than communities. I think it's essential [to protect both].

So researchers need to make two checks in their minds and documents: one to respect the individual and another to respect the community. What might protect a community at one time in history might not be protective in the future. Being clairvoyant would be a researcher asset, but trying to think into the future, given the past, helps.

Susan Rodgers, an anthropologist researching in Indonesia, was well aware of the need to protect the names of communities as well as participants while researching high oratory in Batak communities. She said:

> In the process of living with Batak families and doing this work, which is not just conversational Batak but the high oratory, people tell me all kinds of things. They're either gossiping about a relative or talking about Indonesian-level politics, and those stories might put them into a situation of vulnerability. I was very cautious about assigning a person's name and location to a particular story. You have to be constantly on the alert on what the situation is with the intelligence police, and we never use people's real names or the real name of the place. There is a kind of political horror story: During the Vietnam War, the US military forces found that they needed maps of some of the highland villages for their bombing campaigns, and the best source, most unfortunately for the discipline of anthropology, were old PhD theses moldering away in some university's collection. As a junior anthropologist, if you were doing your first fieldwork in a village, you drew a map. In anthropology, we realized that we can no longer be naïve. Should you want to falsify a map and tell your readers why you're doing it? You should approach it with situational ethics.

As stated in the introductory chapter, anthropologists are now sensitive about any of their work being utilized by the military. David Carey Jr., a historian from the University of Southern Maine, also knew that he needed to think of the history and future of the community when making decisions about his care of data.

> In places like Guatemala, there was a [history] of tension around information. If you were to say the wrong thing to the wrong person, you could have ended up dead. In terms of the individual consent, most of the folks I interviewed are illiterate, so that made that a little more problematic. But I was explaining to them what the project was, and I really insisted on using pseudonyms because I was still unsure how stable Guatemala was going to be. Some people certainly wanted to have their names in there. I was really uncomfortable with that. Previously in the '70s and '80s, anthropologists' research had led to people being killed. I have all these oral history interview tapes that I would like to leave in Guatemala, but I am still not comfortable doing that, and it's not just because of the conditions of community archives.

Knowing the political circumstances in the region in which you collect data is important to communities, community archives, institutions, and individuals. Some researchers have found that locals on research teams can provide knowledge that allows build-in protections for their communities. Further confounding the issue, several researchers talked about the ethical dilemma of feeling committed to protecting a community when they thought that individuals within the community didn't deserve protection. In talking about the research done for films, Philip Morrissey said:

> In one film based on a book, they had an Aboriginal consultant. They tried to meet the needs of the community, which turned out to be quite diverse and quite difficult. The film deals with things that the community didn't feel should be dealt with and that they didn't want popularized. It does show the complexities of community, with revelations of domestic violence, forms of sexual abuse, including abuse of children. One wonders, if you are a researcher, how you would research that. Should communities control all information, even about things that should be open for discussion and judgment by the wider community? Revelations involving elders, people who have enjoyed their power, could be serious. How on earth would they ever be uncovered unless they were brought to the attention of a wider community? Sometimes people are making sure that no one knows about offenses and actually use the power of traditional authority to do that.

As Jaggar (1998) notes: "Members of subordinated groups may not wish to discuss problems affecting their community with members of more powerful communities, especially if the powerful communities already claim cultural superiority" (p. 20). Furthermore, as Sluka (2007, p. 124) says, "Today, the communities with which cultural anthropologists do research are nearly always stratified, plural, and internally divided, and relations have to be maintained with different factions and interest groups who may be in conflict or competition with each other."

The juxtaposition of the quotes above manages to show just how complicated the researcher's and/or collaborator's position can be. This comes back to doing no harm, most recently addressed with communities: Does the researcher tell the truth and jeopardize a community and/or an individual in the community? Or does the researcher protect the anonymity of both, letting socially disturbing events continue? Is this a case for researchers to deal with, or does it need to be referred to those able to make interventions? Furthermore, given community divisions, where does one place protective measures? Here is yet another place where this book presents as many questions as answers, but at least it puts forth the issues.

Smith's stage three: when research is complete

As I sat in Karin Tusting's office at the University of Lancaster, UK, she was thinking about finishing up with participants. She pointed to her window sill:

This is a card from one of the people that worked with us closely. I will keep in touch with him because I feel like there is a sort of a friendship there. I worry that he doesn't understand fully the [research] reason I was there. You talk [to them] on a regular basis about their lives. And then he writes, "I like you very much," and he underlines it, and he puts quote marks around it. And I just feel very uncomfortable. But maybe it doesn't really matter that there is a disconnect between my life and his. Have you found people who also said similar things?

And my answer was "Yes!" Many researchers were feeling conflicted with the maintenance of the relationships they forged during research. Linda Tuhiwai Smith described this phase of research as being just as important as the ones that came before: "Building the relationship is regarded as a third of the task. Then there's the interview, which is like a moment, and then there's this long-term relationship deemed to be the third stage of research."

Julie Canniff talked about the multiple roles she fell into with the Cambodian families involved in her research:

There was this tension about whether I was still collecting data or just enjoying their company. I wrote a paper for a conference about the different roles that you can take on as an ethnographer. So one of the roles is researcher, one of the roles is as a cultural broker, and in another I am perceived as an elder. I am older, I am educated, and, therefore, I receive a certain amount of respect and authority. With one young woman, if her mother couldn't explain something or couldn't discipline her, then her mother saw me as a back-up "mother." At one point after the book was published, I was talking to my primary informant about his son. He told me that his son had written a letter to a senior monk requesting permission to spend three months in the temple as a novice monk in order to honor his parents. I was so moved because this young man had never considered this "rite of passage" expected of the oldest Cambodian son before my interview with him years before. I thought about asking for a copy of the letter and writing an article showing how he valued his bi-cultural identities, but then decided this would be opportunistic, like taking advantage of our friendship. So I stopped.

If researchers have encouraged a relationship with a participant, they may not want to disconnect, but as Rachel Hodge, researcher at the University of Lancaster, UK, points out, there are other life pressures:

There are all sorts of issues around withdrawing from research as an ethnographer. I'm still in touch with participants, trying to advocate with solicitors, going to immigration centers, even financially, socially. And I hardly can cope in some ways. My family will say, "Well, you can't keep bringing people home." I found out that one young Angolan woman wrote her own proverbs in Portuguese. And I was really interested. By the third interview, she translated one of these proverbs, something like "You meet many people by chance, but not everybody becomes a friend." And she said, "That's like you and me. We met by chance, but we talk together so nicely, and now we're friends." And this is an issue. It's always a delight to see her. But in another way, I'm aware that I've spread myself increasingly thin. I think that these things just have to be considered carefully and negotiated. A methodology book can raise the issue, but it can't spell out a right and a wrong.

Karin Tusting, the ethnographer with the card on her window sill, said of another relationship:

> Eventually I had to leave [the research site], knowing that nobody else was going to take my place. And it was going to have quite an impact particularly on one individual. I promised her I would keep in touch, but she moved. Funding was not continued and the clarity wasn't there from the beginning. I'm starting to think that there aren't really any external ground rules beyond being open and honest with people and respecting their lives and boundaries and your own.

She articulates what most researchers were trying to work out for themselves. Though some still craved rules that would give them confidence in the way in which they were being with participants when the research was over, most had realized that hard-and-fast rules don't exist. Tusting described her approach as a sort of situational ethics: open, honest, and respectful of their lives, a bit different than the concept of the third interview above, but caring.

Whereas many researchers talked about maintenance of relationships with participants, Brian Street gave one example of how respecting participants and keeping them from harm meant severing a relationship. As a researcher, he needed to make the decision based on the situation:

> As I left, a revolution happened in Iran; we reached a point where it wouldn't have been good for them to be receiving letters from England. It began to become apparent during my last year there. The revolution began building up, and the [presence of] an unclean non-Muslim living in the village [might have been perceived as] contaminating, by some people.

Openness, honesty, respect, and care seem to be qualities that have worked best for researchers as each situation brought its own complications.

I have maintained long-term relationships with participants, and my involvement in lives and schools gets increasingly complicated. I worked to bring Julian Cho's wife and sister-in-law to the University of Minnesota to complete degrees, and I have complicated feelings about how that has changed their lives. Cho's wife has a new life, living miles from her family. His sister-in-law has completed her degree and has returned to Belize to complete the very land-rights work that her brother-in-law started. I have respect for the way they have shaped their lives, and I don't want to absent myself from those lives. I visit regularly, as I continue to bring student teachers to Belize where they are still appreciated. While this program widens the lenses that the student teachers have on the world, the Maya family focuses my lens on the richness they have brought to my life. Last year the father proudly toured me around his farm to show me every new addition, and, as always, we visited the mahogany trees that he and Julian Cho planted years ago. More and more I understand their humor, the complications that the world presents to them, and the love in their lives. And more and more I understand myself through the richness that the juxtaposition of our worlds brings.

World traveling

In discussing respect of research participants, Grbich (2004) presents Mikhail Bakhtin's (1990) statement that mutual respect should be quite easy to fathom if, as Bakhtin holds, the other is already a part of oneself "as one of the many voices absorbed during identity formation." Indeed, as a researcher, one must stretch to tap the "other" within the self, and, in the best sense of empathy, to do right by one's own crowded self and that of the participants. Issues of respect were constantly on the minds of the researchers whom I interviewed; they had reached deep within themselves to proceed with empathy, sensitivity, and respect for the strengths in the "other." When working across cultural borders, whether of race, class, ethnicity, generation, gender, religion, language, or any other type between ways of being, acting out of an informed and loving approach gets perhaps the closest to the kind of respect needed in research, especially when the issues are complicated. As already mentioned, Lugones (1987) suggests what she calls "world traveling" as a "loving way of being and living" (p. 390). She makes the distinction between loving versus arrogant perceptions in relationships with others and sees love as revealing plurality, "the plurality of selves" within a person that can connect with others.

8
Complexities of Analysis in Cross-Cultural Research

> You can find multiple ways of being clever when you collect data and sensitive and ethical, but what you do with that data is another layer of ethical responsibility.
>
> (Martin Nakata, Torres Strait Islander, University of South Australia)

Postmodern researchers have long recognized that knowledge, the analyses that led to it, and, hence, the actions that come from it are filtered through the researcher's way of viewing the world. What humans see and hear and feel and even sense is affected by present circumstances and past experience. If we come in from outside on a cold day, the inside can feel very warm until we sit still long enough to realize that it isn't quite warm enough. Our experience of reality is situated in place, in culture, in gender, in time. Truth is seen through our complicated bundle of identities and resultant standpoints. I used to wear a light sweater as a grown woman on a cool day and still bundle my infant granddaughter, whose circulation was no doubt better than mine, in a number of blankets, until some knowledge about circulatory systems and logic intervened. My initial grandmotherly lens on an infant's need for wrappings might have been absorbed from my mother and her grandmother, until logic and the viewing of lightly wrapped children in other cultures intervened. And with, for instance, a poem, an important part of what meaning it initially makes for us has to do with its consonance or dissonance with our own experience, experience that reflects, infects, and affects our sense of its meaning. It is often when others with different experience weigh in on the same poem that our perspectives can grow and readjust. Thus it can be with data analysis. Stuck in our own standpoint/perspective, our ability to analyze can be limited.

The whole purpose of research is to generate the knowledge upon which participants, practitioners, researchers, and policy makers can act. Because each discipline has its own set of analytic methods and its own disciplinary lens, discipline specific analytic procedures will take less emphasis in this chapter than broader cross-cultural issues related to analysis and those who work more qualitatively. Questions that will be considered in this chapter are: Can the concepts of the situatedness of knowledge, identity, power relations, positionings, and collaboration, presented in previous chapters, help us through the morass of thinking about analysis? Can we fully know, understand, and represent the positions and experiences of people from different cultural positions?

In cross-cultural social settings, our analysis of data is complicated and enhanced because we gather points of view from those who are differently positioned. Our liability is that when we hail from the dominant culture, our take on truth may be fed by default layers of unrecognized or unscrutinized assumptions, until the search for alternative interpretations and deep-reaching logic intervenes. Willis et al. (2008) quotes Hall (1982) as saying that misassumptions can explain "the failure of dominant concepts, definitions, and models as explanations for the Underserved" (p. 30).

All that said, coming up with something to report and act upon from our research is essential. When researchers come to the "saturation point" (Liamputtong, 2010), the point where no new data is arriving and the point at which discrepant data has been further probed, the time for analysis has arrived.

Is there a truth with so many positionings possible?

In the behaviorist scheme of understanding human behavior, if you introduced controlled input, human reactions were predictable, but Lev Vygotsky's (1978, 1986) work on social mediation of thought complicated those considerations. Humans consider the messages, the symbols, and the sensual experience that comes to them, and they construct and act on their ever-changing theory of the world. Blumer (1969) sets out premises about interpretations of human behavior: because humans act on the basis of meanings that they ascribe to what they experience and on interactions with others and with society, the meanings themselves are a part of their interpretive process and are mediated by both symbols and signification. He terms this "symbolic interactionism." In that we create meanings through symbolic interactionism, the question arises: Is there a truth to be had with so many perceptions of what is true? As Stryker et al. note (2000, p. 26), "A symbolic interactionist frame assumes that humans are actors, recognizing the possibility of choice in human life" based on developed meanings.

As researchers in social settings, we seek truth, but is it objective truth that is important or is it our understandings of other's truth that is important? Most Western legal systems depend on a search for "facts" to provide justice: proof from witnesses, physical evidence, and logic assist judges and juries in making "judicial" decisions. Western forensic science pushes for objective truth, scientific evidence, beyond what witnesses might contribute, as witnesses might well have past experience and resultant perspectives that affect what is seen, mediated, for instance, by media images. But there is cultural difference in what is deemed to be just in a dispute. Laura Nadar (1990; see also Nadar and Metzger, 1963) wrote about the legal system in two Mexican communities where it was not necessarily the "truth" that was needed. Whether the legal system discerned what actually happened was not the focus; more important was the reconciliation and restoration of social relations (see also McCaslin and Breton, 2008, on restorative justice).

Research journals have assumed that what is published gets closer to the truth. But, as Stanfield (1994, p. 166) says, "It has become quite appropriate in America to question authority in places once considered sacred, whether in the areas of business, medicine, law sciences, religion, or the profession of teaching." Indeed, for researchers in social settings, a healthy skepticism has developed, and that skepticism is necessarily extended beyond truth to what is moral or ethical. Some of this skepticism arose as researchers began to acknowledge differences in men's and women's ways of knowing (Belenky et al., 1986), and in thinking through controversy over male and female moral development generated by the Kohlberg/Gilligan debate (Flanagan and Jackson, 1987). Further research on cultural differences in what is moral and on moral development have further complicated views of morality (see Miller, 2001, for more on this topic).

Postmodern relativism furthers this discussion by considering the encoding of thought through language. As Grbich (2004, p. 47) says,

> Knowledge is viewed as unreliable if it comes solely from language. History, and the discourses they have been a part of, influence meaning. There is no absolute truth beyond or beneath the text. Reality is fragmented and diverse, and analysis has tended to highlight texts, language, history and contextualized cultural practices.

In a way, skepticism is one of the strengths of cross-cultural research because, in leaping out of one's context, one can see things differently, and one can open up the possibility of others viewing things as differently true.

Though researchers who hold on to a positivist stance have believed objective reality to be paramount, postmodern thinking from both quantitative and qualitative researchers has begun to look at the complexities of truth and its situatedness. As Renato Rosaldo (1993) says, "The truth of objectivism—absolute, universal, and timeless—has lost its monopoly status" (p. 21), and as Lather (1991) says, "The mantle of objectivity which largely shielded the sciences from such questions has been irreparably rent." Given multiple perspectives, conscious and unconscious bias (and interests served by bias) must be scrutinized. Even in research reports, it has become common to acknowledge issues that might have muddied clear analysis and to determine implications for further research to clarify what needs greater scrutiny. This is especially essential when there are borders to be crossed. Local theories of truth from a declared time and context stand a better chance of portraying a reality for those in that reality.

In research across cultures, then, we necessarily look for things that hold across data and explanations of data (Ember and Ember, 2009), fully knowing that truth is evasive.

Acknowledging experience and its effect on dynamics in social settings

Research in social settings often examines what motivates or what reduces motivation—for instance, to participate in school learning, or to explain why certain groups of people choose certain areas in which to live, or to explain why some people follow "law" and others veer from its strictures. Research in social settings has long acknowledged that experience frames the way humans see the world and act upon it. Research seeks explanations of human behavior. Tess Moecke-Maxwell, Māori identified researcher in New Zealand, talked about such considerations:

> All the perceptions of the women I researched might not necessarily correlate to any truth in the outside world. What's meaningful and important is that this is their truth, and they have a right to it. Once there is access to this research, maybe some people will find a part of themselves reflected. These stories are the truth-telling of some people. How I got round the whole "if you can't measure it, it's not valid" thing is that these are stories, and it's not about trying to prove the stories, it's about trying to appreciate these stories, and use them in a way which may explain. You don't have to measure stories.

In cross-cultural analysis of research done in social settings, it is important to take up such complexities. David Carey Jr., a historian at the University of Southern Maine, talked about a complexity in discerning truth in Guatemala:

> People would start to talk a lot about the spiritual stories and myths, and I would redirect the conversation towards history because I saw the two as being distinct, whereas for them there was this kind of natural flow between the two. We view history in the US as that which definitely happened in the past. But there is not that clear division between the natural and spiritual worlds in these Mayan communities. There are stories such as the one about the Siwanaba, this woman who lives in the canyons in the Maya highlands. By turning into a beautiful woman, her goal is to entice men into the canyon and kill them. So I thought, well that's not really history, but they hear her crying and screaming in the middle of the night. And sure enough one night I woke up, three in the morning, and I heard her, and my room was at one end of the courtyard and the

bathroom at the other, but there was no way I was even going out in the courtyard. So at that moment she was very real to me, but I didn't include her in the book. Others would look at that and see that not as history but as a myth.

The "natural flow" between spiritual and historical truth for Maya people affects their actions. The actions are a reality. And even researchers who consider the fearsome existence of Siwanaba to be illogical can see how such a belief affects behavior.

Besides conflicting views of reality in different cultures, researchers also confront the problem of being told purposeful untruths because of lack of trust, based on research that disserved a group in the past and/or based on political and economic savvy of why truth might disadvantage the participant in the future. Roy Young gave an example: "If we ask about income, we use a range. That way respondents feel more comfortable because they may otherwise think the researchers are doing it for income tax purposes, or they may want people to think they are doing better than they are." Susan Rodgers talked of these dilemmas in Indonesian survey research:

> With survey material in many Indonesian contexts, if you ask an Indonesian farm family how many children they have, and they really have seven, but only three are showing in the house, they'd pretty much say "four" because even though you told them you're a researcher from the US, they think you're the taxman or the taxwoman. Or they kind of psyche out what they think is the answer you want in some sort of open-ended or yes/no questions. And they're not lying, they're just being polite, they're just being nice.

The juxtaposition of these quotes, each from a culture distant from the other, gives the researcher cause to search for careful, strategic motives behind answers, which may be given out of politeness or self-protection. Researchers who spend a good amount of time within the community can be canny in their understandings of where representations of truth originate, and again there is value in cross-cultural teams of researchers who can scrutinize the data, problematize participants' motivations, seek explanations for discrepant data, look for unstable language, and see the fluidity in meaning.

In analysis of data from research across cultures in social settings, it can matter less what the truth or untruth is and matter more how a person's take on experience affects their actions.

Dealing with the danger of simplistic analysis

In most experimental research, variables are controlled, evidence is gathered, statistics are applied, reliability and validity are determined, logic is applied to results, and articles are written. Analysis in cross-cultural research in social settings becomes a more complex adventure. Once data are collected there is reliance on insight, juxtaposition, collaboration, and logic, and researchers have generated further ways to increase accuracy of their understandings of the motivations behind human action, and, hence, the future benefit of their findings. Before formal analysis even begins, those who research across cultures often find themselves flexibly adjusting their research questions, methodology, methods, tools, and analysis strategies.

In etic research that compares cultures, efforts to further improve what can't be deemed experimental research are evolving because of the inability to randomly assign participants to different cultures. In a chapter on methodological issues in quantitative cross-cultural research, Leung and Van de Vijver (2006) describe two approaches attempting to eliminate a single culture's dominating research question selection and biasing results. The authors discuss the consilience approach that develops quasi-experimental research with strengthened validity of cross-cultural causal influences. The value of multiple methods, multiple sources of data—as is suggested in this book—is supported in this approach. Leung and Vijver acknowledge that "the interpretation of the meaning of research findings is crucial but evasive, because cross-cultural research is essentially different from true experiments... In our opining, the best approach is to formulate a number of rival hypotheses on an apriori basis and design studies that are able to rule out alternative explanations" (p. 251). More and more sophisticated methods of analysis are needed and are being developed to work with this etic, versus emic, cross-cultural data. Leung and Vijver continue to say "but in this globalizing world, we cannot afford to be blind to cultural similarities and differences... for productive and enjoyable intercultural contact" (see Leung and Vijver, 2006, and Ember and Ember, 2009, for further discussion of methods for analysis of etic comparison of cultures).

Though structuralists, in an attempt to move beyond simple data collection, stressed using binary oppositions as a way to inform classification systems in analysis, researchers have since argued for more complex coding systems. Simplistic analysis is always a danger. In the analysis stage, my collaborative team found, for instance, that, in coding transcripts, we added many additional codes when quoted material didn't fit neatly into one category, more than doubling the number of originally conceived codes. Healthy discussions within our team, based in part on age, gender, and culture, moved us to more complex systems of coding and, hence, both more careful shaping of what we might say from the data and prevention from missing out on what was buried in the data for one or more of us. Willis et al. (2008) term "traditional categories of analysis as part of a system of oppression" (p. 62). This process can be started by thinking about the data and its discrepancies from multiple points of view. For instance, there is always the danger of inadvertently taking a deficit emphasis in looking at results, focusing on weaknesses instead of on the compensating strengths and resilience that individuals in another culture develop in meeting the standards that the dominant culture holds dear (see also Dey, 1993, and Seidman, 2006, for more discussion and critique of "coding").

Michael Rosberg talked on several occasions of looking for the logic in cross-cultural situations: "Saying to yourself: 'What is going on here,' as opposed to saying 'It's wrong.' 'What is the logic behind it? In what way does it make sense?' Everything that a person does has some kind of logic to it." He validated researchers' ability to think analytically and to think past the historic and dominant culture's reasons for things. Negotiations over meaning in research teams, teams comprised of those within the culture being researched and those trained in the analysis strategies of their discipline allow the teams to step beyond former understandings to meaning informed by the culture and the context of the research setting.

Moving *inductively* from examples of participant behavior, survey responses, or statements to understandings can also get analysts to see beyond traditional interpretations; this requires starting with the data instead of a theory. This grounded or inductive approach to analysis is different than that which is begun with a hypothesis. It results in new insights and new questions that may be asked about the data and topic.

Furthermore, John Arthur talked about preventing his Western-oriented academic training in sociology from getting in the way of his analysis in his study on African immigrant groups:

> In some of the activities I attended, I noticed gender role differences. When I went to a child-naming ceremony or a party, I found the men segregated here, the women there. I noticed the men were served first. The women were congregated in the kitchen area while the ceremony took place. Things were sent to the men. My first hunch was to look at the non-egalitarian relationships that were visible to me. The sociologist in me wanted to understand the gender roles in labor, from a Western point of view. But in the in-depth interviews with the women, that was never an issue, and with the adolescents it wasn't an issue at all. So my sociology was reading into this interplay. What had seemed to be the case was not. The women were seen as better able to protect themselves and the children by having these gender roles clearly defined. The outsider looking in thinks that there is a marginalization of women and children. I realized they see their role as one to ensure the security of the family, to allow the men to be what they want to be, as they allow the women to be what they want to be. Also something that emerged was the role of matriarchs in coming to help with childrearing and in serving as a bridge connecting the husband, wife, and children, and helping with other problems—with elderly care, immigrant experiences, those

struggling with being transplanted here without friends. Some take ESL courses just to learn English at 75–80 years old, so they can facilitate that matriarch role more effectively.

Dealing with the danger of simplistic analysis can be discipline specific and culture specific, but the place of reflexivity in preventing this from happening is further discussed at the end of this chapter.

Grounded theory and beyond: complicating the search for thematic patterns

I asked Shirley Brice Heath how a researcher can seek patterns in data without overgeneralizing:

> First and foremost, human beings cannot exist without reliance on patterns simply because our brains are not otherwise capable of managing the chaos of our world. So at a neuroscience level, [the researcher's mind will seek] patterns. In a youth-based organization in Boston in which I've worked for years, any social scientist entering that site for the first time would be likely to say: "This is chaos. How do you ever sort out what the patterns are?" That is an issue, but within the patterns there are individuals, contextual features, and leadership issues that play in and with those patterns. You can't just take a single lens and go in and say: "I'm going to see this group through this lens." I don't criticize people who do that, so I shouldn't say you can't. I would say *I* can't. I need to move across a lot of circumstances and keep my eyes open and think: "What were the patterns operating in *this* situation? What were the patterns operating in *that* situation? And how do I fit in? And where do I learn not to carry something from here over to there?" People who want to make the post-structuralist or the critical argument, or the feminist argument or the Marxist or any single one, miss much that may seem random but is actually structured.

Lightfoot and Davis (2002) describe the effective researcher as one who "gathers, organizes, and scrutinizes the data, searching for convergent threads, illuminating metaphors, and overarching symbols, and often constructing a coherence out of themes that the actors might experience as unrelated or incoherent" (p. 185). Much of pattern seeking in qualitative thematic analysis of cross-cultural research comes to us from the grounded theory of sociologists Barney Glaser and Anselm Strauss (1967). They deem that validity comes from how well "a researcher's understanding of a culture parallels that culture's view of itself" (Kellehear, 1993). Kellehear warns:

> The central meanings attached to objects or relations should reflect the beliefs that the insiders hold about these. The analysis may go beyond these meanings, but if those meanings are the starting point then they

had better be valid ones. Validity here begins with the convergence of researcher and the subjects' ideas about the subject's view of the world. In the case of interviewing, of course, one can check back with respondents about the themes which emerged from the interview. (p. 38)

Cross-cultural collaboration in all phases of research, but definitely in analysis, increases the likelihood of the data reflecting the beliefs and realities of participants.

The process of looking for patterns in qualitative data is both intuitive and inductive. It may start by taking its categories from the data and from field notes. Simplistic categories slip away when new patterns are seen or patterns within patterns are discerned. Participants' participation in this process can help. Themes that seem important to the researcher may be quite different from those important to the researched and their different ways of viewing things. The frequency of data in categories themselves does not affect validity or reliability. Post-structuralist analysts push grounded theory further by querying omissions and inconsistencies. Patti Lather (1991) warns of declaring patterns without critiquing them from multiple perspectives:

> The category systems we devise to "explain" empirical "findings" are re-inscribed by post-structuralism as strategies of legitimacy where exactitude and certainty deny the unthought in any thought, the shadow, supplement, alterity, the structuring absence inherent in any concept. Conceiving useful categorical schemes as provisional constructions rather than as systematic formulations, focus shifts to how data escape, exceed and complicate rather than how to impose a specific direction of meaning on the unfolding of the narrative. (p. 125)

Given this way of thinking, it is no wonder that collaborative teams move one more reliably from data to theory. Categorizing is a form of power in research; when research involves differently cultured people, there needs to be a space for them to be involved in that process. This brings us to the value of recognizing standpoint in the determination of patterns and in analysis.

The agency of standpoint

Having seen the kinds of unexamined assumptions and embodied response that can get in the way of observation, one can understand why contemporary research in social settings has long criticized the claim for objectivity. The standpoints, the subjectivities from which the researcher and the researched hail, need to be problematized as data are considered. Martin Nakata talked poignantly about the necessity of recognizing the agency of the researched in the analysis of data:

You go out and collect data, whether it is ethnographic research or quantitative calculations or accumulation of numbers or stats, or the qualitative interviews that you may do. Then you bring the data back, and you have a standpoint from which you can deal with the data. In today's world of doing research, that standpoint is not necessarily named. In cross-cultural research, standpoint theory is really all important if we are to give primacy to Indigenous people and their knowledge. Ethically, you cannot read data with the kind of contexts that make them victims of the dominant situation, or victim of a masculine paradigm. They actually have a different kind of agency that can surround the data you are collecting.

Researchers need to scrutinize their own responses to the data they collect and recognize the agency of the researched. Vicki Crowley was considering issues of gender as she considered her own response to an interview:

A Greek man had told me a story. As a young boy, he had to go with his mother to a surgeon because she was miscarrying all the time, and he had to translate. The gynecologist showed diagrams—this was an eight-year-old boy—of ovaries and said to him, "Doesn't your mother know we did a partial hysterectomy?" So the Greek man is telling me this story, and I was interested in how he understood the workings of gender and sexuality. And I asked: "Do you think gender is an issue in terms of racism?" He says, "Oh, no, no, no, no." Now my response was probably like yours when I first heard this thing, so I kind of thought: Why do I respond like this? My response was profoundly a gendered one. But it also made me think: "What am I hearing here?" I heard a child speak, I heard an adolescent speak, I heard an adult man reflecting, and maybe he would tell his story differently the next day. All of these responses are happening inside our own constructions of racism. Had I been responding to this particular story in this way because I had been married to a Sicilian, whose experience had been to translate for his parents all the time? I was keyed into why his story disturbed me so much, why it was both familiar and strange, and it was partly my own. So a way of dealing with my ethical dilemmas was to kind of work it out in thought. One response was an embodied response, which is not the response of the person who is telling it. [As researchers], we actually can acknowledge those responses, those standpoints.

Crowley's reflexivity was a part of her research process. She interrogated her own responses, problematized them, and sought understandings for her own responses or interpretations of data by focusing in on the things that bothered her about her own responses. Reflexivity to recognize one's researcher standpoint is an important part of what researchers need to do when analyzing data and again when reporting them. Other researchers talked about the value of having research teams who might weigh in on data from other standpoints, collaborating in the analysis of data. Having analysis come from multiple perspectives can bring to light otherwise unexamined interpretations brought about because of your own past experience or socialization. Saavedra and Nymark (2008) talk about the positive contribution of those who, because of their hybrid identity, offer double consciousness in analysis. "As a tool, methodology, epistemology, and a way of existing, borderland-mestizaje feminism embodies a hybrid mode of consciousness that challenges researchers to rethink new ways to know and to be" (p. 269).

Some steps in discerning standpoints are as follows: allowing viewpoints within the data and viewpoints amongst team members to argue with one another; deconstructing inconsistencies and discrepancies in the data; interrogating generalizations to extricate specious conclusions and complicate the reporting of results; thinking in terms of discourse analysis to uncover hidden agendas; and reading against the grain of any textual sources or data. All these strategies are enhanced by having culturally different viewpoints at the table, and most importantly recognizing the agency of those researched, hence the next section.

Seeking multiple positions of analysis

> Above all, the stories that we bring back in other women's words for translation on our side of the border need interpretive homes that will not turn out to be prison houses with yellow wallpaper.
>
> (Ruth Behar, 1993, *Translated Woman*, p. 272)

Nakata urged recognizing and honoring the agency of the standpoint of the researched in analysis, Crowley urged reflexivity in examining standpoint, and many other researches advocate collaboration to make sure that there are multiple positions of analysis and that the standpoint of the researched be applied to collected data, problematizing researcher's initial interpretations. Shirley Brice Heath went so far as to say: "I won't advise graduate students if they were going in with a predisposition toward proving their viewpoint." By actively seeking multiple positions of analysis, one eliminates the potential for prior predispositions to drive analysis, even unconsciously.

Renato Rosaldo (1993) puts forth a strong argument for seeking multiple positions of analysis: "Each viewpoint is arguably incomplete—a mix of insight and blindness, reach and limitations, impartiality and bias—and taken together they achieve neither omniscience nor a unified master narrative but complex understandings of ever-changing, multifaceted social realities" (p. 128). Seeking out multiple positions in analysis is a postmodern shift, the shift from emphasis on theorizing to attention to the problems of interpretation. Even the attempts to define postmodern validity are to be critiqued. Grbich (2004, p. 59) cites Lather (1993): "Any attempt to define postmodern validity is problematic and must be viewed as a link back to the power structures which attempt to control and frame research within particular objective parameters." Researchers, however, note the value of cross-cultural teams and/or transdisciplinary teams working toward more ethical analysis. Barbara Rogoff offered an example of seeking out additional standpoints during analysis:

> One of the kids who was in the first study that I did in Guatemala grew up to become my grad student and now is a professor. The first research project that we did together involved looking at four tapes each of toddlers and caregivers in San Pedro and the US. I didn't tell him what I thought I saw in it. I thought, well, this will be interesting. I asked him to just write down what happened in each of those tapes because I had already written down what I saw happening. We compared them. I saw it as an exercise in how our perceptions differed of the same events from each of our communities. I had spent enough time in San Pedro and he had enough familiarity with the US that there were surprisingly few differences, but they were interesting. By having those who have backgrounds that give them some insights from personal experience in what we are studying in Indigenous communities of North America or Central America, they could say, "Yeah, I see what you are trying to say, but it's a little bit more like this." Then I might say, "Okay, I follow what you said there, but let me see if I can describe what you just said." Then together we come up with ways of saying it better. We might base ideas on different experiences and use those different experiences to figure out how to articulate it. This crucial, collaborative attitude I learned partly by hanging out in San Pedro.

In analysis it is also important to recognize that data represent simply a metaphorical minute in time and place. Vicki Crowley returned to weigh in on this:

> Having been a research subject and seeing what I said printed in a way that was totally out of context has made me refuse to participate in some research. So I know what it's like to see one line put in a context for the researcher's agenda. When I was doing research and I was traveling overseas, Catherine Hall said to me: "What gives you your eyes and ears for this particular research?" And I gave her an answer, and she said to me, "Well that's not good enough." So that has stayed with me, about why the constraints with which I am able to see and hear have an effect on what I do with the data. Whatever comes out of that time is never a once-and-for-all statement; it's in a particular moment, in a particular time, and framed in a particular setting. So I guess I'm trying to honor that; that in some way seems to me a question of ethics.

The shift in postmodernism urges the scrutiny of one's conclusions and the utilization of alternative viewpoints, transdisciplinary and/or cross-cultural.

Analysis that benefits from juxtaposition

As researchers, we can juxtapose data drawn using different methods and learn where the conclusions from one data set complicate, replicate, or evidence themselves as discrepant. For instance, in quantitative work, researchers can look for both convergent and divergent validity to further inform analysis. In qualitative work, researchers may juxtapose the stories of many participants and learn from those stories how they replicate each other and develop themes, or complicate each other, or evidence themselves as discrepant. Qualitative and quantitative researchers can look at studies done by different researchers or teams of researchers, and once again see where the studies replicate, complicate, or evidence themselves as discrepant. And we can juxtapose the data from archives and juxtapose them with oral histories as Carey has done, or juxtapose narratives with social historical structures as Black (2009) has done with that same process.

As mentioned above, selecting several methods, before data collection even starts, is apt to allow researchers doing cross-cultural research different takes on the research question. But after data are collected, there are further ways to juxtapose data, again, to problematize results. Psychologist Barbara Rogoff evidenced this:

> Once I was about 10 or 15 years into each of two different projects, and I realized I was learning a similar thing from both of them. You have to get hit over the head sometimes to learn your lessons. I started my work puzzled as to how kids can learn without being taught. The question came up in the Mayan setting where children do very complex things. I would ask their moms how they taught their daughters to weave, and they would say: "We don't teach them to weave, they learn." And I couldn't understand that because I had this idea that people have to be taught in order to learn complex things because they can't invent it on their own. And that was a dichotomy that just didn't work. It was my preconceptions, probably based on the extent of schooling that I have myself experienced. But I was learning the same thing in the innovative US elementary school where I was doing research. And I had thought that these were totally different projects.

In juxtaposition, the researcher can see similarities that might point to the possibilities of universals in human nature; differences might point to the effect of culture on the development of certain skills. Juxtaposition can offer fascinating possibilities, enabling researchers to better see where their own cultural orientations might predispose them to see data from only one standpoint.

Juxtaposition of narratives, sometimes termed as collage or montage—as often done in qualitative research and as done in this text with research stories—has its advantages and disadvantages in cross-cultural research. Ellis (2004) says that though stories may be true in the present, if representation of truth is your goal, it's best to have as many sources and levels of story recorded as possible. Additionally, though the reader of research can add their own analysis, it is the researcher who selects what is to be juxtaposed and in what order the juxtapositions are placed, trying as hard as possible to take cues from the narratives, but, thus, directing the readers' sequence of thoughts. As Bella Graham, oral historian, then interviewed at the University of Waikato in New Zealand, said:

> I take responsibility for cobbling it together; it's more like a director of a TV show where you've actually selected this bit and this bit and this bit. It is a collage, but there's a point to it, and so that point is mine. I'm wanting to show there are some political agendas there ... but I'd like to think that a political agenda that I'm putting forward is put forward by the informants, that it is actually a tribal political agenda not just my own personal belief where I am an insider. And I become an outsider when I stand out of their directive. I'm trying to cobble together, and I am trying to subdue my own personal statements and find the commonalities of the informants.

The strength of such juxtaposition is that, with limited author intervention, the data can speak for themselves with openness for readers to do analysis of their own. Often juxtaposed narratives, oral histories, research reports, or data groups provide productive friction, enabling both the researcher and the reader of the juxtaposed cases to sink into their own analyses and discover new questions for scrutiny. Valuable is the critical edge honed on juxtaposition.

Participant involvement in analysis and representation

> I learned more by allowing Kaqchikel to interpret their history than I would have had I hoarded the data and analyzed it without their insights.
>
> (David Carey Jr., 2003, p. 104)

In the past, by the time a researcher arrived at the analysis phase, face-to-face involvement in cross-cultural research was often non-existent. Though using participants' own words in research reports has become a mainstay of qualitative research, used as a way of minimizing the researcher's mis-representation of participants, participant involvement in actual analysis is beginning to be seen as productive.

Daphne Patai (1988) has been both articulate and wise, however, about the intrusion of the researcher when working with oral histories, personal narratives, and interview material which, she notes, do "not necessarily come to us in unadulterated form: people speaking their souls directly into our ears." The interviewer as mediator collects and then even juxtaposes interviewee's words affecting the individual's words, and then sometimes juxtaposes that interviewee's words with those of others. These become one version of a people's stories. Patai continues by saying that even the resulting participant tapes "must be seen as a point of intersection between two subjectivities— theirs and mine, their cultural assumptions and mine, their memories and my questions, their sense of self and my own, their hesitations and my encouraging words or gestures (or sometimes vice versa), and much much more" (p. 2). Bella Graham, recently deceased Māori oral historian from the University of Waikato in New Zealand, said:

> What I often see is that in the process of writing things up or presenting things, it is the researcher's own position that takes over again. I've researched and worked on major exhibitions of oral history, looking at the Tainui tribes in this region. The selection of what is going to be used wasn't selected by the interviewees. There are photographs and things like that, and even the selection of the colors of the written words were done by the art designer. So after the gathering of the information, the thing becomes removed.

And here I am presenting her words, here and above. There is irony that she will be unable to personally edit her words, as have others, to limit the very remove she described in them.

Though written reports of the findings to the community have become commonplace, these reports, as Carey says, are often not as valuable to the researcher or the community as is the discussion about those findings (Delva et al., 2010). Most recently, community or participants have been involved in actual analysis steps as a way to validate the realities of groups from the perspectives of some members of that group.

In Chapter 7 the case was made for respecting participants by giving them editing rights to their contributed data; this section describes further involvement of participants in analysis. The approach solves some heavy issues around interpretation and representation by allowing participants or the community to weigh in on the perspectives that researchers or research teams have used to inform conclusions. This process, of bringing a number of participants into analysis when the words of many more have been gathered, has also been critiqued; nevertheless, it is a step in the right direction. As a side product of this process, participants may gain from this more emancipatory approach: "The goal of research is to encourage self-reflection and deeper understanding on the part of the researched at least as much as it is to generate empirically grounded theoretical knowledge" (Lather, 1991, p. 60). A number of interviewed researchers combined transcript checks with having the participant reflect on what they said initially. I began to see this as a layered process of analysis. Christine Sleeter allowed participant reflection and a deeper analysis:

> I haven't analyzed data in the more traditional qualitative research way. I have constructed portraits of teachers who do interesting things with multi-cultural education. One set of them is in the multimedia book *Culture, Difference and Power*. I had a graduate student videographer, and we went into classrooms and videotaped the teachers, and then I transcribed interviews with them. And then I put together a vignette of the teacher and showed it to her for her feedback. Some of the teachers added some information; some of them didn't like their transcribed words. One said: "No, no, no; I am cleaning that up." Another said: "Let's go show this to the principal to show her I'm not crazy."

Sleeter's interactive portrait process with teachers allowed the multicultural teachers to feel comfortable with the way they were presented and allowed the principal and teacher audience to see the value in what they were doing.

Community involvement in analysis

This community involvement in analysis can also be important to both self-determination and the development of what Mary Hermes terms "intellectual infrastructure." She used strong language:

> Don't take analysis out of the community. In the analysis, you're producing knowledge, thinking through it together. If the community doesn't have a strong hand in that process, there are isolated islands of thought at the university that are not connected back to and amongst communities. Knowledge is power; it can come from conversations and analysis amongst Indigenous people. Without that there is a sort of brain drain. The thinking goes to the university where you're often one of a kind. We will have elders in the community. Without them and discussions, it is not connected enough to the heart. That analysis, the theoretical, might not look like what we do when we write papers, but it is there.

Meanwhile, on the other side of the world, Daryle Rigney said:

> I want to find out what we need to be a politically literate community, using cultural knowledges, applying them, and using them to shape ourselves, establishing our own agenda, and using that framework as a strategy to critique policy analysis. I wanted to pick up on the bridge

issue [see Chapter 3] as a case exercise in political literacy, so that we are actually engaging in our own political development. Most communities are dealing with the same sorts of issues [needing to apply cultural knowledges] around health-related matters, or land rights, native title matters.

When I interviewed Rigney, he was working across the Tasman Sea with Linda Tuhiwai Smith and Graham Smith. Linda Tuhiwai Smith added:

As an Indigenous person or a minority person, you always are involved in that sense of being engaged with the dominant group and its knowledge. In all my training the assumption was that I belonged to the dominant group, and this is how you did research with others. I spent a great deal of time deconstructing why that didn't work for me [see her seminal work *Decolonizing Methodologies*, 1999]. As an Indigenous woman who is a minority in the academy, you have to negotiate your entry back into your own community as a researcher or as an educator. Most of my work is in the cross-cultural domain. I've tried to work inside my culture and recognizing that culture is complicated. It raises up enough of its own issues to keep me busy for a while!

As an outsider anthropologist, Joan Metge talked about mentoring young Māori researchers and urging them back to their elders:

I said to them: "Go back to your grandparents and your elders. Consult them." But then a lot of them call me "Aunty" because I have been cast in their own parental and now grandparental generation. Māori elders decided I was worth teaching and took me under their wing, fed me like a baby bird, but I think there is an obligation to respond to any requests for help and advice by stressing that they must go back to their own grandparents, aunts, and uncles and seek their ideas. You have to stand aside and let them develop their own ideas.

The knowledge and perspective of community elders and their collaboration is important in analysis. Though they may be without tertiary education, their presence in research can be essential in building success and trust, and they can offer local knowledge and insights about all steps in the research process (see also Delva et al., 2010). The epitome of fostering self-determination is to step aside when community researchers are ready and able to do analysis on their own behalf, but even then a set of "outsider" eyes on community-owned and analyzed data might well add clarity from possible dialogic conversations related to the data. And, as will be further discussed in Chapter 9, the "outsider" researcher may be able to give good advice about dissemination to the public policy makers.

Dialectical considerations of data

Fiona Cram also poses the following question: "What happens, for example, if the researcher's interpretation of the findings is at odds with the participants' interpretations or the participants are unable to agree among themselves? Whose account is privileged within a final report?" Cram (1997) and G. Smith (1990) noted that contradictions can be decreased if the researcher is fully immersed in the community. Nevertheless, there is important value in the dialectical conversations and dialectical thinking that lead cross-cultural teams to deeper considerations of the data.

Dialectical considerations cross-culture and discipline can take place on four levels: within the cross-cultural research team; between team researchers, participants, and community members over analysis of a single study; between differently disciplined and/or multicultural researchers coming from different paradigms but studying the same or similar topics (Delva et al., 2010); and then again at a professional level with practitioners in the field and/or at international conferences and/or in international partnerships or symposiums over both research in progress and completed and reported research. International partnerships are now using technology that expands these possibilities. Psychologist Barbara Rogoff used dialectical discussions at a local level, checking how what she saw in her data (videotapes) resonated with those in the community, she conferred with her research team, she had reflexive conversations with herself to find comparable dynamics between her own studies, and she conferred dialogically with other researchers. A growing number of researchers are studying comparable themes and subjects, using technologies with free international communication, like Skype, across cultures and geopolitical spaces. Databases of ethnographic research are being compiled as an ongoing resource (see reference to the *Ethnographic Atlas*, Singleton and Straits, 2010).

But back to disagreements: usually dialectical considerations of data work toward clarity, but if there are no resolutions, there is always the opportunity to describe the unresolved issues in the research report. And while some groups or teams find consonance in their preliminary conclusions, other groups of scholars might well come together and discuss contradictions that can come from partial understandings, working through the cultural and other contradictions in what Lather (1991) terms "the process of ideology critique" (p. 63) and "deliberate ambivalence" (p. 163).

It is inevitable that these dialectical modes of analysis deepen understandings or show the researchers that they have more work to do, raising questions for further research in the great shared puzzle quest of research.

From analysis to theory: from the cultural inside out

While I do believe that close contextual work is the lifeblood of theory, I also believe there is something useful to be said across cultures and historical epochs when our focus is narrowed by structural similarities.

(Scott, 1990, p. x)

An outcome of the intrinsic motivation of curiosity is humans' search for patterns and then theory as a result of what is observed. My father's elderly acquaintances around a dinner table are full of stories and theories as they work to make sense of their world travels; they are full of theories about human universals and cultural specificities.

Durkheim broke ground in the field of sociology in developing methods for moving from facts to theory in cross-cultural study, attempting to make the process both scientific and objective. He called for impartial observation and comparison of observations as opposed to settling theory on individual observations as untrained world travellers might. These were positive steps and positivist steps. Following on, Kuhn (1962, p. 40, as cited in Singleton and Straits, 2010) adds: "It has been shown that disciplines may adhere to theories for long periods in the face of much contradictory evidence and that major theories are displaced only after prolonged 'scientific revolutions'" (Singleton and Straits citing Kuhn, 1962, p. 40). As we move on to postmodern times, Grbich weighs in: "Meta-narratives or grand theory as an overall explanatory tool become less useful, as linearity and prediction disappear, as boundaries shift, and as feedback loops make causality impossible. Local explanations linked to chaos and complexity become more useful" (2004, p. 61). Some believe that the actual word "theory" may have lost some of its usefulness (Dey, 1993; Seidman, 2006).

Given the insights and accompanying skepticism of postmodern, post-structural, and postcolonial scholars, getting from data to theory has become a more complex endeavor. Indeed, analysis of each set of data is apt to produce unique results, dependent on the particular time and place and with particular relationships of power between people. And then criticisms of postmodern and post-structural approaches come along and usually focus on concerns of nihilism, the concern that nothing much can be said given the fact that everything is relative to situational factors: unique to every set of data, to the context in which it was collected, and relative only to one moment in time. Yet, theory may lead to new understanding or to new hypotheses, and alternative theories suggest more research and, at best, another piece, however tenuous, put into that metaphoric puzzle about life and behavior in social settings.

Yet, developing theory is the attempt to make sense of the world even though there are contradictions and indeterminacies. As Spivak (1987) says, having theory is "a way of holding at bay a randomness incongruent with consciousness" (p. 78). Brian Street pointed out the irony in the necessary role that university researchers have in taking research beyond the confines of collected stories—for instance, to theory:

It may be slightly dishonest to pretend to the locals that you're simply going to tell their story as they would want to tell it. That isn't what a doctoral dissertation is doing. It's telling their story through their eyes to some extent, but ultimately you are framing it as your contribution to knowledge. You can sure give back and say: "I'll take my reframing of your experience so it can actually contribute to the field and maybe put your questions in a different light, for instance, challenging neo-liberal positions." There are standard stories to be told, and the whole point of research is to get them beyond the standard stories. If all we did was reproduce them, that might be fine for the locals, but I don't think it would be much help for them either. It wouldn't be giving anything back. It would just be reproducing what they're already saying. I think there has to be a dialogue rather than privileging one or the other. A dissertation is contributing to knowledge and moving theory up. Locals may not want to do that in that same sort of way.

Theory rarely resides in one story, or one data set, and in some inquiries doesn't derive from one culture. Stepping back in analysis, looking at what you have, what meaning you have, juxtaposing different sub-sets of data or similar or discrepant studies or stories, seeing where things don't fit, rethinking the things that don't, considering the center of the evidence, deconstructing the center as a possible red herring, thinking beyond your discipline, looking at the data from multiple standpoints, and—important in cross-cultural research—making sure all voices are present: all these processes taken together are what allows us to move toward theory. Cultural geographer Joseph Wood went through some of these processes as he tried to theorize how Vietnamese refugees worked to shape a sense of place, especially around a shopping center called Eden Center, named after a shopping district in Saigon (1997, 2006):

I had journalistic reports as well as interviews, so I was compiling all of this, trying to make sense out of it as a geographer. I stepped back, instead of trying to retell the story of other researchers, creating a new concept. I arrived at the concept of place-making, the creation of a set of places that, in effect, were sort of buffers for the process of acculturation, allowing some concentration of familiar activities even as people were dealing with change. Then I realized that's what Chinatown was doing. I started looking at the recent literature on deconstructing the concept of Chinatown, constructs as much in the eyes of people outside as in the eyes of insiders. At the same time I also realized that more people from the dominant culture began to go to Eden Center restaurants that had been written up in *The New York Times*. It was a two-way acculturation process: people were becoming familiar with having Vietnamese restaurants or Vietnamese jewelry stores, just as immigrants began to imagine and understand what it was to live in the suburbs. The place-making was the facilitator.

Each discipline is apt to have methods that work for that discipline and well-used means of analysis to use with data. Most importantly in cross-cultural research, many researchers and teams are also beginning to take their lead in analysis and theory building from those cultures which are being studied, developing theory from the inside out. Russell Bishop talked about analysis moving toward theory using Māori metaphors:

> When people talked about doing research, they used the Māori metaphor of the ritualized meeting or coming together, to explain analysis. People talked about weaving things together...a very Māori metaphor...instead of teasing things apart. Instead of analyzing things to find essential kernels of truth, they were weaving things together to create a home. People talked about time in terms of looking backwards to see the future. They would then look at their research in that sort of process. The imagery that we have in mind is how we construct the world; the world we construct is through our images, and the images are reflected in a language, and the language that reflects them most vividly are the metaphors.

Is coming to theory actually that weaving together of the metaphoric puzzle pieces that Durgunoğlu and Rogoff have referred to? Taking a metaphor of the culture seriously moved Sharon Kemp into a more culturally relevant way of analyzing her data:

> I started out with the research question of how women in India talked about production and reproduction. I was mostly interested in how women viewed themselves. I did 100 interviews of women across castes. One woman said to me: "Women and bullocks do the most work, but the name of the man is praised." I couldn't get that out of my mind. So I went back and started looking through the interviews. And in the third interview, there it was: "Women work like bullocks." So I started asking Western academics about this, and they said that it is not possible in a gender-segregated society such as India to have women think of themselves as castrated male animals. But lo and behold, I found a short story written about a farmer whose bullock died, so he hitched his wife to the plow, and at the end of the story, he is massaging her feet, which is something a man would never do for a woman because it is a sign of respect. Then I found a folk song: "God gave me the life of a woman, but oh that I were a bullock, honored for the day." I asked an Indian academic from that area. He said: "Oh, yes." My dissertation was restructured: wives, Mothers, Bullocks. Things started to fall in place. If women are not married, they are considered dangerous. Bulls unless castrated are dangerous. It was an image that was all over the place. The religious system structures

women's lives on the importance of being a wife; the family system structures women as mothers, the role they feel most honored in; and the
economic system structures women as work animals. The minute I found
that verse, everything fell in place. Of course, I came back and had to
convince Western academics that this was Indian women's point of view.
Had I continued with the structure of production and reproduction, it
would have been a Western perspective that was shaping Indian women's
experience, a Marxist perspective.

Kemp actually reconstructed her research analysis, moving away from the
Marxist approach she had originally intended, taking her key from cultural
metaphor.

Finding the center of one's data and its analysis, inductively if grounded
theory is applied, is one way of moving to theory. Moving through cultural metaphor or cultural world views is another enriching mode of
reconstructing theory.

A good thing about the advent of post-structural, postcolonial, decon-
structionist thinking is that in reporting research, the researcher can describe
the complications that exist, keeping us from reporting pat theoretical
pronouncements and reporting in a way that is consonant with the community's understandings. Researchers still strive to generate theory while
acknowledging its possible contradictions and the holes that need examining in future research.

Nevertheless, when the researcher or research team strives to do research
with egalitarian purposes, research that will make a difference, there is probably disappointment when there is an inconclusive conclusion. However,
research that doesn't generate pat theory and propound broad generalizations will be "closer-to-truth" research from which future researchers will
work. Perhaps one researcher's inconclusive theory is precisely what builds
breadth and depth in a future inquiry. Furthermore, a postmodern reaction
against reason and logic does not mean that postmodern researchers don't
use those thinking strategies for analysis. Those human tools help us see the
holes in our thinking as well as possible things to say from our research,
both to those who act on research and for those who need the attentions
and resources that research may bring.

Issues of power in analysis

If the dominant culture enjoys the power base and its benefits, controls the
funding agenda, and controls what is deemed as knowledge, those not in
that group are disadvantaged. The 20th- and 21st-century disillusionment
with power structures and the recognition of the depth at which they are
embedded have resulted in awareness of inequitable and unethical social
structures and socially constructed breaches of human rights. Since the
mid-20th century, researchers, with privilege and without, have taken up an

agenda to right the scale by rejection of simplistic explanations, which support both inequitable policy and depend on antiquated forms of analysis. Nevertheless, those in power tend to stay in power. Change comes slowly. Funding agencies are not without their agendas, and government entities and economic powers are apt to want to perpetuate the policies that might make them look good or that maintain power. Researchers have begun to act on the inequities they see in a variety of ways. Researchers from three continents talked about the way in which power structures authorized some representations while blocking others. Shirley Brice Heath spoke passionately about the misreading and misuse of research by powerful agencies:

> This is an ethical issue, but it can become deeply personal: I really like punching holes in theories that have actively punished or repressed the young, the poor, and members of minority groups. Often I do this when I'm angry with shoddy, wrongheaded information piling up and then being turned back and dumped on the heads of those least able to defend themselves. That's when I roll up my sleeves. That's why many of the foundations in this country have little use for my research. I've rolled up my sleeves over a number of issues that are precious for them and their silos.

Heath went on to discuss the misreading of her own work by agencies that then want her assistance. The irony is that those agencies control funding. From the other side of the globe, Barbara Comber talked about the stifling of research findings that didn't make schooling look good in Australia:

> I tried to show the ways in which poverty and race had a major impact on what was going on in schools and how that happened. We had both the ethnographic and the quantitative data, and I was able to look at what was making the difference, referring to specific cases strategically, to get things noticed. And that's probably why it [the research report] didn't get released. The schools didn't look good. We're trying to resist simplistic readings of race, simplistic readings of class. But they tried to change our conclusions and our recommendations, and they've deleted parts. That's why I'm already starting to write.

Groups of outraged researchers have also opposed erroneous meta-analysis that has informed public policy in the USA. An example of this is described below (Cleary, 2008):

> The National Reading Panel, which informed the No Child Left Behind legislation, was based on a meta-analysis of only experimental research done on five topics: phonemic awareness, phonics, fluency, vocabulary, and comprehension. Left unexamined was the valuable qualitative research, which offers understandings of reading in real and diverse

settings (including research in Indigenous settings), and research on other topics essential to understandings of reading success (such as motivation). Both NCTE (National Council of Teachers of English, 1998) and IRA (International Reading Association, 1998) have deemed the summary of the report (upon which the legislators acted) to be a limited representation of even the "scientific research" that the panel reviewed (Krashen, 2005). The limitations of the report, translated into instructional recommendations on only five discrete areas of reading, have fueled and funded instruction that is often scripted and non-strategic drill.

Brian Street talked about the similar skewing of research summaries based on the exclusion of all results that weren't "control-tested":

> They looked at a particular topic and did a survey of all the literature on that topic that they could find from the last five years but used the criteria of being control-tested. I was at a seminar and 120 articles had been reviewed and only three counted. I mean, none of ours, our work would have been in the 120. It's not just about ethics; it's about ideology and power. That ethics is not just some universal moral efficient way of being good, it's preempted by power as the inclusion and exclusion of what counts as knowledge.

Even evidence-based research results require critique, as do qualitative data, especially when researchers measure non-dominant cultures on the basis of the dominant culture without regarding culturally bound values and socially constructed motivational factors. Researchers are frustrated but not naïve when their research does not align itself with the agenda of those in power. Using an educational example, with big business so focused on getting well-prepared workers to the workplace, the chance for the impoverished to use literacy as a critical means to understand the economic power structures is limited, further entrenching those very power structures. How much power will researchers, focused on righting wrongs for the underserved, have in their attempts to equalize power? Thinking through modes of dissemination (see Chapter 9) may be one avenue that researchers have.

Analysis of your analysis: the meta step of reflexivity

Drawing participant interpretive stances into the analytical process disperses the researcher's authority; nevertheless, there will always be effects on research that we can't account for in all aspects of research, including analysis. Ian Anderson said:

> There is no such thing as a risk-free practice. We are fooling ourselves if we think we can get our actions to a point where we can completely

eradicate our presence on our practice. So it's a continual process of balancing the judgments, the consequences of doing something vis-à-vis the consequences of doing nothing. A critically reflective practice is the kind of practice I want to encourage in researchers.

Consequently, Peshkin (2000) calls for a "series of metanarrative reflections" on research that he calls "problematics" (p. 5). His self-reflective method is first to identify a pattern that he sees in his data (I do this through initial coding) and to follow with critique of his own analysis of it (I do this through both critical reflection on the coding, conferral with cross-cultural research partners, sending back quotes to participants, consideration of those quotes that are discrepant and those that have a different take on the topic). A second step that Peshkin suggests is to problematize the researcher's own sense of identity and how that might "intertwine with their understanding of the object of investigation." Pillow (2003) states:

> One of the most noticeable trends to come out of a use of reflexivity is increased attention to researcher subjectivity in the research process—a focus on how does who I am, who I have been, who I think I am, and how I feel affect data collection and analysis...

Reflexivity takes a constant vigilance on the part of the researcher (I often assign this vigilance to my reflective research journal and dialogic discussions with team members). This process involves for Peshkin "the interplay of subject and object, self and problem" (p. 6), and he sees it as a series of "formal internal tests." This conscious endeavor to reduce biased actions in analysis and in selection of the conclusions to be presented is particularly effective if the members of a cross-cultural collaborative research team all involve themselves in the process.

The sole use of reflexivity as a means to validate, legitimate, and question qualitative research practices and representations has certainly been called into question. However, it does take the researcher one more step closer to being confident about the analysis process. A further endeavor should be to draw on other standpoints, especially on the standpoint of those researched, ensuring that we have meaningful things to disseminate, which is the next step in the research process. Lather (1999) quotes Yeo (1989, p. 10): "In these anti-foundationalist times, in which seemingly the ground is being swept from under our feet, perhaps it is timely for beings with legs to talk about how it is possible to take a stand—and whether it is impossible not to."

9
Dissemination: Reciprocity as an Imperative for Action

> You can pick up books where sacred, restricted information is made available to everyone, one of the most hurtful things for Aboriginal people. Knowledge for knowledge's sake had its origins in academic pursuit. Social Darwinism supported that stance: "We're superior, gathering knowledge about lesser people." Information was given to others with little concern for Aboriginal people. The damage is done. There's no going back.
>
> (Ken Ralph, Aboriginal, Australian Catholic University)

But there certainly has been a going-forth.

Obviously, disseminated cross-cultural research has advantaged the researcher's career and increased available knowledge about cultural universals and specificities, and, in the best-case scenarios, has informed policy makers. In the 21st century, however, there is an ethical imperative to return knowledge in accessible forms to those researched and to go beyond that. Now many researchers feel that the ends—those reports to policy makers and implementation of findings—are what justify the means of research and the efforts of both researchers and participants. While respecting participants' self-determination over their own knowledge, there needs to be a deliverable result accessible both to the researched and to parties that can leverage action for the researched. Following through with dissemination is a matter of reciprocity, a matter of conscience. Ken Ralph went on to line up the venues for responsible reciprocity and dissemination:

> You've got to ask yourself: "Who are the stakeholders?" First of all, you have to give feedback to the community in plain terms, not a chart in standard deviations—in terms that might generate some discussion about the implications or answers in a community. So, the next responsibility is to the broader community, as long as the specific community researched agrees. It might go into university libraries, but it shouldn't go where it would end up in the garbage. It should go to vocal people who have responsibility to take action, whether for legislation or for their ability

213

to act upon things in the community—for instance, housing authorities. Then research could make all the difference.

Thus, Ken Ralph delineates the parameters of effective dissemination:

- accessible local reports to the community;
- addition to the knowledge base in academic articles or books;
- strategic delivery to those in a position to act on the results: to legislators, housing authorities, principals and education agencies, clinics, social agencies, and so on.

This chapter will look both at issues of respectful dissemination and at quandaries that arise in its delivery.

Representation

> I use "ethics" to signal the workings of an ethos of responsibility to one's object of inquiry, a responsibility opposed to hegemonic domination and representational violence.
>
> (Shemeem Black, 2010, p. 3)

As stated in Chapter 2, concerns arise about representation in every phase of research, but in respectful dissemination, the issue of representation demands very close attention. I quote Dewes' despair over irresponsible representation: "I am sick and tired of hearing my people blamed for their educational and social shortcomings, their limitations highlighted and their obvious strengths of being privileged New Zealanders in being bilingual and bicultural ignored" (cited in Cram, 2001, p. 36). Research reports can perpetrate stereotypes of participants, portraying people as abnormal or deficient when they are judged by Western norms. A real danger in dissemination is allowing images of failure—a blaming of the victim—to supercede possible portraits of resilience and success in the face of odds (see also Lawrence-Lightfoot and Davis, 1997, pp. 8–9).

Theorists like McConaghy (2000) call for critical analysis of representation. In interview, Russell Bishop said: "We need to seek representations that are legitimate in the eyes of the person who is speaking." Discussions about possible dissemination in initial community negotiations start the process of participants' weighing in on how they want results to be presented beyond their own world. But when initial reports are in progress, participants need to have a chance to compare the reality presented with the reality that the participant lives. And in using narratives, even these considerations are complicated by considerations of whether the reality of more than one person is presented. Lather (1991) says: "Narrative realism, hence, is but one of many textual strategies with its assumption of the transparency of description;

such realism is challenged by the crisis of representation which is, in essence, an uncertainty about what constitutes an adequate depiction of social reality." Though representation becomes easier to get right when monitored by collaborative research teams, constant vigilance is important, no matter who the disseminators or their intended audience.

Reporting back to those researched

Disseminating preliminary results to the community early on can allow a check on analysis before the researcher or research team begins to write up reports for publication. This also allows full debriefing after research (Goldstein, 2000). Jenny Barnett talked about the need to offer multi-modal presentations to some communities as a way to insure understanding and even as a way to gather new data, do a check on data, and/or receive community feedback on analysis. As in the layering described above, Barnett's plan makes very distinct phases of research obsolete:

> I think putting it [data] into a play, performing and re-performing it would actually be a way of making new data. Psycho-drama. You present, you talk your way through it, and then they play it back to you, and if the community plays back to you what they're hearing from you, then that becomes part of checking that you have it right.

The reporting back can actually be a celebration of the strengths of those who offered up knowledge. Discussions of what is learned can prompt local action, the avenues for which may not have been discerned before the research.

Thus the returning of information is often so interesting to the community that it can be one of the most satisfying aspects of research for the researcher and/or collaborative team. Two factors are particularly important in this process:

- that language and content are accessible to the community while respecting their ability to understand;
- that participatory sharing increases the community's willingness to listen as well as increasing their own self-determination and intellectual infrastructure in relation to the topic.

Researchers can learn more from what is most interesting to participants in the process of reporting back.

Language, social distance, and resistance
The use of accessible and respectful language and the contextualization of the results in the participants' lives are means of decreasing the social

distance between the researcher and community. Brian Street described how his team found ways to reduce social distance between researchers and teachers by avoiding too much formality:

> There are dilemmas: some of the teachers are female and the professors are mostly white and male, so status differences might be perceived. Giving feedback to schools on our findings has proved to be fairly complex. It may be practical things, not just abstract ethics. So, at the interpersonal level, we might just talk to a teacher after class, walking down the corridor to the staff room, having a cup of tea. At the next level, we used our research funds and took all the teachers to lunch at a pub. And it was just a relaxed thank you, but they would ask questions, and we might ask as well. The next layer has never happened because they are all so intensely busy and because some of our findings are not so favorable, making a dilemma for us in full reporting. The schools and teachers will often see the local community, especially the working-class local community, as impoverished, deprived, ignorant, and not having literacy practices. As researchers, we challenge all of that while looking at local literacy practices and the richness the students bring.

Figuring out how much to prolong your presence after research is complicated. Psychologist Aydın Durgunoğlu proffered the following advice:

> It has to be their choice how much they want to interact with you after the research. They can say, "Share the information with me, and I'll do what I want to do." But you can't say: "I am going to continue being in your life, so I can change your behavior." That's more patronizing than just leaving because it implies: "I know what's good for you better than you do." If they ask: "What should I change?" then that's a different story. Or if they invited you and then said, "Here is the situation, or "Is it working or not working?" then reporting back and offering advice is not patronizing.

Reporting back can also be influenced by funding issues. Jenny Barnett described the issues of accessibility and funding that her team faced:

> We had wanted to include broadsheets with a fold out so you could pin it on the wall, a miniature poster, with dot points [bullets] laid out to catch the eye, in language that was neither intimidating nor patronizing and voiced to the communities, using the pictorial devices that those communities use for themselves. They needed that presentation of findings because there is nothing else available except in academic tomes or school reports to tell communities what their options are. But you need to put in another funding application for presenting your findings to the community.

Barnett's plan to insure accessibility and close cultural distances was solid though limited by funding. Often researchers find mid-project that they hadn't budgeted for the different forms of dissemination that they need; others are forced to be quite inventive due to lack of funds.

Being aware of community and generational politics

Another level of social distance that can complicate research reports may be generational or political. Western researchers are not always fully aware of the status that elders hold in a community, but as Māori researcher Sarah Jane Tiakiwai said, "If I couldn't take it back to the old people and explain it to them, then it didn't mean anything; it was just an academic piece of work." Acknowledging the wisdom and knowledge of elders and including them as important recipients of results and participants in discussion is essential, but as the reporter, one also needs to be aware of the political situation between groups in a community. Bella Graham said:

> You have to remember that the elders are not some sort of universal group. They have their own personalities. And you might have some elders dismissing the statements because they are made by young people, or perhaps by an elder they don't like. You have to be careful you are not playing one elder off against another.

Such situations are yet another reason why cross-cultural team members with a presence in the community are provident.

Multi-modal presentations

Acknowledging participants' potential to understand research findings, findings initially informed by their own experience, is respectful, but finding ways and words to make sure they understand is essential. For example, some researchers have suggested different sorts of performances leading to both understanding and positive social transformations, allowing for both self-determination and reclamation of culture.

Multi-modal presentations or "performances of research" (Denzin and Lincoln, 2000) results may not only increase accessibility but also open the hearts of wider public audiences to hear what research has to say, audiences that may otherwise be resistant. Multi-modal presentations of analysis allow engaged understandings, lessen social distance between the participants and the reporters, decrease the academic jargon that might get in the way of both local and public understanding, and still allow the opportunity for critical thought (Madison, 2008). Video presentations can provide powerful images that expand understandings, both to participant/community audiences and to wider public audiences. Resources are always an issue, but such technology has become much cheaper in recent years. We have all probably experienced the value of film in reporting researched circumstances.

While studying indigenous literacy some years ago, I happened to be in Melbourne for the opening of the Australian film *Rabbit Proof Fence* in the city. The narrative line and the courageous children portrayed in the well-researched film provided diverse Australians with a perspective on their history that many hadn't experienced from the inside out. The sounds of weeping in the theater were not coming just from the Aboriginal attendees; there were cross-cultural and cross-gendered tears. As Grbich (2004) says, "There are various ways of capturing readers' attention and bringing them into an active and emotionally empathetic dialogue with the text, and to a greater or lesser extent with the writer/people who wrote the text" (p. 95). Film, plays, and images offer some of those ways. In 2002 I happened to be in Auckland when *Whale Rider* opened, and that film had a similar response from the audience, as had the much critiqued *Dances with Wolves* in the USA. In all three cases I was taken with the power those films had for those around me in the theater, people who came together to watch films about a regrettable past. Wendy Holland, Aboriginal researcher at the University of Sydney, said:

> *Rabbit-Proof Fence* affects the many non-indigenous people as diverse as that group is, not just white Australians, but Greek Australians, Italian Australians, Lebanese Australians, Vietnamese Australians, Chinese Australians. It takes that kind of level of dissemination to actually get the message across, awakening the ignorance in people. Until a nation acknowledges its past, it can't begin to heal, let alone move effectively into the future.

Of course, such a film to report research can be cost prohibitive, and though films can be critiqued as having little to do with native intellectualism (Cook-Lynn, 2008), my purpose above is to relate the power of images for public audiences. Liamputtong (2010, p. 227) quotes Tedlock (2008, p. 155): "Theatrical performance is often used as a form of political analysis, catharsis, and group healing by indigenous peoples who have experienced ethnic, cultural, and social displacement; grinding poverty; and horrendous acts of violence." Vicki Crowley talked about her difficulty some years ago of reporting her research back to participants, and how years later she found a way to do so:

> My dissertation was hugely contentious. I didn't even send it to people who participated even though I was going to. That will weigh with me forever and a day, and is consistent with people's criticisms of academics furthering their own interest, but there is a climate now for the research I did then, except the data is out of date. What I did was to dramatize it, condensed it in order to put it out there as something that I could think about too because I needed some distance. The arts present a way

of making such an intervention. If it's an art product, you can put it out there, and we can talk about it without necessarily being: "Whose side are you on?"

She went on to talk about more recent multi-modal presentation of data:

> I've just been this morning to see about having an art exhibition based on a conference presentation, "Inner-sanctums Bifurcating Selves: Navigating Cultural and Educational Contexts," shocking title, I know. I couldn't actually perform it, so I did a slide show from a photo shoot. I'm using photography in order to document and to look into the kinds of questions that are there. It's getting honest with the research. I can put something out there that provokes another series of questions.

Bella Graham, in her outsider persona as researcher and her insider Māori identity, talked about the effectiveness of multi-modal presentations:

> In 1996 I was asked as an oral tribal historian, an academically trained historian, to help the tribe [present a legal case]. I taught them processes of sorting out information that would probably be required, then helped put it in a package that we could present. The biggest problem they had was the presentation, the write-up of a report, so we ended up using a multimedia Powerpoint presentation, finding ways of saying things that just couldn't be articulated in words. One part was a documentary of the process by which the tribe was to provide a collective narrative and an analysis working from what the interviewees had said of *iwi* identity and how we are connected to this and that tribe. Some narratives were left out that didn't conform to the discourses of law rationality because a legal counsel said, "You can't say that," or "That's going to take too long."

Grbich (2004) offers a list of multi-modal ways of presenting research that sometimes blur the boundaries between the presenter/actor and the audience to "deconstruct discourses that might have created misinformation and non-empathetic attitudes" (p. 97). The suggested modes of innovative dissemination invite the audience in with their own critical minds: "juxtaposition, layering, pastiche, vignette, literary, and dramatic approaches." She includes creative visual forms, such as "photography, paintings, videos and computer imaging," and aural forms, such as "music and other sounds." Denzin and Lincoln (2008, p. 7) discuss a

> commitment to democratic politics, an ethics and aesthetics of performance . . . These performances reflexively use historical restagings, masquerade, ventriloquism, and doubly inverted performances involving

male and female impersonators to create a subversive theater that under-mines colonial racial representations...This is a utopian theater that addresses issues of equity, healing, and social justice.

Rachel Hodge gave a good example of her use of photography in research which allowed young people to own and to voice their own experi-ence (a form of what Grbich (2004) calls "photoethnography" and what Liamputtong (2010) and Delva et al. (2010) similarly term "photovoice"). Hodge related its benefits and a consequent problem:

Their culture is very different than mainstream young people. They pro-duced their photos with writing around their photos, but they didn't want their photos and writing to be identified with their names, so we decided together that we'd make an anonymous display. We were ever so pleased with ourselves. It was extremely powerful in relation to what they wanted to represent. Then the manager phoned me sounding extremely frosty, though I had a good relationship with her. "The display is just so negative." The young people's voices were very volatile and nega-tive, and they used expletives. As researchers, we're linguists, so we don't write those things out. I quickly could see the difficulty for her. As a manager she was desperate to secure funding to respond to the needs of the young people and needed something much more positive and polite to present to funders. Our work had been very individual-centered rather than organization-centered. Recently I gave a presentation at a seminar on what I called issues of representation, re-presentation, and self-representation. We all agreed in that seminar that how we use actual images is something we need to think about. I don't say it's resolved in my mind.

Above is an example of the complications that can come with visual images. What might be winning with the participants might cause resistance in another audience—for instance, those who fund research. As a researcher, allegiance can be divided.

As powerful as visual images are with an audience, there are critiques of use of multi-modal modes of presentation. As Grbich (2004) notes,

The major concern here is that the information gained often comes from those of a different class/culture from that of the researcher, and in turn-ing narratives gained in the research context into performances there is a tendency to trivialize, simplify or ignore the depth and contexts of cultural differences.

(pp. 95–96)

Those who find images used in reported research to be trivial are often of a different mindset than the researchers and those researched. Therefore, presenting data in multiple ways, from academic discourse to "performances," is still important.

Presenting to wider public audiences

In April 2006 at the annual American Educational Research Association conference, Michael Apple warned of danger in "reporting research only to ourselves." Henry Giroux (2010) took this even further:

> Even many leftist and liberal academics have retreated into arcane discourses that offer them the safe ground of the professional recluse. Such academics seem unconcerned about writing for a larger public and inhabit a world populated by concepts that both remove them from public access and subject them to the dictates of a narrow theoretical fetishism.

Though single-author publishing in academic journals has traditionally been an academic goal of the researcher, more recently cross-cultural researchers have seen value in making results known to wider public audiences with participant partnership in determining content, purposes, and mode of representation. Mary Hermes noted that:

> Writing for academic journals is just a small slice of what is needed. Writing things that are more popularly read can have a bigger effect. Academic writing is so narrow, but then you never know. When I wrote an article, "The Gut Wrenching Years," my mother gave it to her priest, and that really made a difference. Different writing reaches different people. What I feel best about is what I've written in a narrative way—for instance, when I've tried to sort out my own issues with internalized oppression. I had the tribal graduate cohort read that this year. It was important for them to see that you could write narrative and still address some very salient issues, often edited out in academia. It shows how layers of oppression can stop us from getting where we need to go. Writing that way really deconstructs. So, different presentations of material reach different people. That's why we are making these films of people learning their Ojibwe language.

In publishing results, collaborative groups must be strategic. Nevertheless, it may be that knowledge about academic discourse and access to international audiences are an important part of what the researcher contributes. Stephen May declared the need to share internationally:

> There are audiences that I have access to as a result of my international work. I think that work can contribute to what happens back here because it's important that those other cultures' stories are heard and told within the context in which they are useful for Māori. The indigenous people's movement itself is an example of this kind of approach, so I'm not alone.

There is a strong argument for cross-cultural research in a sense that cross-cultural researchers have different audiences where information can go.

Even writing about methods that work cross-culturally is important. Fiona Cram reported:

> We're trying to be more politically astute around publishing. Some used to pooh-pooh peer-reviewed publications. I have come full circle around and have thought: "Well, we need to publish quite widely because the knowledge we have is in the methods we use and how we use them, and we need to be telling people about that."

Journalistic reportage, multi-modal presentations, and academic tomes all have a place in disseminating the results of cross-cultural research, as have new forms of writing that are more multi-voiced, dialectic, and dialogic, proffering more complexified thinking than thesis, support, and conclusion can contribute.

Journal articles and presentations at academic conferences

> From my own experience, I can say that, very often, a problem seemed settled, everything fixed and clear, till I began to write down a short preliminary sketch of my results. And only then, did I see the enormous deficiencies, which would show me where lay new problems, and lead me on to new work.
>
> (Bronislaw Malinowski, quoted in
> Sluka and Robben, 2007, p. 512)

Vygotsky (1986) notes that in the process of turning from thought to writing, we learn more than we thought we even knew. So, even when all the data are analyzed, further considerations often take place in the very act of writing. Filtering our thoughts, our results, through a projected audience help us consider how an audience might take what we say, and that, too, adds a perspective that we may not have considered. And even in consideration of that projected audience, we need to think of both our representation of others and the politics of reportage. bell hooks sends us a warning:

> When we write about the experiences of a group to which we do not belong, we should think about the ethics of our action, considering whether or not our work will be used to reinforce and perpetuate domination.
>
> (1989, p. 42)

Some past reports of cross-cultural research in academic discourse allowed representation of the lived experience of other cultured participants to further marginalize them or to reinforce stereotypes. As researchers, we are challenged to represent silenced participants in academic space. Given the discontinuity between culture of the academy and the culture being represented, researchers are still doubly challenged in both relating research findings to academic audiences in ways that assert one's scholarship while preventing the re-marginalization or re-colonization.

Nevertheless, even in many academic journals and in presentations in academic settings, there is new openness and resilience. Whereas previously, editors were looking for pat research findings, publications are open now to honest descriptions of what results were inconclusive and to meanings drawn inductively from narrative (Cleary and Peacock, 1997). Now many editors, and their readers, respect reflexivity that declares itself with the deconstructions of past research, problematization of current findings, and the presence of ambiguity. The times are changing.

If a researcher is working with a cross-cultural research team, decisions about written articles and conference presentations can be negotiated, and the researcher can work with the team about what needs to be said and why it might need to be said in a certain way for certain audiences. Sociologist Judith Stacey (1991, p. 115) talks about these issues in terms of ethnographies:

> Like feminists, critical ethnographers eschew a detached stance of neutral observation, and they perceive their subjects as collaborators in a project the researcher can never fully control ... Here they have attempted first to acknowledge fully and own up to the interpretive authorial self, and, second to experiment with dialogic forms of ethnographic representation that place more of the voices and perspectives of the researched into the narrative and that more authentically reflect the dissonance and particularity of the ethnographic research process.

Ted Glynn, again, provided a good example of collaboration:

> I will go back to the team and ask them if they want to share this, and with whom, and they'll say, "That's fine." Or, the older people might say: "If you are talking about this [topic], say this," and they will tell me what to say. And they'll say: "Remind people that this is an initiative from our *iwi*, our tribe, because we don't want Pākehā people to get an impression that this will work anywhere in the country just because it's been worked through one tribe. It probably will work for someone else, but they need to work it through." From a Western point of view, we might see this as tribalism. From a Māori point of view, it's more about not stepping on the toes of another tribe, who have their own right to decide things for themselves, and their own ways of doing this.

Thinking through audience issues can be huge in cross-cultural research. Taking presentations abroad, for instance, can bring on a new set of difficulties, often related to language and audience conceptualization of word meaning. Brian Street weighed in again about the illiteracy/ignorance dilemma that crops up in translations:

> You do have to tailor the story to the person you're talking to and the language you're using. I was in China a while ago giving a talk. I started talking about literacy events and literacy practices, and realized this wasn't easy to translate, so I always try to talk to the translators in those situations. Very interesting people translators: obviously they have a linguistic awareness. They were intrigued by the difference between talking about literacy/illiteracy, and literacy events and practices. We had long debates and that became part of the conference discussion. How do you translate these terms? What are these funny guys from England talking about? And the same actually happened in Cairo. So in any situation, one needs to ask: "What's the social relationship you're engaging?"

Ted Glynn went on to talk about the difficulties and the progress in transferring thoughts to another culture and internationally:

> It is more difficult to publish internationally. The audience may have a traditional positivist empiricist orientation; that's a problem New Zealand has anyway. And if we send something to an American journal, by the time you are finished defining what we mean by each and every Māori construct, and words that have specific meanings in our country, or by agreeing that our word is really just the same as someone else's word (when it isn't quite), you end up thinking: "Is this our work anymore?" Fortunately, indigenous people are establishing their own publication outlets with their own conventions. Over the years I've witnessed a huge change. Within the New Zealand Association for Research in Education (NZARE) the whole nature of the annual conference has changed from one of resistance, through regarding it as (paternalistically) quaint, to now starting the conference with a bicultural welcoming ceremony. It's worth investing the energy because you can turn things around.

The problem of speaking for "others"

> The prerogative of speaking for others remains unquestioned in the citadels of colonial administration, while among activists and in the academy it elicits a growing unease and, in some communities of discourse, it is being rejected. There is a strong, albeit contested, current within feminism that holds that speaking for others—even for other women—is arrogant, vain, unethical, and politically illegitimate.
>
> (Alcoff, 1991, p. 286)

As Ted Glynn said, "Because I am the researcher, I can't assume that I have the right to speak on behalf of the group. It's a collective thing." As a member of the cross-cultural research team, he seeks guidance in dissemination. Researchers struggle over whether to even speak for others, but those with team assistance at least have insider advice about representation and research results.

Using the participants' own words or narratives to get meaning across only partially takes care of the problem. Australian researcher Stephen Muecke used a montage technique and raised the issues of cultural differences in narrative and of translation:

> You have a so-called universality of narrative; we know that narratives are common to all societies, but that generalization can only go so far. What is really interesting is the particular differences. It's open to interrogation about where narratives can take us and where one narrative sort of bumps up against a different narrative from another culture, and what happens in the presence of translation. Do you turn their story into something else? Do you merely juxtapose story A with story B and not comment, or a kind of montage technique, where you say between A and B there is a possible third space which will remain undefined? Do you leave it for the reader to make their own leaps of imagination?

In juxtaposition of narratives, the researcher, in the very act of juxtaposing or ordering quotes, is complicating the meaning of what has been said. In dealing with this problem, I have given material back to interviewees in the context in which it will be published for revision.

But researchers do feel compelled to speak for others, especially when they realize the need for those who normally are unvoiced to be heard by those unlike them and even by others like them who haven't articulated their like experience. Respect for the voices of others can be complicated. Tess-Moeke-Maxwell-Maxwell said:

> I am very selective about the voices that I bring through. It's important that knowledge gets told and shared with other people who cannot find the words for what they are doing or want to do, but it's also really important that the women are not exploited in the process.

Attributions

Ted Glynn commented on just how complex attribution can be and on the need to be assertive with editors when it comes to the acknowledgement of collaborators' contributions. These attributions might seem trivial to the publisher but they may be deemed as extremely important to research teams.

When you hand in your article, you get editors saying: "You can't have eight authors." And Māori people will identify themselves as people connected to, and so belonging to, their *iwi* (tribes) and *hapu* (sub-tribes), and not just to their institution and their particular job descriptions. They want their tribes listed, and they might have four grandparent lines; their identity is in terms of the collective. Other Māori people may be slow and careful about letting you include them. And usually it will be the elders. Once they've committed to it, they don't want to be anonymous. It's not a show-off kind of thing; it's just that they've chosen to give their *mana* to the work, which is like saying that part of their lived self has been committed to this project.

What cross-cultural researchers come to know is that attribution needs to be both negotiated and culturally significant so that collaborators are fully honored for their contributions. Different cultures, generations, genders, and so on will have different modes of honoring contributions.

You can't go it alone

Often researchers are the ones asked to give presentations as the academic on a cross-cultural team. I did this once alone due to team members' schedules, and I realized the hollowness caused by the missing voices of others on the team. A week later I was in Australia talking to Ted Glynn, and he gave me a good line to send to folks in Wyoming who were, just then, also wanting to limit cost by having only me as an upcoming presenter. He said: "I say I can't stand and present other people's stories, even if some of my stories are woven in. As a researcher, you've got a legitimate space in there, but you can't present the whole story." A year later, Celia Haig-Brown talked about a similar invitation. She said:

And they would have been open to my partner's joining me, except for the airfare, but in those cases they often come around if they see there is no other choice from my point of view. It becomes my command after the invitation. I can no longer go it alone.

Issues of power in dissemination

Following research, academics can be silent even when it is realized that myths need to be debunked. John Arthur, sociologist, gave a good example:

There is a myth amongst the populace and policy makers in the US that the poor are poor because they fail to make the effort for gainful employment. The knowledge that researchers have, that the working poor still need assistance, may not reach the policy makers or general public in ways that elevate the well-being of our respondents.

Disempowered cultures often feel the sting of unutilized research—research that had no consequential benefits. Ken Ralph again articulated the agonizing frustration of many Aboriginal academics:

> Why do you have to come to an academic finding when we've known it all along? We've had that many deaths in custody, stolen generations. It's all been written down, for more than 30 years. But if it's needed, we'll do it again, but we're skeptical. It may have been ahead of its time in 1982. Now we have to convince the bureaucrats who need paper and figures. Research has a few realities that bureaucracies and politics affect.

So the frustration builds, and, as already reported, governments may only want "good news" reports. Some researchers realize what is released is not what researchers originally reported, or it is never released at all. Barbara Comber related that several of her reports were buried. She held up reports that she had written, one by one:

> In this one they tried to change our conclusions and our recommendations, and they've deleted a number of them. That's why I'm already starting to write other papers. And we did this one with six schools, and because they wanted it all to be good news—and it was only *partly* good news—they never did release it, so we did a two-document report and the website. We made sure that some people doing related research had copies of this one, but they knew there were restraints on citations. Finding audiences for reports that have not been released or implemented can still have an effect, though not the policy-changing effect initially desired.

Power also resides in the academic researcher position in reports. The academic researcher can limit the power of the researcher position—for instance in writing—by providing questions as well as answers, opening up space for readers' critical minds. Dispensing results and further questions to other researchers and readers enables them to find their own ways to use the research. If the writing decenters the author's voice or juxtaposes it with other standpoints, the reader can make the text their own to critique and implement.

Researchers and participants can support one another in becoming politically savvy by advising each other about ways to get results from research. Nevertheless, as it is often the researcher who has a recognized name, who has seniority, and who understands the mainstream structures of power, it may be that person who can best leverage that power into action. Understanding the politics of power to get research where you want it comes with experience and with being mentored. Linda Tuhiwai Smith gave an example of how her experience helps her to make decisions about the research she chooses to do:

> Now there's some research that I have done with them [the ministry] where they've pretty much given me freedom to do what I wanted. But there are other projects that I haven't even put in a proposal because I thought: "This is just going to be too political, too constraining." They pretty much dictated the method, the tools, the timeframe. They want the name and connections, and they've already figured out the answer. But sometimes it's worthwhile going through that process with the ministry to get it inside the school system; that's the goal.

Beyond dissemination to action: research with your feet on the ground

> Therein lies the trap into which American society has fallen and into which we all unknowingly fall. There is an undefined expectation in American society that once a problem is defined, no matter how, and understood by a significant number of people who have some relation to the problem, there is no problem anymore.
>
> (Deloria, 1969, p. 93)

> Involvement in activities which have the effect of opposing or amelio- rating cultural domination and/or empowering disadvantaged groups to regain management of their own culture is a legitimate and necessary part of the anthropological enterprise. To refrain from offering professional insights and expertise is to contribute to cultural domination, because it sustains imbalances in the social order and in access to power and resource.
>
> (Clifton, 1990, pp. 58–59)

As you can see from the quotes above, the cross-cultural researcher and teams in social settings have to think hard about the next steps related to dissem- ination. Following critical reflection on the research and its results, it's time to consider how to leverage for change, based on what has been learned. Research may lead us to understandings, but there is a need for a research team to do its part with what Swadener and Mutua (2008) term "critical, culturally-framed praxis," and with what Ladson-Billings and Donnor (2008, p. 25) see as "multitextured political strategies that go beyond traditional legal solutions to issues of racial justice." They use the term "street-level research in ivory towers" as researchers "situate themselves to play a more active and progressive role in the fight for equity and social justice."

Some researchers who work in social settings integrate action into the research plan from the beginning and feel committed to disseminate research results to those who might have the power to implement them. There are many terms for this—for instance, "action research," "participatory action research," "community-based participatory research," or "research for social change." Susan Rodgers talked to me about anthropologists' concern with whether or not to act and gave me a new term for such action:

> Many anthropologists would say "No intervention" because we tend to style ourselves as the observer, but if you have a situation of violence where you could possibly protect a vulnerable person, that's another issue. Nancy Scheper-Hughes's book *Death Without Weeping* (1995) makes the point that anthropologists need to move beyond our old-fashioned classic "we're just here to write and do scholarship" mode to do what she calls "anthropology-with-its-feet-on-the-ground"—research that is ethically engaged. Others think we shouldn't because we can cause more problems than we can solve.

In her own words, Scheper-Hughes (1995, p. 418) states: "Seeing, listening touching, recording can be, if done with care and sensitivity, acts of solidarity. Above all, they are the work of recognition. Not to look, not to touch, not to record can be the hostile act, an act of indifference and of turning away."

Researchers and/or research teams do not want their work to end up on dusty library shelves or as government reports recycled in the refuse stream. Allowing that to happen might be acts of indifference, yet problems that ensue from good intentions have other researchers cautious, noting that good intentions can go awry. Those researched may have difficulty in knowing how to implement findings, or they may be in a position to advise the researcher about what can go wrong. In collaborative teams, counterparts from both cultures are sometimes able to inform each other about needed action and possible consequences. Most important, letting the impetus for action come from the community after discussion of the results allows self-determination to replace prior feelings of helplessness. And always a warning: if the academic researcher in a team tries to be too helpful or too directive, resentment might build even when good intentions were the researcher's only motivation. When participants or participant communities take up their own self-determination in combination with the researcher's knowledge of the mainstream world dynamics, the researcher's paternalistic position is lessened in action based on research findings.

Some cross-cultural researchers start out as practitioners and make the move to research often in order to redress inequalities between those who have privilege and those who do not, inequities that may come from structures so entrenched in society that they are hard to see given the "meritocracy" that hides them. "Why do people who work still need assistance?" "Why can't people rise to positions of privilege if they work hard?" As researchers in social settings, we have long understood the hidden injuries of class, gender, ethnicity, and so on, and the systemic problems with getting meritocracy to actually work, but those in power might not see clearly enough to understand those dynamics (Sennet and Cobb, 1973; Bowles and Gintis, 1976). Yet, as Lareau (2010, p. 7) says, "Studies show that Americans 'generally believe that responsibility for their accomplishments rests on their individual efforts' as opposed to recognition of the effect of race, culture, gender, or class."

I learned in Paolo Freire's seminar in 1985 to see the social world as something to be analyzed and approached with the skepticism of a critical consciousness. One thing he said that seemed especially important was something like: "Unless one constantly challenges hegemonic structures, institutions holding power are given license to proceed as they have in the past, conscious or unconscious of the iniquity in the very systems that perpetuate inequality and inequity." As budding researchers sitting in his humble presence, we had already looked at the unfairness of things in educational settings, but what Freire gave us good reason to do was to look beyond the unfairness and think about how we might implement change. Many of us saw our role as writing and teaching, the two things we were already doing in the institutions of the day. When many of us left the university, involved in our own research and teaching in academic settings, a more active way of working with our research began to be evident. The stories that Freire used in his teaching went away with us. As Ojibwe storytellers say at the end of stories, *"Mi i iw."* And we all went away from graduate school thinking.

There can be a tension between cultural traditions and human rights. What should cross-cultural researchers' response be to cultural practices that are neither equitable nor fair. As Sluka notes (2007, p. 259), "About two-thirds of countries routinely resort to human rights abuses as normal aspects of political process to control populations ..." Nancy Scheper-Hughes (1992, 1995) confronted issues of infant neglect in her fieldwork and advocates and exemplifies interventions. What is clear is that studying a situation carefully before entering into the politics of others is essential for the protection of those you are trying to assist and for your own protection. Though those within a culture may assume oppression to be, as bell hooks has said, "just the way things are," those without may see the systemic issues more clearly. So does a researcher enter into moving cultural others from victims to agents? Martin Luther King Jr. said: "Injustice anywhere is a threat to justice everywhere" (King M.L., 2000). Several researchers entered into this conversation with examples. John Arthur gave an example of research-informed action that went beyond writing:

> For me it is a matter of policy implications. With what I came to know, I tried to work with some of the national immigration organizations and support the activities of the organization—for instance, compiling a list

of immigration attorneys who would work pro bono and trying to find ways that some of the immigrants can gain some power. During the last November elections, we provided information to immigrants about some of the issues that were at stake. For instance, some of the political power brokers in St. Paul [Minnesota state capital] were going to issue different drivers' licenses for non-citizens, inserting a microchip on the license so that when it was swiped it would give information about visa or immigrant status. We formed a grass-roots mobilization, identifying those who would be sympathetic. As an academic researcher that is a benefit I can give. I made a presentation at the immigration service. And I learned you have to be careful in reporting data when a funding agency expects a simplistic bulleted report when you know it is much more complicated. Also, I'm not sure if this is just an African trait, but if you are a sojourner with the temporality that you have, you are not supposed to meddle in the affairs of the host culture. I think that some of the immigrants are seeing their presence here as temporary, so you have to tread cautiously if you encourage action.

Two weeks ago I was at a US airport going through security. I asked the man checking ID what the little flashlight-type instrument was that he used to scan my driving license. He said that many states' licenses had chips in them to monitor certain statuses of those flying, but, he said, "Not in Minnesota." Were the missing chips in Minnesota what Arthur's grass-roots mobilization forestalled? Many researchers used their knowledge of the present system of power and privilege to inform ways to take action for participants, a mode of reciprocity. Linda Tuhiwai Smith, a leader in Māori research, talked about the activism:

A lot of my job is being seen and talking about research. There's a lot of oral presentation. You've got to work with the audience of ministries and the officials if dissemination is to proceed, and you have to work with the researchers. We can get locked up in our jargon and our framework, and sometimes we lose sight that we need to talk about research in ways that connect with what people are really doing. Another part of dissemination is [determining] how you create research that makes difference for communities, by disseminating the research to them, then almost help them use the research. That's a missing part. Such conversations about next steps for research are another avenue that can take place even with policy makers.

In the UK, Adrian Blackledge's team worked on issues in children's services. He said:

We've asked some senior executives in children's services in different parts of the country to reflect on the findings, and that is not only a really good focus for their conversations with each other but it's a form of dissemination. It is also a way of generating new questions related to ongoing research and analysis.

There are times in one's career when, as a researcher and human being, you feel you need to take more action than you can through publishing articles. Shirley Brice Heath talked about when and how she has chosen to use her leverage as a researcher.

> In South Africa in the months after Mandela was released, I worked on the streets with children. When I saw their glue and petrol sniffing and witnessed the effects, I marched right into the office of the head medical policy makers. That's where I think that senior anthropologists, in particular, who have reputation and some acceptance, may feel compelled to ask hard questions. I went in and said: "Where is the research in your medical journals about the brain effects of petrol and glue sniffing? And to what extent do you have research funds dedicated to finding substitutes that will not cause the extent of brain damage that we know to be real? You're not going to make the problem go away." Well, they looked at me as though I'd lost my mind because, of course, it hadn't occurred to them that was their responsibility. They were working on all of the "rich people's diseases." My own view is that it is wrong for researchers to inspire local people to see themselves as change agents in what is either physically or politically or economically a vulnerable environment. Instead, what is much more appropriate for outside academics is to go to the source of the difficulty for those with whom you may have been working, personally, politically, and strategically, and certainly legally. This is the route many archeologists, geologists, and environmental scientists are taking. They go in through what they call the policy route. You work to get greater knowledge spread at the power level.

This complicates the notion that cross-cultural researchers should only support those in the culture to act through their own self-determination. Laura Nader (1995, p. 426), in an interesting response to Scheper-Hughes, said: "How come, if you are interested in misery, you don't study up more, go to the source rather than the victims?" Heath gave me examples of "acts of solidarity" both taking the policy route and supporting participants in their own self-determination.

I could bring forth many examples of researchers, as above, who have "their feet on the ground," those who find ways to disseminate to the policy makers who can make things happen, those who reflectively go about research with outcomes designed by and for those who collaborate with them. Involving participants in dissemination decisions solidifies the base upon which one swings into action. Just as participants have given you information about their culture and circumstances, so you can give them the information they might need in order to guide collaborative action. A researcher may not be in such an experience, as are Linda Tuhiwai Smith and Shirley Brice Heath, but he or she can confer about next steps with participants or elders.

Weaving dissemination into staff development

> In each study, there are opportunities for researchers to address intersections of oppression sustained within multiple structural domains, albeit our focus is educational systems and areas where structural domains of power obstruct or impede equity and social justice.
>
> (Arlette Ingram Willis et al., 2008, p. 65)

I have a huge respect for researchers who have dug in to do what they were able to do, beyond dissemination at a local and more global level; many have done so through staff development in social agencies or in school systems. Most of these researchers wrote their academic articles, but they didn't stop there; they generated staff-development materials "with their feet on the ground."

Developing materials for use with prospective or current practitioners

Christine Sleeter talked about her motivations for research and resultant materials:

> When I create a book, a lot of times it's actually because I need it. The book that just came out, *Unstandardizing Curriculum*, was for the course "multicultural curriculum design." I needed the book so I'd have the tools to use the next time or when I am doing workshops. Before I was critiquing practice, but now I research multi-cultural curriculum to show effective curriculum. I've done reviews of the research on preparing white teachers for multicultural teaching, and the whole theme of white resistance comes through loud and clear. In multicultural teacher education you are trying to get at some very deep-seated beliefs. With white teachers, sometimes you see these guys, usually in the back row with their chairs tipped back like this, not even looking at the screen. That's an example of what white resistance can look like.

Christine Sleeter and I talked on in a heartfelt discussion about resistance during staff-development sessions. We both found less resistance when we turned to positive examples. The week before, I, too, had met up with resistant teachers at an in-service near a reservation. We enlisted the school's theater director to rehearse Blackfoot students to present stories from our recently published book *The Seventh Generation (2003)*. In the morning session we went from the native students' heartfelt school stories, to faculty discussion of what was needed for the students to feel less alienated in their school, and then on to revising both approaches to native students and their curriculum. All teachers were involved; none seemed resistant. In the afternoon session the Blackfoot students told me they were sorry, they had thought they were only needed for the morning and had a community obligation in the afternoon. In that afternoon's session I gave up on the stories; I knew my voice behind the students' stories just wouldn't work as well. Instead, I talked of the results of our study and tried to go through the same process. But there they were, the three teachers, in the back of the room, chairs tipped back, with discomfiting laughs and comments amongst them, the same resistant scene that both Sleeter and I had experienced before. Ted Glynn had said the year before in interview: "You might only have five percent of resisters, but they are very powerful. You can't stand only on your professional knowledge base. You have to understand their knowledge base." Later, the in-service organizer apologized: "You saw the difficult ones this afternoon." I'm sure that might have been true, but I knew those resistant teachers were taking what I said, my knowledge base, as criticism, without the earnest voices of the students to disrupt their knowledge base.

Again: recognizing the power of narrative

Since reading *I, Rigoberta Mehcu: An Indian Woman in Guatemala* (1984) in the mid-1980s, I have been impressed with the ability of the first-person text to portray the struggle evident in the repression-memoir. The use of native student narratives challenges teachers to think differently, disrupt stereotypes and binaries of identity. Sleeter's multicultural teacher demonstrations and case studies challenge traditional classroom scenarios and give teachers some models for multicultural work. They open channels for new ways of thinking. Looking through the perspectives of others pushes practitioners behind their own perspectives. This is the humanizing characteristic of literary narrative, of co-constructed participant narratives, and of case studies and demonstrations. Narratives allow less resistant discussion of uncomfortable subjects, alternative points of view that are consonant with the real lived world experience, as Vicki Crowley said, raising questions without pushing the question: "Whose side are you on?" For instance, Mary Hermes juxtaposed interviews and academic readings as curriculum materials for staff development, an activist aspect of her research to "honor not only written academic discourse around Indian education but the community dialogue as well." She said:

> The model I used was inspired by a model of editing a video tape (Bordowitz, 1988). By taking different but related "clips" of writing— stories as told by myself or others, analytical writings and quotes, and examples of practices at the school—and creating a montage, sometimes

with smooth transitions, sometimes jarring juxtapositions, I hoped to capture some of the detail and complexity of the voices that exist around the competing ideas of "school." Further, Bordowitz's video production model is most compelling in that it brings together different perspectives, side by side, without resolving tensions or making sweeping generalizations.

Adding the juxtapositions to the dissemination of her research, Hermes lowered resistance in her work with practicing and pre-service teachers, and the discussions dove into the heart of the matter. She wasn't the staff developer who preached from her knowledge base; instead she involved others in problem discovery, using the strengths in the practitioners to work through the issues and into solutions that they could own.

Working with the strengths of practitioners and those with whom they work

After reporting back, working with the skills of those researched can often guide self-determined implementation. I return to a shortened quote from Russell Bishop used in a prior chapter:

> Somebody might have expertise in one area, another in other areas. We recognize each other's strengths, and you can explain that again in terms of Māori metaphors because that goes back to that *powhiri* again. In a *powhiri*, what you do is you get up and you say, "I recognize you, *tena koe*," which, some people say, means "Hello," a formal way of saying hello, literally means, "There you are. I recognize you, I acknowledge you." And everything else that's done in a *hui* is all about that: I recognize your particular strengths, and your particular power. I am not saying I "empower", "empowering" is not an activity I am interested in. I am saying: "Recognize the power they have already." You don't have to give them power; they already have the power. You are just going to recognize and implement it.

He went on to talk about a research project and its implementation:

> Using a collaborative storying approach, which involved a sequence of in-depth, semi-structured interviews and conversations with over 70 Māori students, I was able to develop a profile of what effective teaching for Māori students looked like. The students told us volumes. They were extremely articulate and clear about problems and solutions. We used this profile as the basis for a professional development package, and when teachers were supported sufficiently, the problem behavior that was facing teachers diminished, the learning difficulties that students had been facing diminished, absenteeism diminished, and Māori students'

educational test scores have gone up. For the first time, we are really getting down to making a difference for Māori kids, cracking the egg.

Bishop was trying to get the funding to keep the staff development going that began in research. He added with determination: "I'll just keep going and going and going and talking and saying, 'Look, we are getting the answers. We need you to start prioritizing your money and continue this.'" Since then, in an article published in 2008, he says that such an education was one "where power is shared...where culture counts...where learning is interactive, and dialogic...where connectedness is fundamental to relations...where there is common vision: There is a common agenda for what constitutes excellence for Māori in education" (p. 445).

Wrapping research and staff development back together

Multiple but linked studies (one weaving off the other and evaluating its implementation) give extra benefit from the initial time spent in developing meaningful and respectful relationships, and bring rewards for both the community and researchers:

> I work with teacher practitioners. We involve the Aboriginal Education Workers [AEWs/assistants], who are hugely important in educating the white teachers because there is extreme teacher turnover. We set up practitioner research projects: everyone can be both researcher and subject. It has been difficult for the AEWs to take the researcher role, but they have been sitting in class and getting that beginning level of understanding of what school-based research can be about: observing something, recording it, discussing it, and then thinking about it, and starting a cycle of action on what was observed. At the community level, we aren't talking too much about the contributions of AEWs because being singled out or being praised would have a shame factor. Projects can be praised, the idea as a whole can be praised, the effort can be praised, but the individuals: no.
>
> (Jenny Barnett, University of South Australia)

In professions, now such action research, practitioner research, teacher research is being used as staff development. Practitioners raise their own questions, use research methods to gather data, collect preliminary answers, implement those results, and make other rounds of inquiry as they examine the results of their implementation. The reports of this research are beginning to be taken more and more seriously in professional journals. Barnett's quote above is particularly interesting given the cultural sensitivity that is also wrapped into the process, but what may be issues of acknowledgement and shame in one culture may be quite the opposite in another. Wrapping back around to research from staff development can often be an almost two-way proposition. In sociolinguist Stephen May's initial research site, he found the school staff had wound themselves into his research:

> The school's response to me as a novice researcher was interest in what I was doing, but at the same time they also wanted me to participate actively by giving whatever knowledge I had. One of the key characteristics of the school was that it was a theorized approach to education where staff meetings might go five or six hours every week, and they would be discussing theory in relation to how they would apply it in the school— rather fantastic. I was catapulted into that engagement. The kinds of ideas that I was developing were discussed and critiqued within that kind of very engaged staff development. So it was a wonderful process.

As researchers: where do we put our energy?

We've seen how dissemination, implementation of research in social settings, and consequent activism can weave into research itself, but the question that academics often have is: "Where do I put my energy?" How do you balance your teaching, your research, with the added imperative of dissemination?" Barbara Comber, a well-published researcher, is strategic with her time:

> Our biggest problem is that we've often got too much on the go. Do you put your energy in getting this out to the academic community, or do you put your energy into working with those on the ground? Where do you have an impact given limited time and resources? I work to create teacher researchers, really working with teachers around issues of racism, around what culturally inclusive pedagogies look like. It needs to be negotiated locally with people, but it is about trying to get a re-intellectualized profession with strong ethical standpoints. And for me it's trying to both theorize and describe teaching that makes a difference in culturally diverse communities, and about the strengths kids bring to literacy. I do a lot of public speaking, so I tell a lot of these stories.

Does activism take you too far out of academia for your own good? Do you get tenured and promoted on the basis of activism? Often not, but institutions are beginning to value activism based on research; that, of course, is institution-dependent. Academics at different stages in their careers also have different priorities. Early-career academics may need to put a good amount of energy into publishing, but many academics, as described above, have found ways, even in their early career, to wrap dissemination back into further research.

Care of participants in dissemination

For some the dilemmas in dissemination are intense. The possible identifica-tion of people and sites in research reports bothered Howard Groome. This is true in all research, but multiple cultures present in the research site further complicate issues of dissemination:

> I love doing qualitative research, but there are real hazards in the process. You need to locate your subjects in time and space by saying, for example: "This is a mother of five children in Farragen Park." Those who know the area then might say, "Yes, that must be so and so." When you have small communities, you can't protect them. So what do you do? Distort the data? Not acknowledge the institution? Another instance: in a small school, Aboriginal staff members would just blow their top at "the bloody deputy," so you'd try to sensitively talk about school leadership, but if you actually said what was said to you, you'd blow the school wide apart. In cross-cultural research, essentially you are giving some power to people who are powerless, but what happens to those voices is critical.

The dilemma: respecting participants may mean that research goes unpub-lished or disguised in ways that distort the results; yet again, published research may advantage a whole group of people who have less voice and power in a situation. For the good of many? For the care of one? Allow-ing participants to reconsider pseudonyms, letting them see how your acknowledgements might make them vulnerable, and making sure they can understand the potential results in the mainstream world of reporting their data—all these steps can allow participants some self-determination in their own protection. But inevitably, hard decisions come the researcher's way. The more forethought, the better the collaboration, and the richer the understanding of both the researched culture and the culture of the tar-geted audience make the research safer; nevertheless, care of participants in dissemination needs serious consideration.

Even delaying publication can have its own negative results for partici-pants keen to have their voices heard. Henry Amoroso related a dramatic example:

> A local research event was to occur, and I talked with the prison warden. I thought that the most articulate man in the program, one who had deep insight into why he was willing to share his story, would have an impact on the research audience. The dean and the warden agreed that he was a low-risk prisoner, and he was allowed to go to this conference with me. We went to the conference, and before I could introduce him, he said, "I want to tell the audience something about you," and he [turning to me] said, "You promised me that these stories would be read by others."

And he said some stronger words, and he was right: I hadn't yet taken it to the next step [publication]. That's a universal: we have obligations to our subjects.

Though Amoroso brought his research directly from the participant to an audience, it wasn't yet in the written form the participant expected. His work with prisoners, however, did inspire the foundation of *Voices*, a journal in Canada about adult literacy.

Research has an implied imperative of dissemination, but many researchers go through dilemmas when no way seems perfect, and as Celia Haig-Brown said below, dissemination may end up with an edge to it:

> In native-run institutions, funding is hand-to-mouth. This administrator was a high-energy guy, dedicated to critical pedagogy. He saw that my study would give legitimacy [to the school] by having a scholar studying it. I did say to him: "You need to know that I am not doing any kind of glory story; I am coming here to look at what taking control means, problems as well as the benefits." And he was fine with that. Immediately apparent were the complicated relationships between the administrator and the teachers. He had a strong personality and was powerfully committed to critical pedagogy. He went from one classroom with himself as teacher to building a lovely building for about 350 students, lots of teachers, but the struggle around control undermined the critical pedagogy. In the study, some perspectives on his style of leadership came to the fore, which he found hard to take. I did some massaging of things so it wasn't undermining what he was doing. There was no question that he did an amazing job, but at the same time I couldn't erase things. I did give him an opportunity to read the whole thing, and I took out a couple of things. The school is still doing its work, but he left. I never wanted to make a person feel bad, and I don't know what he thinks. So, it's a good book that has an edge to it for me.

To be rigorous in research, particularly in caring for cross-cultural research participants, can be complicated. To research is to learn, sometimes to learn solutions. Researchers can feel "edges" to what they are doing while simultaneously feeling the commitment to doing it. One can do everything that is deemed responsible and respectful and still feel an edge, and, actually, the ability to feel and fathom that edge is a strength in and of itself.

Barbara Comber believed that the imperative of dissemination continues beyond published articles to leveraging for the implementation of the research:

> Make sure that no harm that you can stop happening happens. But continuing to publicize the work: that is making a difference. A researcher

who was working in the largely Aboriginal school in Western Australia found things that he couldn't do anything about. What can you do about alcoholism in the community? What can you do about the fact that teachers don't want to stay there? You can try and explain the complexity of teachers' work in these situations and explain how Aboriginal children are progressively disadvantaged by the education system? You have to write it again and again.

Comber uses the privilege of her university position, her writing ability, and, hence, the power that she has to leverage in care for others with less power. This is truly respectful of what she has learned from participants. Part of the care one gives to participants is in dissemination and beyond.

Dissemination in cross-cultural research means finishing with the same respect and trust as when negotiations started. Reflexivity over the following questions may help in resolving dilemmas that present themselves:

- How does one tap the power of participant stories, especially if the purpose of one's report is to gather enough empathy for action without having participants' feelings of privacy or even desired anonymity jeopardized?
- How do you use data without them being what was termed "fodder for people's stereotypes"? As your data conflict with stereotypes, is that the time to make sure that data are disseminated?
- How does one talk about community problems in reports without exacerbating dissent within a community, between elders or amongst other divisive community groups?
- How does one report research and engender positive action while maintaining the dignity of participants, without "po-thing-afying" participants, sensationalizing, or misrepresenting participants?

Stephen Muecke offered a very straightforward and simple answer to most of these questions: "Your responsibility is to clear with them just how they want to make that public and if they want it to go into print or not. If they say 'Yes' and seem to know where it's going and who's going to read it, then that's what they've decided to do." His mode of checking with participants adds a logical solution and conclusion to this chapter, for he argues for care of participants in terms of anonymity and representation through providing their own shared determinations in dissemination.

10
The Two-Way Bridge: Doing Cross-Cultural Research with Integrity

The metaphorical bridge which one travels in doing cross-cultural work is a two-way bridge. As described in Chapter 6, we often concentrate so hard in crossing that we are myopically unaware that those on the other side often must do the same thing and often with less power, longer sojourns, and higher stakes. Moving one way or another can offer fascination with different ways of being, but it also engenders discomfort. Though those who have been colonized may be more used to moving across the bridge and may have a wider angle from which to consider human affairs, yet their time on the other side of the bridge can cause understandable feelings of resistance. Mainstream researchers, too, experience discomfort crossing into cultural discontinuity, often with those on the other side scrutinizing their intent. Though rarely addressed in books about research, the pressures and emotional aspects of culture disorientation and inequity are better acknowledged below than ignored.

The discomforts of researchers from marginalized groups

Cultural discontinuity

Those from marginalized groups who pursue education and a future as a researcher often feel a keen sense of isolation in those pursuits. A researcher who wanted to remain anonymous with the following quote described his entry into academia: "Academia is a very lonely, isolated place for Indigenous people—for one person going off and pursuing their study. And the structures that are required, the linguistic requirements, scare us. Our qualities come with speaking; as incredible teachers; we can hold people through our talking." In interview, he went on to speak about his difficulty in academic writing (Chapter 5). Beyond feeling isolated, getting along in two cultures requires complex code-switching and a tugging of values. Many learn to do that with both confidence and integrity, but often still with discomfort. Thomas Peacock (Cleary and Peacock, 1998) called it a kind of "acting" that he does. He acts with a second consciousness as he operates in the university theater. Tom Chee described the added strain in entering the dominant culture: "There is constant shifting, 'double clutching'... If you know who you are and maintain your world view, you can go through all the hoops of the dominant society and come back and reconnect. It becomes easier with age to shift gears" (as quoted in Harvey-Morgan, 1994, p. 10).

Meeting other cultural norms and isolation

Additional stress on researchers from marginalized cultures is the unrelenting pressure from dominant culture to meet dominant cultural norms (Dunbar, 2008. p. 91). The double clutching and discomfort are in part about academic discourse, the language expected in academic articulation of thought. Nakata (1998, p. 4) notes:

> One of the difficulties facing Indigenous scholars is that any challenge, contestation or even expression of unease must be conducted within the framework of Western understanding, logic, and rationality. In argument and debate where opposing or differing points of view are proffered and extended, an Indigenous scholar is still bound to academic convention and must substantiate the argument within the academic corpus. Though not always problematic, it is essential for meaningful intellectual communication and for inclusion within the academy.

And just as researchers from marginalized groups may feel the strains of isolation and different cultural norms and discourse, they also can feel a burgeoning sense of being misunderstood in their own communities. Mary Hermes said:

> People [in the community] assume that the university is the most leisurely place in the world. Then you do this thing called research. People think that if you are in academia you have privilege, and in some ways we are lucky to do this work. But how isolating it is; what a struggle it is to figure out the right thing to do, and then to put it all together to fit in with the bureaucracy. There are just layers and layers for us. At the same time what you are doing has other meanings too: publishing is going to help other researchers on the ground to do research as American Indians.

Researchers from marginalized groups often talk about having feelings of illegitimacy in mainstream culture even though they are well qualified and well published, and simultaneously some feel resentment from those of their own culture. Pipi et al. (2002) note that there is the need for Māori researchers to "Be humble in your approach. Don't flaunt your knowledge" (p. 22), and added that Indigenous researchers will quickly be corrected if they are not humble in their community. Archibald (2008) talk about the academic divide as a chasm: "But becoming educated in mainstream institutions can create a chasm between the person who is university-educated and others who are not educated in this way...Being university educated, I have to work hard at showing others of my community that I still share their cultural values and that I am still at heart a First Nations person—that I have some form of harmony and balance" (p. 40).

Research pressure and tokenism

In the well-intended desire to right past wrongs, researchers from dominant society want to include researchers from marginalized groups in research and other endeavors. The researcher who wanted to remain anonymous said: "There is this hunting down of people to take on research projects. Here you can count the Indigenous on two hands. We put our hearts into teaching, but we get research pressure from our institutions." On the flip side, Karen Swisher (1998, p. 196) says:

> It is difficult to take a selfish stance and say no in the university experience when it means an Indian presence or perspective will not be included. My Indian colleagues and I feel a strong sense of commitment, and the urgency to do something for our people overpowers the desire and time it takes to write.

Furthermore, even as those from the mainstream faculty seek out those from traditionally marginalized groups to repair the previous lack of representation on committees, that very committee work can add additional discomfort for some because the needed for "speaking out" may not be a cultural way of being. And because the numbers of academics of color are still low, as Mary Hermes says, "Native people get pushed up beyond their skills too quickly. In the naïveté of white liberalism, they are manipulated to move forward."

Well intended as the pressures may be, they add up to a new form of coercion. Eleanor Bourke offered an additional perspective:

> There could be an element of tokenism: mainstream faculty want to see Indigenous people succeed to the extent that faculty might let them do what they want, regardless of criteria. There are such a small group of Indigenous people at the university level. And at the opposite end of the spectrum, Aboriginal people can be hard on those that follow them. The Indigenous mentor may have been mainstream-schooled, trained to do it this way: "I had to do it, so you do too. If I can do it, anybody can do it."

In addition, several researchers talked about the pressure they felt to do research on their own cultures when they might have strong inclinations to do research related to their disciplinary interests, irrespective of culture.

Liz McKinley said: "Criticism might come from Māori: 'Oh, look, here is Liz who is a Māori researcher, who isn't doing anything particularly Māori right now.'" bell hooks (1984) adds: "Just as racisim may mean that a black woman's scholarship on black women may be seen as less than definitive, she may also receive no validation for writing on subjects that do not pertain to race or gender" (p. 45).

Working through frustration

Though often working toward balance and harmony, non-mainstream academics have needed to work their way through anger and frustration, wanting to stand their own ground. Sarah Jane Tiakiwai talked about how she resolved some of the strains she felt as she began her career:

> Having the PhD letters attached to my name make a huge difference in the eyes of Pākehā colleagues. People put me into little boxes, and I'd like to think that I can straddle different spheres. Also, there's the whole notion of how to say something without being disrespectful. I've had issues, maybe because I am younger and a woman, and so I've talked to my aunty to try to get some understanding. If I have the older people to go to for advice, that really helps. I do it in a triangle: if I have an issue with a person that I don't feel comfortable to confront, I try to find somebody else that I trust to advise me on how to do it.

Like Tiakiwai, many other Indigenous academics and academics of color have had to work through frustration in working in the academy. Hermes said:

> I understand why Indigenous people are pissed at white people, but I've seen people leverage anger and power to get somewhere personally. Even in the university system, I've seen native people who are very angry and white people who are actually trying to do the right thing. I've been there myself, but I've decided it's really destructive to write off entire groups of people even with the consciousness that bad things have happened. I know how self-destructive it is to carry so much anger. Some people have an easy time of letting it roll right off. I have to get some of that. Sometimes I wonder if there was work I could do that would be easier.

Having elders to consult and being conscious of the dynamics involved were strategies that helped Tiakiwai and Hermes to work with an understandable frustration.

Stresses on mainstream researchers

Though the study of the culture, history, politics, and power differentials may help mainstream researchers intellectually with crossing over cultural borders, many still feel stress, frustration, and discomfort. The degree of discomfort is, in part, determined by what Ward and Chang (1997) term "cultural fit," the consonance between the culture of the researcher and the culture of the researched.

Frustration when the time isn't right

Howard Groome was not alone when he talked about the frustration when his team's research preceded interest in Aboriginal affairs.

> I worked with an Aboriginal man from Tasmania, and we did a national survey talking with Aboriginal kids about what they saw as factors in their success and failure. We tried to represent the tremendously confused identity of so many Aboriginal kids to the readers. That was a great thing, but I don't know what benefit those Aboriginal kids got from that research. Somehow the research seems to get buried if it doesn't fit the current political objectives. I heard that someone completely replicated it and came up with the same "new" answers.

Coping with anger

Just as people from marginalized communities feel anger about residue from past colonization and its more recent remnants and reincarnations, mainstream researchers may need to cope with that anger. Having traveled to present with my research team at an International Indigenous Conference in Hawaii, I felt a deep sting when the keynote speaker urged that United Airlines fly all white people back to the mainland. It wasn't so much the speaker as the uproarious response and applause given to her that made me shrink in my seat under its weight. Anger has a counter-strike power of its own, and the very sensitivity that enables cross-cultural researchers to work with some integrity may also heighten their sensitivity to anger. Though there may always be the sting, many mainstream researchers have gotten much better at:

- understanding the anger that has fueled the needed reclamation of knowledge and cultural pride;
- seeing anger as a result of bad past research and oppression;
- finding active ways to deal with its cause in research through reciprocity and collaboration in question, method, and mode of dissemination choices;
- taking the anger seriously but realizing it wasn't necessarily them that set it off.

Career path

Some institutions still penalize scholars who work with time-intensive cross-cultural research; other institutions encourage it. I asked David Carey Jr., historian from the University of Southern Maine, whether a commitment to cross-cultural research affected one's career path:

> To get a good sense of historical perspective, I went back to Maya people, and they critiqued what I had. It made my work sharper, getting closer to what they would recognize as an authoritative history of their people, but it took a longer time, but it's not clear to me that people recognize the time that foreign scholarship takes.

Collaborative cross-cultural research often takes more time, but the more time taken, the better the results, and the greater the gratification for those who take the time—and once the initial relationship-building time is spent, multiple studies can come from the initial effort.

Multicultural educational researcher Christine Sleeter arranged her career so that she could do the kind of research that she wanted:

> I have chosen to work in places that have not been "research one" institutions because I wanted to work with more diverse students who tend to be at the state institutions. But when I needed to get tenured at the University of Wisconsin, Parkside, I was paying a whole lot of attention to what the institution said I needed to do to get tenured. After, my orientation started shifting away from what the institution was demanding of me, and toward what I wanted to do. Actually, at present I am retired from California State University Monterey Bay, mainly because the full-time university work was making my research and mentoring work difficult. So I retired from the university in order to continue doing my "real" work. For example, a recent book (*Teaching with Vision*) involved coaching the teachers themselves in writing chapters about their own teaching— a continuation of the trajectory of moving from blaming teachers, to co-constructing portraits of excellent teachers with teachers, and now to mentoring teachers in writing their own stories.

Actual danger

On occasion, the misunderstanding of a culture and its environs can put the researcher in physical discomfort or even danger. The best way to avoid such dangers is to collaborate and live with people in the community; not only can they inform you of possible dangers but your presence in their lives is a protection in and of itself. I have strong memories of cultural and geographic misassumptions I made, and when danger was averted by those near me:

- of being diverted from going across the street from a fenced-in teachers' lounge to talk to potentially violent, adolescent petrol sniffers (tin cans suspended from their ears so their sniffing could be continuous);

- of not picking up on polite warning signals from a village principal before accepting a ride back to town with a drunken driver, but being protected by his teacher wife, in a standoff that is too long and distressing a story to relate;
- of being advised to take a dog with me on an Aleutian Peninsula trek because the dog would get early scent of bear and flee when I, too, still had time to flee.

Without local advice and assistance, my lack of knowledge would have put me in jeopardy.

These are dangers resulting from lack of familiarity with the culture and region. Anthropologists have been forthcoming about researcher dangers (see Howell, 1998; Sluka, 2007, pp. 234–244). Sluka notes that "about one-third of the world's countries are currently in warfare and about two-thirds of countries routinely resort to human rights abuses as normal aspects of political process to control populations..." (Sluka, 2007, p. 259). I've summarized some of his suggestions for minimizing researcher danger in such settings (pp. 259–269):

- Think ahead about possible danger and determine actions that might decrease or increase it.
- Continue to consider the dangers and ways of minimizing them during research.
- Be aware of and accept the possibility of having to terminate the research; develop an exit plan upon arrival.
- Consider the source of funding and how it might offend the participants.
- Be honest about your research question and methodology.
- Be aware of the possibly negative definitions that participants might have of you.
- Enter observing and listening, without asking questions, while you become oriented to the issues and power structures.
- Protect participants' anonymity and research data from others who might make things difficult or dangerous for them. Remove identifying materials from where you work or live.
- Be aware that you may not be able to publish your findings if they might increase danger to the participants.

Beyond the tugs of empathy and sensitivity to action

In the summers I have long lived on a coastal river in southern Maine. When I work in my garden, I find more clam shells than can be naturally explained. When I first started thinking about Indigenous literacy in preparing teachers, I was just beginning to understand that Abenaki people had lived where I grow zucchini and harvested what the field, river, and ocean had to offer.

As the land around the river mouth was settled and developed, the number of Abenaki who made the mouth of the river their summer home decreased. When I arrived in the 1960s, Abenaki came only to sell sweet grass baskets and to pick blueberries. One older town resident told me: "They were eased out." The clam shells make me sad for those who left the land that I now call my home of heart; I know how dear that land can be to those who care for it. "Eased off" is a euphemism that doesn't tell the truth. Yet guilt is what Fine et al. (2008) call an "appropriation of pain," saying: "We urge our readers and remind ourselves to resist the appropriation of pain . . . of Indigenous peoples and other oppressed peoples" (p. 157).

Though some of my forebears did colonize lands of Indigenous peoples, limiting their resources and freedom, and causing internalized oppression, there are important differences between guilt and empathy. Guilt or appropriation of pain is non-productive. What is productive is the action.

Distinguishing it from guilt, researchers did talk about the tugging of emotions when they saw egregious injustice. Shirley Brice Heath, for instance, spoke of having to leave when emotions ran too high. "I tell my students, for example, I cannot work in societies where children are mistreated, where children are tortured or where their legs are broken to make them better beggars." The toll that researchers feel in their empathy is sometimes inevitable. Aydın Durgunoğlu, psychologist from the University of Minnesota, said in relation to her literacy research:

> In Turkey, even though I speak the language and I am from the same culture, the culture of poverty is so different. When somebody says, "My husband is out of work and I don't work," it's very hard to understand how they're making the ends meet, so those things are really hard things to deal with, and then I feel awkward asking them to do some literacy task when they have much more basic concerns than whether they can read the passage or not.

Fathoming the complexities of doing no harm is a continual concern for the sensitive researcher. John Arthur varied his research method as a result of this tug of empathy:

> Normally I would take notes, but when I interviewed these immigrants, I had to put down the pen and listen, relying on memory. When you hear people recount the leaving of home, crossing the Sahara, sleeping at night in the desert, stopping to make money in Mauritania, Tunisia, paying a fisherman, heftily, to get to Spain or Italy, I couldn't take notes. Most of them saw this as a family project, a bonded trust. If you arrived in Palermo, even paid as a migrant worker, you would send some money back. I learned a lot about the human spirit, the lengths they went to

make that trip. Instead of always taking from them in writing, I was attending to them.

Another kind of sensitivity is that which makes you feel like a trespasser on another group's turf, feeling an almost unbearable exclusion and having to figure out what that means for research. On other occasions, participants can feel pride in your interest in their way of living.

Sharon Kemp once told me: "I think that researchers need to get used to the notion that people will laugh at you." I laughed myself when she said it because I remembered figuring out that things were going pretty well when those in a community laughed and when you could enjoy their laughter or benefit from its cause. When I was plagued with bug bites, an elderly Maya woman laughed, muttering something about Maya "warry" ticks' attraction to my white skin, and then telling me about soothing lime juice while giggling between the words. Ah, that lime juice and laughter could always heal the sensitivity that researchers have. It helps to have a hard and soft shell simultaneously: hard enough to let what should be directed at others, past or present, roll off your hard shell, and soft enough that you are sensitive to when you are overstepping or harming. Yet, you can still be confused at any given moment about which shell serves best.

Reciprocal mentoring

One thing is for sure: the stress of researchers from both sides of the metaphorical bridge can be moderated by the knowledge and support they can receive in cross-cultural collaborations and thoughtful relationships. I look forward to a time when cross-cultural collaborations can look at questions with equally skilled researchers, when the richness of the research draws from the multiple perspectives available in partnerships, when paternalism in mentorship is long gone, and when new methods and methodologies are developed as researchers become increasingly open to cross-cultural ways of knowing and understanding.

As that is happening, there is a profound need for what I term reciprocal mentoring, with both skills and perspectives. Reciprocal mentoring comes from both directions and is especially imperative when a mainstream researcher hasn't a good handle on the culture being entered and/or when one researcher is being judged or promoted on another culture's theoretical, discourse, or value system. Part of reciprocal mentoring is giving the researchers from both cultures the ability to understand both the approach needed to benefit those researched and the discourse needed for action. Reciprocal advice enhances the initial reporting back, then the discussions that prompt internal change, and finally the leveraging of benefits that can come from academic and public policy publications, staff development, and other actions.

This may sound simple, but collaborating parties need to dig deep for understandings. Fiona Cram said:

> I have found mentoring quite challenging in the past year. It requires me to unpackage what I am doing, so I can share how I work. I've got to think aloud so that they can have input, and if you're not used to thinking aloud, or are not sure quite how you think, it's complicated. One of the project managers with whom I've worked closely has been very good at getting me to unpackage how and why I do what I do, so she can learn from me and engage with us.

Sarah Jane Tiakiwai talked about her mentor and the need to share knowledges reciprocally:

> People find him as an authority, but a lot of people challenge his lack of lived culture. I'm grateful because I've had this opportunity to work for him and with him. I've learned a great deal, and I'm hoping he's learned from me in a mutual relationship: a concept of *tuakana teina*, that's sort of older sibling, younger sibling; although it's not actually based on age. He would be my *tuakana* in terms of the academic context, but I might be his *tuakana* in terms of the cultural context.

In reciprocal mentoring, mutual respect and careful relationships are essential. Howard Groome said:

> My aim was to shrink my participation, and I helped them to pick up skills. In all Aboriginal issues, the relationship is the key thing, and if we hadn't had a good relationship, it would have damaged the research. We got into a lot of situations where we were able to disagree quite intensely about what was being said, and I could see the point of view of my Aboriginal colleague: I wasn't reading the situation right, or the student didn't mean that, but you don't get to that stage until you know each other very well.

For years, Groome managed to do what Holland termed "staying on the journey" as previously quoted in Chapter 6:

> It is often challenging for many 'non-Indigenous' Australians to 'stay on the journey' with 'Aboriginal' people. Working with others who may be culturally different from one-self might mean that plans may be disrupted. It is important to have patience, to 'stay on the journey', even when it might get a little tough. There needs to be a preparedness on the part of the researcher to be open to new ways of thinking about and 'doing' research particularly with those culturally different from one-self. It must be a respectful and negotiated process.

Those who stay on the journey are often those who have taken the power differential out of the cross-cultural relationship. Reciprocal mentoring demands full recognition of the strengths in the other.

To do or not to do

Some years ago, a professor at Harvard University set up a conference call between his graduate class on research in the Native American Program, and Thomas Peacock and me at the University of Minnesota Duluth. A student at Harvard asked me what I thought the role should be of a non-native researcher. My immediate response was that one should make one's role self-destruct. I added that there were many young Indigenous researchers in that very Harvard classroom ready to take on Indigenous research. A native student piped up, saying something like: "Some of us already talked about this. The teachers our kids have to work with are mostly white; you know both the teachers and the issues. We need to figure out how the white teachers should best work with native students. We need the double perspectives you have developed." In part, my work on this book has helped me question whether my initial words about my role as a cross-cultural researcher, heartfelt at the time, fell too easily from my lips. In the bi-cultural research arena, was there still a place for me?

Can a researcher from the majority culture do cross-cultural research with integrity? Though few discussions of cross-cultural research address the stress of the researchers, many talk about whether or not cross-cultural research should be done. Most are careful in acknowledging both sides of the question. Alcoff (1991, p. 288) complicates it:

> Adopting the position that one should only speak for oneself raises similarly difficult questions. For example we might ask, if I don't speak for those less privileged than myself, am I abandoning my political responsibility to speak out against oppression, a responsibility incurred by the very fact of my privilege? If I should not speak for others, should I restrict myself to following their lead uncritically? Is my greatest contribution to move over and get out of the way? And if so what is the best way to do this—to keep silent or to deconstruct my discourse?

In creating social change, researchers note that support is still needed for some groups of people. Ann Diver-Stamnes, researcher at Humbolt University, USA, wrote the following email to me some years ago:

> If the only people who have the right to write or edit books about specific groups are those from the same ethnicity or life experience or culture, then Michael Harrington never would have written *The Other America* because he wasn't poor, and Kozol would not be able to write such books as *Rachel and Her Children* (he wasn't homeless) or *Illiterate America, or*

Amazing Grace, and I certainly should not have written about inner-city kids of color living in Watts in *Lives in the Balance*. [Not participating] is a fallacious argument, and one that alienates precisely those people who are needed in the battle against racism, classism, and ignorance. The only way change will occur is if we work together; there are not enough of us who are like-minded that we can afford to factionalize in this manner. We also need to recognize that multiple voices and perspectives only enrich the discussion.

Vicki Crowley also spoke of support needed in research and dissemination for the GLBTIQ$_2$ community:

I confronted this issue at a roundtable where they were reporting research about sexualities. There was a person doing research on lesbian teachers who did not identify as a lesbian. Her research was totally fabulous, but, of course, it's the whole question of who should be doing the research. I would want people to do research regardless of their sexuality because there's so much that needs to be done. We can't do it alone; it takes community support to allow us rights, and people who are not gay and lesbian need to support it. Now that might be a rationalization, but that does seem to me the reality.

Need is the main argument that is extended, but the native teacher at Harvard extended what for me was another rationale, that multiple perspectives might be needed, for some years to come, on social issues that cross cultural borders. Kincheloe and Steinberg (2008, pp. 154–155) hearten us, noting that "intra- and intercultural knowledge traditions can inform one another…These encounters reduce the ugly expression of epistemological zenophobia and the essentialism it spawns—whatever its source…Different ways of seeing can illuminate problems in unique ways and should be understood in this manner. Stephen May examined residual tensions:

I don't agree with essentialist positions that say: "Māori should be the only ones who research Māori." My intellectual frame of reference is bilingual research, and yet, I also have to acknowledge the real lived experiences of people and the way that colonization has framed research. There's an ongoing tension between trying to be open intellectually while at the same time conducting oneself personally and professionally in ways that are not replicating past problems. I am not by any stretch of the imagination, nor will I ever be, an expert on Māori medium education, but I am in the area of language and bilingual education. This position allows me to enter those debates from that perspective. I need to ensure that research is appropriate, accountable, beneficial. I need to be relationally engaged, trusted and respected. However well informed we are, we can simply go down the wrong road. All relationships require ongoing negotiation.

All this said, some mainstream researchers have branched away from their cross-cultural work, some because they have taken seriously the kind of thing that bell hooks (1984) has said:

> I was discussing this subject with another black woman professor and she said: "There was a time when we black people needed other people to speak for us because we could not always speak for ourselves. And though I am very grateful to white historians and the like who worked to inform people about black experience—we can and do speak for ourselves. And our struggle today is to be heard."

Experienced researchers from the majority culture depend on the impetus for cross-cultural research to come from those who feel its need. Barbara Comber said:

> I always feel like it's up to an Indigenous researcher to make the invitation. Whether that's wrong or not, I don't know. I don't feel like I want to be invading other peoples' territory. I also don't want to avoid responsibility. What I think I've decided to do is always respond, like the unfunded project with an Aboriginal school community which had received a state award for how well they were doing. As part of them getting this award, they said they would like to work with our research center. And I was over the moon about that.

Researchers whose track record in cross-cultural research is well established often have cross-cultural teams that keep them going on questions raised in past studies. While Celia Haig-Brown decided she would begin research now "by invitation only," she also described a way in which those new to cross-cultural research might begin:

> People invite you because you can contribute something, and quite often it's something specific. But, the thing is, you have to start somewhere because people can't know you're useful until you are known. One graduate student was in an Aboriginal area as a teacher, and he had some positive connections with some young men through hunting. He's been invited to come back now. With the Native Ed. Center, I put myself in a place where they could make an informed decision about whether they wanted me around. But now, for me, it is working by invitation. I have more work to do than I can imagine, and I love it.

Sometimes it is up to the beginning researcher to make the first move. It may mean scoping out those who need the kind of expertise that the researcher is developing. Knowing the paths to collaboration described herein will ease the path to initiating research.

Whether to do cross-cultural research or to supportively step aside is a question the many experienced researchers were asking themselves. And, of course, this comes back to some of the initial questions in the book: Whose question is the focus of research? Who benefits? Who has control over intellectual property? But are those the only questions that need to be asked?

Looking into the future as globalization continues, there may well be escalating pressures for the less powerful cultures to cave in to those holding dominant power, and the dominant power holders may well change. More needs to be understood, more needs to be respected, and those in non-dominant cultures (or those in now dominant cultures that may become non-dominant) will need to be thinking hard about culture in the world. I do believe, as the native Harvard students gave me the insight to believe, that multiple perspectives are a large part of why cross-cultural research should continue. I have come to believe that whenever one culture meets another, whenever one culture presses against another, reciprocal consideration of others' perspectives across a two-way bridge will be the way to maintain respect and cross-cultural understandings.

The richness of cross-cultural research

We learn a good deal about ourselves while working to understand others. This self-discovery does not concern only our hitherto unsuspected resourcefulness and resilience; it is also that, by beginning to understand other people's complexities, we are brought face to face with our own (Cohen, 2007).

One of the richest results of my own experience in cross-cultural research has come from my developing ability to peel away the layers of assumptions fed to me as a child, to critique my own culture's arrogance, to challenge that of others, to recognize and adjust my own lenses, and even to have empathy for those whom I have previously viewed as narrow-mindedly ethnocentric, realizing they might come from lives that haven't had that richness of cross-cultural exposure. Thus, a real gift that comes from cross-cultural research is coming to know oneself in relation to the wider world. Çiğdem Üsekes described her exit and then return to her birth culture of Turkey after being abroad:

> Having lived in the US [for some years], I brought a new perspective back to social, political, and cultural issues in my life in Turkey. When I came here I did not have a pro-Kurdish sentiment, and I think having seen what goes on in the race relations of the US, gave me a new perspective of what goes on for the Kurds in Turkey, in a country that for many years

refused to let Kurds use their own language publicly. I learned to look at the old with a fresh perspective.

A friend once told me that I became a more interesting person when I began articulating my deeper ways of seeing things from foreign travel and research. I thought about this most recently when my six-year-old grand-daughter said: "Tell me again about the time you were asked to eat the witchedy grub and the sugar ant, you know, where the kangaroos live." She was interested in other worlds, in my experiences of being in them, but most interested that you could actually eat a sugar ant and that it was, indeed, sweet, wiggly, and crunchy in your mouth. Hence, my newer, deeper understandings spill over into the rest of my life. As researchers, we become more resilient, less wedded to old ways of reacting, and better able to handle complicated relationships. We are open to continual self-construction and develop the means to interact with others creatively. When puzzled, we find ourselves thinking "What's happening here?" rather than offering arrogant knee-jerk reactions. I experienced this a week ago when I was at the gas/petrol pumps getting lawnmower fuel. I gasped at the fuel prices as the attendant helped me open the plastic jug for the fuel. He said: "Dear, you can blame the A-rabs for those prices." I gathered my immediate but unarticulated response back into my mouth. (Years ago it might have been my feminist: "I'm not dear to you, nor you to me," but last week it was more about economic understandings like: "You need to think of gas prices as more complicated than that.") Instead I thought about the gradual conversations I could have with the gas station attendant to further explore the complexities of the low US fuel costs, environmental issues, and political leveraging.

With experience in other cultures, researchers have the luxury of having one foot in what Saavedra and Nymark (2008) call "borderlands," a bit of the "hybrid consciousness" that allows us to better understand others' positions, and that "challenges researchers to rethink new ways to know and to be" (p. 269).

In juxtaposing different worlds, there is also that inductive climb to simpler constructs, coming full circle with what an elder said to me on the Passamaquoddy reservation: "When you start to see things simply, you will come closer to the truth." I have come to see, more simply, that all humans want self-determination, healthy food, healthy lives, and healthy loves. Though postmodern thought urges us to recognize and acknowledge the complexities in research results (not reporting pat answers and five bulleted recommendations), learning, observing, and thinking about multiple cultures can also bring us to the unity in the plurality that makes us all human.

Grounding research in friendship, in *agape*

The Greek term *agape* connotes the kind of caring that is essential in cross-cultural work, an unconditional and universal love for all people. Darder and

Miron (2006) note that love is essential in a just society. *Agape* is an emancipatory love upon which interdependence and collaboration should be built, allowing humans to respect each others' strengths and different ways of being, and looking into history to explain things that might be troubling. In cross-cultural research, researchers are responsible, beyond the discipline or institution to which they belong, and perhaps more importantly to a team and to those who are other-cultured participants. Maria Lugones (1987) talks about this kind of love, "not seen as fusion and erasure of difference but as incompatible with them. Love reveals plurality. Unity—not to be confused with solidarity—is understood as conceptually tied to domination" (p. 390). To love then is to honor difference and strength, not erase it. Given our multiple identities, our plurality of selves, and the resultant and possible connections with people from different cultures, cross-cultural teams and participants can connect with that *agape* kind of love. Lugones says: "I recommend that we affirm this travelling across 'worlds' as partly constitutive of cross-cultural and cross-racial loving" (p. 390).

Nothing stands still: as many questions as answers

In cross-cultural research, our research reflexivity keeps questions coming. In the end, we often end up with more evolved questions as a feature of our answers: the antithetical, the unexplainable, and the discrepant arise. This book offers no formulas, but it does play out the problems as a beginning to solutions. As Spivak (1993) says, "Truth of a human situation is the itinerary of not being able to find it" (p. 77). Nothing stands still, neither time, nor conditions, nor politics, nor the realities of people's lives. Listening to others' research experiences was for me a time when others articulated some of my same misgivings, or brought me to new insights, or brought me to see how these problems won't necessarily stand still. After each interviewee's narrative, I went away (as the Hopi woman told me) *thinking*. We literally cannot stand still and must avoid being paralyzed by the indeterminancy of our analyses.

Afterword

And I am appreciative that my understanding of Julian Cho has not stood still. Several years after I began my inquiry into cross-cultural research, initiated in response to Julian Cho's death, I met Armstrong Wiggens. As the administrator of the Indian Law Resource Center in Washington, DC, he had supported the land-rights work of Cho. We talked of our admiration for the remarkable man, and then he said something like: "I warned him to be careful and warned him that the complexity of those who might want to end his work might not be simple to discern." Wiggens had done what I had not known enough to do, and I was relieved that Cho had taken risks of which he had been well aware. Though warned of danger that he might well have suspected himself, he held on to the hope that he might make a difference.

Many researchers have moments when they despair about what they see as their mistakes, the mistakes, as Larry Knopp said, that might keep them from sleeping well. In light of a conversation we had about our misadventures in cross-cultural research, I told Vicki Crowley about my impetus for this research, Julian Cho. She said:

> I still think it's about doing things in good faith. That you learn by mistakes is, of course, a cliché. Your mistake means that you, now, are asking me these kinds of questions, an incredibly important kind of pursuit, and one that other people will be really interested to hear about. We have to realize that we are part of this world and all of its terrors. Some things will always be painful, but those things make me work harder to know how I can go about my work in a way that does something for possibilities in the future. And that's what has to become; otherwise, I sink with it.

In research, as in all things, we need to keep hope alive: "Hope is an ontological need" (Lather, 1993, p. 163).

List of Quoted Researchers

Henry Amoroso, Associate Professor Emeritus and researcher, founder of journal *Voices*, University of Southern Maine, USA.

Ian Anderson, Director, Cooperative Research Centre for Aboriginal Health, University of Melbourne, Victoria, Australia.

John Arthur, Professor of Sociology, University of Minnesota Duluth, USA.

Jenny Barnett, Researcher and Senior Lecturer, Centre for Studies in Literacy, Policy and Learning Cultures, University of South Australia, Australia.

Mere Berryman, Senior Research Fellow, Te Kotahitanga Research Unit, University of Waikato, New Zealand.

Russell Bishop, Professor for Māori Education, School of Education, University of Waikato, New Zealand.

Adrian Blackledge, Professor of Bilingualism and Director of MOSAICS, University of Birmingham, UK.

Eleanor Bourke, Professor, Centre for Australian Indigenous Studies, Monash University, Melbourne, Victoria, Australia.

Celia Haig Brown, Professor, Faculty of Education, Faculty of Graduate Studies and School of Women's Studies, York University, Toronto, Canada.

David Carey Jr., Professor of History and Women and Gender Studies,University of Southern Maine, USA.

Julie Canniff, Chair, Department of Teacher Education, University of Southern Maine, USA.

Julian Cho, Chair, Humanities Department, Toledo Community College, Punta Gorda, Belize—deceased.

Barbara Comber, Professor, Faculty of Education, Queensland University of Technology, Australia.

Fiona Cram, Senior Research Fellow, Eru Pomare Māori Health Research Centre, University of Otago, New Zealand.

Rhonda Craven, Director, Centre for Positive Psychology and Education, University of Western Sydney, New South Wales, Australia.

Angela Creese, Professor of Educational Linguistics,Centre for Research on Multilingualism, School of Education, University of Birmingham, UK.

Vicki Crowley, Senior Lecturer, School of Communication, International Studies and Languages, Research Centre for Gender Studies, University of South Australia, Adelaide.

Ann Diver-Stamnes, Professor and Educational Psychologist, Humboldt State University, California, USA.

Louis-Jacques Dorais, anthropologist, Universite Laval in Quebec City, Canada (emeritus).

Aydın Durgunoğlu, Cognitive Psychologist, Turkish-born, Literacy Studies in the USA and Turkey, University of Minnesota Duluth, USA.

Ted Glynn, Foundation Professor of Teacher Education, Wilf Malcolm Institute of Educational Research, University of Waikato, New Zealand.

Bella Graham, Faculty of Education, Māori oral historian, University of Waikato, New Zealand, deceased—deceased.

Howard Groome, Lecturer in Aboriginal Education, University of South Australia, Adelaide—retired.

Shirley Brice Heath, Margery Bailey Professor of English and Dramatic Literature and Professor of Linguistics and Anthropology, Emerita, Stanford University, California, USA.

Mary Hermes, Faculty of Education, mixed Dakota heritage, University of Minnesota, USA.

Rachel Hodge, researcher at Lancaster University, UK.

Wendy Holland, Lecturer, School of Social Sciences, University of Western Sydney, New South Wales, Australia.

Sharon Kemp, anthropologist, University of Minnesota Duluth, USA.

Larry Knopp, geographer and Director of Interdisciplinary Arts and Sciences, University of Washington Tacoma, USA.

Stephen May, Deputy Dean of Research, Faculty of Education, bilingualism and language rights, University of Auckland, New Zealand.

Dana McDaniel, Professor of Linguistics, University of Southern Maine, USA.

Liz McKinley, Māori researcher, University of Auckland, New Zealand.

Joan Metge, Pākehā anthropologist and Honorary Research Fellow, University of Auckland New Zealand.

Sue Middleton, Professor, Policy, Cultural and Social Studies in Education, University of Waikato, New Zealand.

Jean Mills, Senior Lecturer in Education, University of Birmingham, UK.

Tess Moeke-Maxwell, Research Fellow, Indigenous Mental Health Care, University of Waikato, New Zealand.

Philip Morrissey, Academic Coordinator of the Faculty of Arts Australian Indigenous Studies, University of Melbourne, Victoria, Australia.

Stephen Muecke, Professor of Cultural Studies, University of Technology, Sydney, New South Wales, Australia.

Geoffrey Munns, Centre for Educational Research, University of Western Sydney, New South Wales, Australia.

Martin Nakata, Torres Strait Islander, Director, Aboriginal Research Institute, University of South Australia.

Ken Ralph, Yalbalinga Aboriginal Centre, Australia Catholic University, Strathfield, New South Wales, Australia.

Daryle Rigney, Yunggorendi First Nation Center for Higher Education and Research, Flinders University, Adelaide, South Australia.

Susan Rodgers, Professor of Anthropology, College of the Holy Cross, Massachusetts, USA.

Barbara Rogoff, Foundation Distinguished Professor of Psychology, Culture and Human Development, University of California at Santa Barbara, USA.

Michael Rosberg, economic anthropologist, Director, Institute for Social Entrepreneurship and Equity, University College of the Caribbean, Jamaica.

Flynn Ross, educational researcher, University of Southern Maine, USA.

Ines Sanchez, Professor, University of Belize, folktales and legends, Spanish language.

Christine Sleeter, Professor Emerita, College of Professional Studies, California State University, Monterey Bay, multicultural education.

Linda Tuhiwai Smith, Professor and Pro-Vice Chancellor, Māori, University of Waikato, New Zealand.

Brian Street, Emeritus Professor of Language in Education, linguistic ethnographer, King's College London, UK.

Sarah Jane Tiakiwai, Academic Director, Waikato-Tainui College for Research and Development, New Zealand.
Karin Tusting, Lecturer in Linguistics and Literacy Studies, University of Lancaster, UK.
Çiğdem Üsekes, Professor of English, Western Connecticut State University, USA.
Chris Winch, Head of Department, Department of Education and Professional Studies, King's College London, UK.
Joseph Wood, cultural geographer, Provost, University of Baltimore, Maryland, USA.
Roy Young, Belmopan, Registrar, University of Belize.

Works Cited

Alcoff, L. (1991). The problem of speaking for others. *Cultural Critique* (Winter 1991–92), 285–309.

Alexander, B. K. (2008). Queer(y)ing the postcolonial through the west(ern). In N. K. Denzin & Y. S. Lincoln (Eds.), *Handbook of critical and indigenous methodologies* (pp. 101–134). Los Angeles, CA: Sage.

Alexander, C., Edwards, R., & Temple, B. (2004). *Access to services with interpreters: User views*. London: Joseph Rowntree Foundation.

Allen, P. G. (1986). *Kochinnenako in academe: Three approaches to interpreting a keres indian tale. The sacred hoop: Recovering the feminine in American Indian traditions* (pp. 222–244). Boston, MA: Beacon Press.

Archibald, J. (2008). *Indigenous storywork: Educating the heart, mind, body and spirit*. Vancouver: University of British Columbia Press.

Bakhtin, M. (1981). *The dialogic imagination*. Austin: University of Texas Press.

Bakhtin, M. M. (1990). In M. Holquist & V. Liapunov (Eds.), *Art and answerability: Early philosophical essays*. (V. Liapunov, Trans). Austin: University of Texas Press.

Banks, J. (1998). The lives and values of researchers: Implications for educating citizens in a multicultural society. *Educational Researcher, 27*(7), 4–17.

Bartlett, E. A. (2004). *Rebellious feminism: Camus's ethic of rebellion and feminist thought*. New York: Palgrave Macmillan.

Behar, R. (1993). *Translated woman: Crossing the border with Esperanza's story*. Boston, MA: Beacon Press.

Belenky, M., Clinchy, B., Goldberger, N., & Tarule, J. (1986). *Women's ways of knowing: The development of self, voice and mind*. New York: Basic Books.

Bergstrom, A., Miller Cleary, L., & Peacock, T. (2003). *The seventh generation: Native students speak about finding the good path*. Charleston, West Virginia: ERIC Clearinghouse.

Bernstein, B. (1971). Social class, language and socialization. In P. P. Giglioli (Ed.), *Language and social context* (pp. 157–178). Harmondsworth, Middlesex: Penguin.

Bernstein, B. (1972). *Class, codes and control, Volume I: Theoretical studies toward a sociology of language*. London: Routledge and Kegan

Best, D. L., & Everett, B. L. (2010). The most recent years: Journal of Cross-Cultural Psychology, 2004–2009. *Journal of Cross-Cultural Psychology, 41*(3), 329–335.

Betancourt, H., & Lopez, S. R. (1993). The study of culture, ethnicity, and race in American psychology. *American Psychologist, 48*, 629–637.

Bhabha, H. (1994). *The location of culture*. New York: Routledge.

Bishop, R. (1996). Addressing issues of self-determination and legitimation in kaupapa Māori research. In B. Webber (Ed.), *He Paepae korero: Research perspectives in Māori education* (pp. 152–160). Wellington, New Zealand: New Zealand Council for Educational Research.

Bishop, R., Berryman, M., Cavanagh, T., & Teddy, L. (1997). *Te kotahitanga phase 3: Establishing a culturally responsive pedagogy of relations in mainstream secondary school classrooms*. (Executive Summary). New Zealand: New Zealand Ministry of Education. (where power is shared…where culture counts…where learning is interactive, and dialogic...where connectedness is fundamental to relations...where there is a common vision: There is a common agenda for what constitutes excellence for Māori......)

Bishop, R., & Glynn, T. (1999). *Culture counts: Changing power relations in education.* New Zealand: Palmerston North.

Black, T. (2009). *When a heart turns rock solid.* New York: Pantheon.

Black, S. (2010). *Fiction across borders: Imagining the lives of others in late twentieth century novels.* New York: Columbian University Press.

Blumer, H. (1969). *Symbolic interactionism: Perspective and method.* Englewood Cliffs, NJ: Prentice-Hall.

Boroditsky, L. (2000). Metaphoric structuring: Understanding time through spatial metaphors. *Cognition, 75,* 1–28.

Borofsky, R. (2005). *Yanomami: The fierce controversy and what we can learn from it.* Berkeley: University of California Press.

Bourgois, P. (2012). Confronting the ethics of ethnography: Lessons from fieldwork in central America. In A. C. G. M. Robben & J. A. Sluka (Eds.), *Ethnographic fieldwork: An anthropological reader.* John Wiley & Sons.

Bowles, S., & Gintis, H. (1976). *Schooling in capitalist America: Education reform and the contradictions of economic life.* New York: Basic Books, Inc.

Brislin, R. W. (1970). Back-translation for cross-cultural research. *Journal of Cross-Cultural Psychology, 1*(3), 121–186.

Brislin, R. W., Lonner, W. J., & Thorndike, R. M. (1973). *Cross-cultural research methods.* New York: John Wiley & Sons.

Brislin, R. W. (1980). Translation and content analysis of oral and written materials. In H. Triandis & J. Berry (Eds.), *Handbook of cross-cultural psychology, volume 2: Methodology* (pp. 389–444). Boston, MA: Allyn & Bacon.

Bruner, J. (1963). *On knowing: Essays for the left hand.* Cambridge, MA: Harvard University Press.

Bruner, J. (1990). *Acts of meaning.* Cambridge, MA: Harvard University Press.

Bruner, J., & Weisser, J. (1991). The invention of self: Autobiography and its forms. In D. Olson & N. Torrance (Eds.), *Literacy and orality* (pp. 129–148). Cambridge, UK: Cambridge University Press.

Cannella, G. S., & Manuelito, K. D. (2008). Feminisms from unthought locations: Indigenous worldviews, marginalized feminisms, and revisioning an anticolonial social science. In N. K. Denzin, Y. S. Lincoln, & L. T. Smith (Eds.) (2008). *Handbook of critical and indigenous methodologies* (pp. 45–60). Los Angeles, CA: Sage Publications.

Carey, D. (2003). Symbiotic research: A case for ethical scholarship. *Thought and Action, the NEA Higher Education Journal,* (Summer), 99–114.

Chaudhry, L. N. (1997). Researching "my people," researching myself: Fragments of a reflexive tale. *Qualitive Studies in Education, 10*(4), 441–453.

Cleary, L. M. (1991). *From the other side of the desk: Students speak out about writing.* Portsmouth, NH: Boynton/Cook Publishers.

Cleary, L. M. (1996). I think I know what my teachers want from me now: Gender and writing motivation. *The English Journal, 85*(1).

Cleary, L. M. (2008). The imperative of literacy motivation when native children are being left behind. *Journal of American Indian Education, 47*(1), 96–117.

Cleary, L. M., & Peacock, T. D. (1998). *Collected wisdom: American Indian education.* Boston, MA: Allyn and Bacon.

Cleary, L. M., & Peacock, T. D. (1997). Disseminating American Indian educational research through stories: A case against academic discourse. *Journal of American Indian Education, 37*(1), 7–15.

Clifton, J. A. (Ed.). (1990). *The invented Indian: Cultural fictions and government policies.* New Brunswick, NJ: Transaction Publishers.

Codere, H. (1970). Field work in Rwanda, 1959–1960. In P. Golde (Ed.), *Women in the field: Anthropological experiences* (1st ed., pp. 142–164). Chicago: Aldine Publishing Company.

Cohen, A. P. (2007). Self-concious anthropology. In A. C. G. M. Robben & J. A. Sluka (Eds.), *Ethnographic fieldwork: An anthropological reader* (pp. 89–100). Malden, MA: Blackwell Publishing.

Cohen, D. (2007). Methods in cultural psychology. In S. Kitayama & D. Cohen (Eds.), *Handbook of cultural psychology* (pp. 196–236). New York: Guilford.

Cole, M. (1991). On cultural psychology. *American Anthropologist, 93*(2), 435–439.

Cole, M., & Scribner, S. (1978). Literacy without schooling: Testing for intellectual effects. *Harvard Educational Review, 48,* 448–461.

Comaroff, J. L., & Comaroff, J. (2009). *Ethnicity, inc.* Chicago: University of Chicago Press.

Cook-Lynn, E. (2008). History, myth, and identity in the new indian story. In N. K. Denzin & Y. S. Lincoln (Eds.), *Handbook of critical and indigenous methodologies* (pp. 329–346). Los Angeles, CA: Sage.

Cram, F. (1997). *Developing partnerships in research: Pakeha researchers and Māori research.* Unpublished manuscript.

Cram, F. (2001). Rangahau Māori: Tona tika, tona pono–the validity and integrity of Māori research. In M. Tolich (Ed.), *Research ethics in Aotearoa New zealand: Concepts, practice, critique* (pp. 35–52). Auckland: Longman.

Cram, F., & Pipi, K. (June 2001). *Rangahu Māori II: Iwi/Māori provider success.* Auckland, New Zealand: International Research Institute for Māori and Indigenous Education, University of Auckland.

Cresswell, J. W. (2003). *Research design: Qualitative, quantitative, and mixed message approaches* (2nd ed.). Thousand Oaks, CA: Sage.

Csikszentmihalyi, M. (1996). *Creativity: Flow and the psychology of discovery and invention.* New York: Harper Perrenial.

Currey, J. (1999). *Regimes of language: Ideologies, polities, and identities.* Sante Fe, NM: School of American Research Press.

Darder, A., & Miron, L. F. (2006). Critical pedagogy in a time of uncertainty: A call to action. *Cultural, 6*(1), 5–20.

Davies, I. R. L. (1998). A study of colour grouping in three languages: A test of the linguistic relativity hypothesis. *British Journal of Psychology, 89,* 433–452.

Deci, E. L. (1985). *Intrinsic motivation and self-determination in human behavior.* New York: Plenum.

deLaine, M. (2000). *Fieldwork, participation and practice: Ethics and dilemmas in qualitative research.* London: Sage.

Deloria, V. (1969). *Custer died for your sins: An indian manifesto.* New York: Macmillan.

Delva, J., Allen-Meares, P., & Momper, S. L. (2010). *Cross-cultural research.* Oxford: Oxford University Press.

Denny, J. P. (1991). Rational thought in oral culture and literate decontextualization. In D. Olson & N. Torrance (Eds.), *Literacy and orality* (pp. 129–148). Cambridge, UK: Cambridge University Press.

Denzin, N. K. (1998). The new ethnography. *Journal of Cross-Cultural Psychology, 27,* 405–405–415.

Denzin, N. K., & Lincoln, Y. S. (2000). *Handbook of qualitative research.* Thousand Oaks, CA: Sage.

Denzin, N. K., Lincoln, Y. S., & Smith, L. T. (Eds.). (2008). *Handbook of critical and indigenous methodologies*. Los Angeles, CA: Sage.

Dey, I. (1993). *Caste and class in a southern town*. Garden City, NY: Doubleday Anchor Book.

Du Bois, W. E. B. (1903). *The souls of black folk*. Greenwich, CT: Fawcett.

Dunbar Jr., C. (2008). Critical race theory and indigenous methodologies. In N. K. Denzin & Y. S. Lincoln (Eds.), *Handbook of critical and indigenous methodologies* (pp. 85–100). Los Angeles, CA: Sage.

Durkheim, E. (1982). In Lukes S. (Ed.), *Rules of sociological method and selected texts on sociology and its method* [Les régles de la méthode sociologique] (W. D. Halls Trans.). (First American ed.). New York: The Free Press.

Ellis, C. (2004). *The ethnographic I: A methodological novel about ethnography*. Walnut Creek, CA: Alta Mira Press.

Ember, Carol R., & Melvin Ember. (2009). *Cross-cultural research methods*. Walnut Creek, CA: Alta Mira Press.

England, K. V. L. (1994). Getting personal: Reflexivity, positionality, and feminist research. *The Professional Geographer, 46*(4), 80–88.

Fine, M. (1992). *Disruptive voices: The possibilities of feminist research*. University of Michigan Press.

Fine, M., Tuck, E., & Zeller-Berkman, S. (2008). Do you believe in Geneva? methods and ethics at the global-local nexus. In N. K. Denzin & Y. S. Lincoln (Eds.), *Handbook of critical and indigenous methodologies* (pp. 157–180). Los Angeles, CA: Sage.

Flanagan, O., & Jackson, K. (1987). Justice, care, and gender: The Kohlberg-Gilligan debate revisited. *Ethics, 97*(3), 622–637.

Foley, D. A., Levinson, B. A., & Hurtig, J. (2002). Anthropology goes inside: The new educational ethnography of ethnicity and gender. *Review of Research in Education, 25*(1), 37–37–98.

Foucault, M. (1972). *Archaeology of knowledge* (A. M. Sheridan Smith Trans.). New York: Pantheon Book.

Foucault, M. (1980). In Gordon C. (Ed.), *Power/knowledge: Selected interviews and other writings* (C. Gordon Trans.). New York: Pantheon.

Freire, P. (1970). *Pedagogy of the oppressed*. New York: Herder and Herder.

Freire, P. (2005). *Education for critical consciousness*. New York: Continuum International Publishing Group.

Friedman, M. (1987). Beyond caring: The de-moralization of gender. *Canadian Journal of Philosophy, 13*, 87–110.

Frye, M. (1983). *The politics of reality: Essays in feminist theory*. Trumansburg, NY: Crossing Press.

Gaard, G. (1993). Living interconnections with animals and nature. In G. Gaard (Ed.), *Ecofeminism: Women, animals, nature* (pp. 1–12). Philadelphia, PA: Temple University Press.

Gearing, R. E. (2004). Bracketing in research: A topology. *Qualitative Health Research, 14*(10), 1429–1452.

Gee, J. (1990). *Social linguistics and literacies: Ideology in discourse*. New York: Routledge.

Geeraerts, D., & Cuyckens, H. (Eds.). (2007). *Oxford handbook of cognitive linguistics*. Oxford: Oxford University Press.

Geertz, C. (1983). *Local knowledge*. New York: Basic Books.

Gilligan, C. (1982). *In a different voice: Psychological theory and women's development*. Cambridge, MA: Harvard University Press.

Giroux, H. A. (2010). "Lessons from Paolo Freire". *The Chronicle of Higher Education, October 17, 2010.*

Giroux, H. A., & Giroux, S. S. (2008). Challenging neoliberalism's new world order: The promise of critical pedagogy. In N. K. Denzin & Y. S. Lincoln (Eds.), *Handbook of critical and indigenous methodologies* (pp. 181–190). Los Angeles, CA: Sage.

Glaser, B. G., & Strauss, A. L. (1967). *The discovery of grounded theory: Strategies for qualitative research.* New York: Aldine de Gruyter.

Goldstein, S. (2000). *Cross-cultural explorations: Activities in culture and psychology.* Boston, MA: Allyn and Bacon.

Grande, S. (2008). Red pedagogy: The un-methodology. In N. K. Denzin & Y. S. Lincoln (Eds.), *Handbook of critical and indigenous methodologies* (pp. 233–254). Los Angeles, CA: Sage.

Gray, B. (1990). Natural language learning in aboriginal classrooms: Reflections on teaching and learning style for empowerment in English, chapter 11. In C. Walton & W. Eggington (Eds.), *Language: Maintenance.* Darwin: Northern Territory University Press.

Grbich, C. (2004). *New approaches in social research.* London/Thousand Oaks, CA: Sage.

Greenfield, P. M. (1997). You can't take it with you: Why ability assessments don't cross cultures. *American Psychologist, 52,* 1115–1124.

Hall, E. T. (1966). *The hidden dimension.* New York: Anchor Books.

Hall, E. T. (1973). *The silent language.* New York: Doubleday.

Hall, E. T., & Hall, M. R. (1990). *Understanding cultural differences.* Boston, MA: Intercultural Press.

Hardin, C. L., & Maffi, L. (1997). *Color categories in thought and language.* Cambridge: Cambridge University Press.

Harstock, N. (2004). The feminist standpoint: Developing the grounds for a specifically feminist historical materialism. In S. Harding & M. B. Hintikka (Eds.), *Discovering reality* (pp. 283–310). Netherlands: Springer.

Harvey-Morgan. (1994). *Native literacy and language roundtable proceedings.* AERA, San Francisco, 1995: The Native Education Initiative of the U.S. Department of Education Regional Educational Laboratories.

Heath, S. B. (1983). *Way with words.* Cambridge: Cambridge University Press.

Heine, S. J. (2011). *Cultural psychology* (2nd ed.). New York & London: W.W. Norton & Company.

Helfrich, H. (1999). Beyond the dilemma of cross-cultural psychology: Resolving the tension between etic and emic approaches. *Culture & Psychology, 31*(3), 131–153.

Hermes, M. (1998). Research methods as a situated response: Towards a first nations' methodology. *International Journal of Qualitative Studies in Education, 11*(1), 155–168.

Hermes, M. (2004). Waadookodaading indigenous language immersion: Personal reflections on the gut-wrenching start-up years. In F. Ibanez-Carrasco & E. R. Meiners (Eds.), *Public acts: Disruptive readings on making curriculum public* (pp. 57–71). New York: RoutledgeFalmer.

Hermes, M., Janelle Dance, L., Gutiérrez, R. (2010). More like jazz than classical: Reciprocal interactions among educational researchers and respondents. *Harvard Educational Review,* Fall.

Heshusius, L. (1994). Freeing ourselves from objectivity: Managing subjectivity or turning toward a participatory mode of consciousness? *Educational Researcher, 23*(3), 15–22.

hooks, b. (1989). *Talking back: Thinking feminist, thinking black.* Boston, MA: South End Press.

Howell, N. (1998). Human hazards of fieldwork. In A. C. G. M. Robben & J. A. Sluka (Eds.), *Ethnographic fieldwork: An anthropological reader* (2nd ed., pp. 234–244). West Sussex, UK: Wiley-Blackwell.

Hymes, D. (Ed.) (1964). *Language in culture and society: A reader in linguistics and anthropology.* New York: Harper and Row.

Jacobson, M., & Rugele, C. (2007). Community-based participatory research: Group workfor social justice and community change. *Social Work with Groups, 30*(4), 21–39.

Jaggar, A. M. (Spring 1998). Globalizing feminist ethics. *Hypatia: A Journal of Feminist Philosophy, 13*(2), 7–31.

Janesick, V. J. (2001). Intuition and creativity: A pas de deux for qualitative researchers. *Qualitative Inquiry, 7*(5), 531–540.

Jezewski, M. A. (1990). Culture brokering in migrant farm worker health care. *Western Journal of Nursing Research, 12,* 407–543.

Jones, A., & Jenkins, K. (2008). Rethinking collaboration: Working with indigene-colonizer hyphen. In N. K. Denzin & Y. S. Lincoln (Eds.), *Handbook of critical and indigenous methodologies* (pp. 471–486). Los Angeles, CA: Sage.

Kashima, Y., Kokubo, T., Kashima, E. S., Boxall, D., Yamaguchi, S., & Macrae, K. (2004). Cultural and self: Are there within culture differences in self between metropolitan areas and regional cities? *Personality and Social Psychological Bulletin, 30,* 816–823.

Kashima, Y., Yamaguchi, S., Kim, U., Choi, S., Gelfand, M. J.. & Yuki, M. (1995). Culture, gender, and self: A perspective from individualism-collectivism research. *Journal of Personality and Social Psychology, 69.* 925–937.

Kellehear, A. (1993). *The unobtrusive researcher: Guide to methods.* Sydney, Australia: Allen and Unwin.

Kendall, F. E. (2006). *Understanding white privilege: Creating pathways to authentic relationships across race.* New York: Routledge: Taylor and Francis Group.

Kim, H. S. (2002). We talk, therefore we think? A cultural analysis of the effect of talking on thinking. *Journal of Personality and Social Psychology, 83,* 828–842.

King, M. L. (2000). "A letter from Birmingham jail" in *Why we can't wait.* London: Penguine Books.

Kincheloe, J. L., & Steinberg, S. R. (2008). Indigenous knowledges in education: Complexities, dangers, and profound benefits. In N. K. Denzin & Y. S. Lincoln (Eds.), *Handbook of critical and indigenous methodologies* (pp. 135–156). Los Angeles, CA: Sage.

Kroskrity, P. V. (Ed.). (2000). *Regimes of language: Ideologies, polities, and identities.* Santa Fe, NM: School of American Research Press.

LaBov, W. (1972). *Sociolinguistic patterns.* Philadelphia, PA: University of Pennsylvania Press.

Ladson-Billings, G., & Donnor, J. K. (2008). Waiting for the call: The moral activist role of critical race theory scholarship. In N. K. Denzin, Y. S. Lincoln, & L. T. Smith (Eds.), *Handbook of critical and indigenous methodologies* (pp. 61–84). Los Angeles, CA: Sage Publications.

Lakoff, G., & Johnson, M. (1993). How metaphor gives meaning to form. In L. M. Cleary, & M. Linn (Eds.), *Linguistics for teachers* (pp. 519–529). New York: McGraw Hill.

Lareau, A. (2010). *Unequal childhoods: Class, race and family life* (2nd ed.). Berkeley and Los Angeles: University of California Press.

Lather, P. (1991). *Getting smart: Feminist research and pedagogy within the postmodern.* New York: Routledge.

Lather, P. (1993). Fertile obsession: Validity after poststructuralism, *Sociological Quarterly, 34*(4), 673–693.

Lawrence-Lightfoot, Sara and Davis, Jessica Hoffman. (1997). *The art and science of portraiture*. Hoboken, NJ: Wiley, John, and Sons.

Leung, K., & Van de Vijver, Fons J. R. (2006). Cross-cultural research methodology. In F. T. L. Leong & J. T. Austin (Eds.), *The psychology research handbook* (2nd ed., pp. 443–464). Thousand Oaks, CA: Sage.

Levine, R. (1997). *A geography of time*. New York: Basic Books.

Liamputtong, P. (2010). *Performing qualitative cross-cultural research*. Cambridge: Cambridge University Press.

Lincoln, Y. S., & Gonzales y Gonzales, Elsa M. (July 2008). The search for emerging decolonizing methodologies in qualitative research: Further strategies for liberatory and democratic inquiry. *Qualitative Inquiry, 14*(5), 784–805.

Lincoln, Y. S., & Guba, E. G. (1985). *Naturalistic inquiry*. Newbury Park, CA: Sage.

Lucy, J. A. (1997). Linguistic relativity. *Annual Review of Anthropology, 26*, 291–312.

Lugones, M. C. (Summer 1987). Playfulness, "world"-traveling, and loving perception. *Hypatia: A Journal of Feminist Philosophy, 2*(2), 390–402.

Lugones, M. C., & Spelman, E. V. (1983). Have we got a theory for you! feminist theory, cultural imperialism and the demand for "the woman's voice". *Women's Studies International Forum, 6*(6), 573–581.

Madison, D. S. (2008). Narrative poetics and performative interventions. In N. K. Denzin & Y. S. Lincoln (Eds.), *Handbook of critical and indigenous methodologies* (pp. 391–406). Los Angeles, CA: Sage.

Markus, H. R., & Kitayama, S. (1991). Culture and self: Implications for cognition, emotion, and motivation. *Psychological Review, 98*, 224–253.

Matsumoto, D., & Hee Yoo, S. (2006). Toward a new generation of cross-cultural research. *Perspectives on Psychological Science, 1*, 234–250.

McCall, L. (2005). The complexity of intersectionality. *Journal of Women in Culture and Society, 30*, 1771–1800.

McCaslin, W. D., & Breton, D. C. (2008). Justice as healing: Going outside the colonizers' cage. In N. K. Denzin & Y. S. Lincoln (Eds.), *Handbook of critical and indigenous methodologies* (pp. 511–530). Los Angeles, CA: Sage.

McConaghy, C. (2000). *Rethinking indigenous education: Culturalism, colonialism and the politics of knowing*. Flaxton, Queensland, Australia: Post Pressed.

McDermott, R. P. (1977). Social relations as contexts for learning in school. *Harvard Educational Review, 47*, 498–513.

Messner, S. F., & Rosenfeld, M. (2007). *Crime and the American dream* (4th ed.). Belmont, CA: Wadsworth.

Metge, J. (1986). *In and out of touch: Whakamaa in cross cultural context*. Wellington: Victoria University Press.

Metge, J. (2010). *Tuamaka: The challenge of difference in aotearoa New Zealand*. Aukland: Aukland University Press.

Miller, J. (2001). Culture and moral development. In D. Matsumoto (Ed.), *Handbook of culture and psychology* (pp. 151–170). New York: Oxford University Press.

Mills, J. (2001). Self-construction through conversation and narrative in interviews. *Educational Review, 53*(3), 285–301.

Morgan, D., Fellows, C., & Quevara, H. (2008), Emergent approaches to focus group research. In S. Nagy Hesse-Biber & P. Leavy (Eds.), *Handbook of emergent methods* (pp. 181–205). New York: Gilford.

Morrison, T. (1993). *Playing in the dark: Whiteness and the literary imagination.* New York: Vintage Books, 1992.

Nader, L. (1990). *Harmony ideology: Justice and control in a Zapotec mountain village.* Stanford, CA: Stanford University Press.

Nader L. (1995). The primacy of the ethical propositions for a militant anthropology. *Current Anthropology, 36,* 409–440.

Nader, L., & Metzger, D. (June 1963). Conflict resolution in two Mexican communities. *American Anthropologist, 65*(3), 584–592.

Nakata, M. (1998). Anthropological texts and indigenous standpoints. *Australian Aboriginal Studies* (2), 3–12.

Nakata, M. (2007). *Disciplining the savages – savaging the disciplines.* Canberra, Australia: Aboriginal Studies Press.

Oakley, A. (1981). Interviewing women: A contradiction in terms. In H. Roberts (Ed.), *Doing feminist research* (pp. 30–61). London: Routledge and Kegan Paul.

Patai, D. (1988). *Brazilian women speak: Contemporary life stories.* New Brunswick, NJ: Rutgers University Press.

Patai, D. (1991). U.S. academics and third world women: Is ethical research possible? In S. Berger Gluck & D. Patai (Eds.), *Women's words: The feminist practice of oral history* (pp. 137–153). London: Routledge.

Patai, D. (1992). Feminist cross-cultural research. In S. Reinharz (Ed.), *Feminist methods in social research* (pp. 109–125). New York: Oxford University Press.

Patai, D. (1994). U.S. academics and third-world women: Is ethical research possible. In S. O. Weiser & J. Fleischner (Eds.), *Feminist nightmares: Women at odds: Feminism and the problem of sisterhood* (pp. 137–153). New York: New York University Press.

Patton, M. Q. (2002). *Qualitative research and evaluation methods* (3rd ed.). Thousand Oaks, CA: Sage.

Pederson, E. (2007). Cognitive linguistics and linguistic relativity. In D. Geeraerts & H. Cuyckens (Eds.), *Oxford handbook of cognitive linguistics* (pp. 1012–1044). Oxford: Oxford University Press.

Peshkin, A. (2000). The nature of interpretation in qualitative research. *Educational Researcher, 29*(9), 5–9.

Pillow, W. S. (2003). Confession, catharsis, or cure? rethinking the uses of reflexivity as methodological power in qualitative research. *International Journal of Qualitative Studies in Education, 16*(2), 175-175–196.

Pipi, K., Cram, F., Hawke, R., Hawke, S., Huriwai, T. M., Mataki, T., et al. (2002). A research ethic for studying Māori and Iwi provider success. *International Research Institute for Māori and Indigenous Education (IRI). The University of Auckland Social Policy Journal Document.* Issue 23.

Pollack, D. (2007). Healing dilemmas. In A. C. G. M. Robben & J. A. Sluka (Eds.), *Ethnographic fieldwork: An anthropological reader.* Malden, MA: Blackwell Publishing.

Quinney, R. (1970). *The social reality of crime.* Boston, MA: Little, Brown.

Rigney, L. (2003). *The first perspective: Culturally safe research practices on or with indigenous peoples.* Unpublished manuscript.

Robben, A. C. G. M., & Sluka, J. A. (Eds.). (2007). *Ethnographic fieldwork: An anthropological reader.* Malden, MA: Blackwell Publishing.

Rogoff, B. (2011). *Developing destinies: A Mayan midwife and town.* New York: Oxford University Press.

Root, M. P. P. (1998). Experiences and processes affecting racial identity and development: Preliminary results from the biracial sibling project. *Cultural Diversity and Ethnic Minority Psychology, 4,* 237–247.

Rosaldo, R. (1993). *Culture and truth: The remaking of social analysis.* Boston, MA: Beacon Press.

Saavedra, C. M., & Nymark, E. D. (2008). Borderland-*Mestizaje* Feminism: The new tribalism. In N. K. Denzin & Y. S. Lincoln (Eds.), *Handbook of critical and indigenous methodologies* (pp. 255–276). Los Angeles, CA: Sage.

Safran, W. (1991). Diasporas in modern societies: Myths of homeland and return. *Diaspora: A Journal of Transnational Studies, 1*(1), 83–99.

Said, E. W. (1985). In the shadow of the west. *Wedge, 7–8*(Winter-Spring), 4–11.

Saroglou, V., & Cohen, A. B. (2011). Psychology of culture and religion: Introduction to the JCCP special issue. *Journal of Cross-Cultural Psychology, 42*(8), 1309–1319.

Schein, E. (2012). *Three levels of culture.* Retrieved 4/1, 2012, from http://www.valuebasedmanagement.net/methods_schein_three_levels_culture.html

Scheper-Hughes, N. (1992). *Death without weeping: The violence of everyday life in Brazil.* Berkeley, CA and Los Angeles, CA: University of California Press.

Scheper-Hughes, N. (1995). The primacy of the ethical propositions for a militant anthropology. *Current Anthropology, 36*, 409–440.

Schutz, A. (1967). *The phenomenology of the social world.* Evenston, IL: Northwestern University Press.

Scott, J. C. (1990). *Domination and the arts of resistance: Hidden transcripts.* New Haven, CN: Yale.

Seidman, I. (2013). *Interviewing as qualitative research: A guide for researchers in education and social sciences* (4th ed.). New York: Teachers College Press.

Sennet, R., & Cobb, J. (1973). *The hidden injuries of class.* New York: Vintage Books.

Shavelson, R. J., & Towne, L. (Eds.). (2002). *Scientific research in education.* Washington, DC: National Academy Press.

Singleton, R. A. J., & Straits, B. C. (2010). *Approaches to social research* (5th ed.). Oxford: Oxford University Press.

Skloot, R. (2010). *The immortal life of Henrietta Lacks.* New York: Crown Publishers.

Sluka, J. A. (2007). Reflections on managing danger in fieldwork: Dangerous anthropology in Belfast. In A. C. G. M. Robben & J. A. Sluka (Eds.), *Ethnographic fieldwork: An anthropological reader* (pp. 259–269). Malden, MA: Blackwell Publishing.

Smith, G. (1990). *Research issues related to Māori education* (9th ed.). Auckland, NZ: Research Unit for Māori Education, University of Auckland.

Smith, L. T. (1999). *Decolonizing methodologies: Research and indigenous peoples.* London: Zed Books.

Smith, G. H. (2003). *Indigenous struggle for the transformation of education and schooling.* Alaskan Federation of Natives (AFN) Convention, Anchorage, Alaska, U.S.

Soin, K., & Scheytt, T. (2006). Making the case for narrative methods in cross-cultural organizational research. *Organizational Research Methods, 9*(1), 55–77.

Spelman, E. V. (1988) *Inessential woman: Problems of exclusion in feminist thought.* Boston, MA: Beacon Press.

Spivak, G. C. (1987). In Forward by Colin MacCabe (Ed.), *In other words: Essays in cultural politics.* London: Methuen.

Spivak, G. C. (1993). *Outside in the teaching machine.* London and New York: Routledge.

Stacey, J. (1991). Can there be a feminist ethnography? In S. Berger Gluck & D. Patai (Eds.), *Women's words: The feminist practice of oral history* (pp. 111–120). New York: Routledge.

Stanfield, J. H. I. (1994). Empowering the culturally diversified sociological voice. In A. Gitlin (Ed.), *Power and method: Political activism and educational research* (pp. 166–180). New York: Routledge.

Stanfield, J. H. I., & Rutledge, D. (Eds.). (1993). *Race and ethnicity in research methods.* Newbury Park, CA: Sage Publications Ltd.

Stonebanks, C. D. (2008). An Islamic perspective on knowledge, knowing, and methodology. In N. K. Denzin & Y. S. Lincoln (Eds.), *Handbook of critical and indigenous methodologies* (pp. 293–322). Los Angeles, CA: Sage.

Stryker, S., Owens, T. J., & White, R. W. (Eds.). (2000). *Self, identity, and social movements.* Minneapolis, MN: University of Minnesota Press.

Swadener, B. B., & Mutua, K. (2008). Decolonizing performances: Deconstructing the global postcolonial. In N. K. Denzin (Ed.), *Handbook of critical and indigenous methodologies* (pp. 31–44). Los Angeles, CA: Sage.

Swisher, K. G. (1998). "Why Indian people should be the ones to write about Indian education". In D. A. Mihesuah (Ed.), *Natives and academics: Researching and writing about American Indians* (pp. 190–190–199). Lincoln, NE: University of Nebraska Press.

Temple, B. (1997). Watch your tongue: Issues in translation and cross-cultural research. *Sociology, 31*, 607–618.

Temple, B., & Young, A. (2004). Qualitative research and translation dilemmas. *Qualitative Research, 4*(2), 161–178.

Temple, B., Edwards, R., Alexander, C. (2006). Interpreting trust: Abstract and personal trust for people who need interpreters to access services. *Sociological Research Online, 11*(1).

Tierney, P. (2000). *Darkness in El Dorado: How scientists and journalists devastated the Amazon.* New York and London: W.W. Norton.

Trimble, J. E., & Fisher, C. B. (Eds.). (2006). *The handbook of ethical research with ethnocultural populations and communities.* Thousand Oaks, CA: Sage Publications, Ltd.

Vygotsky, L. S. (1978). *Mind and society: The development of higher psychological processes.* Cambridge, MA: Harvard University Press.

Vygotsky, L. S. (1986). *Thought and language* [Myshlenie i Rech] (Koz Trans.). (Revised ed.). Cambridge, MA: MIT Press.

Ward, C., & Chang, W. C. (1997). "Cultural fit": A new perspective on personality and sojourner adjustment. *International Journal of Intercultural Relations, 21*(4), 525–533.

Welsch, R. L., & Endicott, K. M. (2002). *Taking sides: Clashing views on controversial issues in cultural anthropology.* Guildford, CN: McGraw-Hill/Dushkin.

Whorf, B. L. (1956). *Language, thought, and reality: Selected writings of Benjamin Lee Whorf.* Cambridge, MA: MIT Press.

Willis, A. I., Montavon, M., Hall, H., Hunger, C., Burke, L. T., & Herrera, A. (2008). *Critically conscious research: Approaches to language and literacy research.* New York: Teachers College Press.

Wood, J. (1997). Vietnamese American place making in Northern Virginia. *Geographical Review, 87*, 58–72.

Wood, J. (2006). Making America at Eden Center. In W. Li (Ed.), *From urban enclave to ethnic suburb: New Asian communities in Pacific Rim countries* (pp. 23–40). Honolulu, HI: University of Hawai'i Press.

Yeo, M. (1989). [Review of M.C. Dillon's Merleau-Ponty's ontology] *Bulletin of the Canadian Society for Hermeneutics, 4*(1), 7–10.

Index

Printed and bound in the United States of America